Faulkner and Chopin

Edited by

Robert W. Hamblin

&

Christopher Rieger

Faulkner and Chopin

Edited by

Robert W. Hamblin

&

Christopher Rieger

Southeast
Missouri State University

Published for the Center for Faulkner Studies
by Southeast Missouri State University Press • 2010

Faulkner and Chopin
Edited by Robert W. Hamblin and Christopher Rieger

Copyright: 2010, by Southeast Missouri State University Press

Published for the Center for Faulkner Studies by
Southeast Missouri State University Press
One University Plaza, MS 2650
Cape Girardeau, MO 63701
www6.semo.edu/universitypress

ISBN: 978-0-9822489-9-7

Cover design: Susan Swartwout and Matthew Long

Acknowledgments

The editors are extremely grateful to Southeast Missouri State University's Office of the Provost, College of Liberal Arts, Department of English, Kent Library, and University Center, as well as the Missouri Humanities Council, for their support of the Faulkner and Chopin Conference that produced the essays included in this volume.

We also extend our sincere thanks to Ashton McFarland, Lindy Lebonick, Amber Walker, and Demetra Perros, research assistants in the Center for Faulkner Studies, for their assistance in corresponding with contributors, managing and editing electronic files, and reading page proofs.

We thank Susan Swartwout, director of the Southeast Missouri State University Press, and her administrative assistant, Donna Essner, for their encouragement, guidance, and support, not only for this book but also for the series of which it is a part.

Our greatest debt of gratitude is to the contributors for their engaging and informative treatments of Chopin and Faulkner, two of America's finest writers.

Contents

Notes on the Conference

On October 2-4, 2008, Southeast Missouri State University's Center for Faulkner Studies hosted "Faulkner and Chopin," a conference devoted to the writings of William Faulkner and Kate Chopin. Supported by a grant from the Missouri Humanities Council, the conference featured presentations by scholars representing five countries and fifteen American states.

The conference opened on Thursday evening, October 2, with a buffet dinner and keynote address. Provost Jane Stephens welcomed the participants and Robert W. Hamblin, the director of the Faulkner Center, introduced the keynote speaker, Barbara C. Ewell, the Dorothy Harrell Brown Professor of English at Loyola University New Orleans, who spoke on "Storm Stories: Chopin and Faulkner in New Orleans—and on the Gulf Coast." Following the keynote address, Dr. and Mrs. Hamblin hosted a reception at their home in honor of Professor Ewell.

Panels and presentations were offered on Friday and Saturday, October 3-4. The papers examined Faulkner's and Chopin's treatments of such topics as New Orleans, race, gender, socio-economic class, the plantation tradition, history, and narrative technique. Special sessions included a panel discussion of "Faulkner and Latin America," organized and moderated by Professor Emron Esplin of Kennesaw State University; "Faulkner Suite," a poetry reading by Sue Walker, Professor of English at the University of South Alabama and the Poet Laureate of Alabama; and presentations on the classroom teaching of works by Faulkner and Chopin.

On Friday evening, October 3, conference participants were treated to "A Salon with Kate Chopin and William Faulkner," a readers' theater program based on the writings of the featured authors, scripted and directed by Dr. Roseanna Whitlow, a published playwright who is Instructor of Communications Studies at Southeast Missouri State University. The dramatic presentation featured Dr. Whitlow as Kate Chopin, Faulkner impersonator Pat Abbott, and, as a surprise guest, Mark Twain impersonator Lester Goodin.

Throughout the conference, Chopin and Faulkner books, manuscripts, and other memorabilia were exhibited in Kent Library. The Chopin exhibit, courtesy of the Missouri Historical Society and Maryville University, was arranged by Dr. Kathleen B. Nigro, Assistant Director of the Institute for Women's and Gender Studies at the University of Missouri—St. Louis. The Faulkner exhibit, from the Louis Daniel Brodsky Collection, was arranged by Dr. Lisa Speer, Southeast Missouri

State University's Archivist and head of the university's Special Collections. Dr. Nigro, Dr. Speer, and Dr. Hamblin hosted a special showing of the exhibits on Friday, October 3.

The conference concluded on Saturday afternoon, October 4, with a historical tour of downtown Cape Girardeau and the Mississippi River riverfront, guided by Professor Frank Nickell, the Director of the Center for Regional History at Southeast Missouri State University.

Introduction

The fifteen essays in this volume were selected from papers presented at the Faulkner and Chopin Conference hosted by Southeast Missouri State University's Center for Faulkner Studies in Cape Girardeau, October 2-4, 2008. The featured authors were paired for this conference because they have both Missouri and Southern connections. Kate Chopin is a native of St. Louis and spent much of her life there; William Faulkner is the focus of the Louis Daniel Brodsky Collection, now owned by Southeast Missouri State University. Additionally, both authors lived in and wrote about New Orleans, and their greatest works are set in a South defined by its troubled history and the impact of that history upon issues of race, gender, socio-economic class, and the environment.

The volume opens with the text of the keynote address of the conference, Barbara C. Ewell's "Storm Stories: Chopin and Faulkner in New Orleans—and on the Gulf Coast." Ewell, writing shortly after the shocking effects of Hurricane Katrina, draws upon the history of New Orleans and Gulf Coast hurricanes to identify severe storms that Chopin and Faulkner would likely have known about, demonstrating how such storms and their consequences influenced the respective authors' fiction, particularly *The Awakening* and *The Wild Palms*. Ewell's analysis of Chopin's finest novel is especially astute, linking the sense of nostalgia and regret in the story to the devastating effects of the Great Storm of 1893, which virtually destroyed the resort community of Grand Isle that was so important to Chopin personally and to her character Edna Pontellier. Faulkner too, as Ewell notes, employs the imagery of storms and floods, particularly in *The Wild Palms*, in which the intense personal conflicts that surrounded the novel's composition resonate in the tall convict's struggle with the forces of nature and Charlotte and Harry's troubled and eventually tragic quest for an ideal love. For both Chopin and Faulkner, as Ewell demonstrates, actual storms generate metaphors for the conflicted emotional states of their characters—as well as for their authors.

Ryan Crider's essay also links Chopin, Faulkner, and New Orleans. In "Miscegenation and the Mystique of New Orleans: Identity and Race Consciousness in *The Awakening* and *Absalom, Absalom!*," Crider examines the ways that the issues of race and the hierarchal social milieu in nineteenth-century New Orleans intersect in a contextually significant manner in *The Awakening* and *Absalom, Absalom!*. Crider demonstrates how both Edna Pontellier's burgeoning sexual freedom and Quentin Compson's confused obsession with the Henry Sutpen-Charles Bon relationship are grounded in the New Orleans environment of an elite Creole class, elaborate quadroon balls, and interracial affairs and offspring.

In "Romances of the White Woman's Burden: Chopin's *At Fault*, Faulkner's *Light in August*, and the Legacies of U.S. Plantation Fiction," Jeremy Wells acknowledges that both Chopin and Faulkner have rightly been celebrated for having transcended the plantation tradition so central to Southern literature from the late 1870s onward. Still, in significant ways, both authors more closely reflect the older literary tradition than many critics have supposed. While several of Chopin's and Faulkner's female characters find themselves liberated from at least some of the constraints of Southern womanhood, they also must contend with being newly "white," which is to say, implicated differently by the discourses of race circulating in the post-Reconstruction South. Focusing on *At Fault* and *Light in August* but glancing at other texts as well, Wells examines what happens when women take up "the white man's burden" and respond differently to the problems and possibilities inherent in mastering the plantation.

Christopher Rieger also looks at both Faulkner and Chopin in relation to the plantation tradition, but he focuses on the pastoral elements, specifically the association of women with nature. In "The Green Breast of the Southern Plantation: Equating Women and Property in Faulkner's *Go Down, Moses* and Chopin's 'No-Account Creole,'" Rieger demonstrates how Chopin's Wallace Offdean and Faulkner's Ike McCaslin equate land ownership with possession of a female body. However, while Chopin's story, according to Rieger, seems to hold out the possibility of a happy resolution of the ownership issue (at least in Offdean's fantasizing), Faulkner's story, written after decades of wanton destruction of the Big Woods, focuses on tragic outcomes. In Rieger's view, what is a feminist concern for Chopin has become an environmental concern for Faulkner.

Julie Kares, in "How Merry Are the Widows in Chopin's *At Fault* and Faulkner's 'There Was a Queen'?," finds commonalities between Thérèse Lafirme, Chopin's widowed Creole plantation mistress, and Narcissa Sartoris, Faulkner's post-World War I widow of the last of the Sartoris line. In both narratives, Kares argues, the widows exhibit determination and practicality, thus asserting their potential autonomy; nevertheless, both continue to be heavily influenced by anxiety sparked by societal pressures. Thus, far from operating beyond the boundaries of societal norms, they remain firmly entrenched within Southern behavioral codes. As a result, Kares concludes, their widowhood serves only to reinforce their conventional female roles.

Gretchen Martin discusses female characters who appear to be more successful in transcending their subordinate gender roles in a patriarchal society. In "Empowering the Pedestal: Unvanquishable Grannies in Faulkner and Chopin," Martin demonstrates how the actual daily lives of plantation mistresses was vastly different from the "magnolia myth" of piety, purity, submissiveness, and domesticity. Such was particularly the case with older women. Drawing upon historical parallels, Martin explains how Granny Millard in *The Unvanquished* and Madame Valmonde in "Desiree's Baby" empower themselves by strategically negotiating a legal and social system predicated on their powerlessness, thus epitomizing the highest ideal of maternal commitment.

Alisa Smith-Riel's essay, "In Search of Agency: Edna Pontellier and Charlotte Rittenmeyer Find Independence, and Death, in *The Awakening* and *The Wild Palms*," treats the female protagonists as "first-wave" feminists of their respective eras. Utilizing Lara M. Ahearn's and Anthony Giddens' definitions of agency as the interplay of free will and social structure, Smith-Riel demonstrates how Edna and Charlotte rebel against the conventional, socially acceptable roles for women as constructed by Southern patriarchy. However, Smith-Riel argues, in the end Faulkner and Chopin present a representation of freedom and independence in death because, in the time frames of the two novels, it is only in death that Edna and Charlotte are able to escape patriarchal oppression.

Jessica Copous finds similarities between Edna Pontellier and another of Faulkner's prominent female characters, Addie Bundren of *As I Lay Dying*. However, in "Failing to Know Their Roles: Examining Parallels Between Addie Bundren and Edna Pontellier," Copous focuses not on the liberating aspects of the women's experiences but on their failures and disillusionments. Having mistakenly entered into loveless marriages that drive them toward solitude and loneliness, and viewing their children as well as their husbands as unwanted intrusions into that privacy, both Addie and Edna seek, first, extramarital relationships and, ultimately, death to escape their unhappiness. For Copous, Addie's and Edna's stories represent not so much a quest for rebellion and freedom as a dramatization of the tragedy resulting from their experiences as disappointed wives and failed mothers.

In addition to the eight essays treating both Faulkner and Chopin, this volume contains four essays focusing solely on Faulkner and three essays on Chopin. Two of the Faulkner essays treat the still-too-much-neglected *A Fable*, a novel that Faulkner greatly admired but critics have typically panned or ignored altogether. Caroline Miles, in "*A Fable* of Labor: Class Struggle, the Specter of Class Consciousness, and Faulkner's Unread Hostility to Capitalism," positions the novel as a materialist examination of "the dehumanizing nature of the capitalist and imperialist logic." Countering the long-held notion that Faulkner is indifferent to labor issues, Miles argues that *A Fable* correlates the military front line with the assembly line, the regimentation of soldiers with capitalist control of the work force, and the battlefield mutiny with a workers' strike. While acknowledging that Faulkner is not a conscious Marxist, but calling attention to the surprising amount of labor imagery in the text, Miles reads the actions of the protesting corporal, his disciples, and the "seething" masses as a Cold War class struggle opposing "the economic logic that governs labor and military combat under capitalism."

Shiela Pardee, in "Deconstructing Immortality and Decay in Faulkner's *A Fable*," also offers a materialist reading of *A Fable*, but she applies it to a reconsideration of the traditional Christian opposition of the body and the soul. In Pardee's reading, Faulkner's novel privileges corporeality over immortality, assigning more value to the corporal's mortal body and even his corpse than to the Old General's empty and facile rhetoric about immortality and deathlessness. Thus, according to Pardee, *A Fable* belongs with other modernist works, such as those by Eliot, Joyce, and Ionesco, that establish a "new dichotomy," setting that which is "natural, subject to decay, and therefore good" against that which is "artificial, everlasting, and poisonous."

In "'You'll Never Find a Woman Who Is Worthy of You': Freud's *The Interpretation of Dreams* and the Effects of Oedipal Impulses in Faulkner's *The Sound and the Fury*," Victoria M. Bryan presents a detailed characterization of Jason Compson based on his near-incestuous relationship with his mother and his extreme resentment and hostility toward his father. Bryan demonstrates how Jason's treatment of the other characters in the novel—not only Caddy, Quentin, and Benjy but also his niece, Lorraine, and Uncle Maury—is grounded in the Oedipus complex as defined by Freud and discussed by him in relation to both King Oedipus and Prince Hamlet. Interestingly, Bryan concludes that Faulkner's Jason is more akin to Hamlet than to Oedipus.

Geri Harmon argues for a different source of Jason Compson's neurotic behavior. In her essay "Some Medical History Embedded in Faulkner's Jason Compson," she explores the widespread interest in homeopathic medicine in the nineteenth and early-twentieth century, as well as the concurrent hormonal research advocated in a well-known book that Faulkner owned, Dr. Louis A. Berman's *The Glands Regulating Personality* (1921). Such medical theories emerged in the practice of the Keeley Cure for alcoholism, to which Faulkner and other members of his family were subjected over the years. Harmon goes on to examine the personality and actions of Jason Compson in light of the homeopathic theory that certain human attitudes and conditions (for example, Jason's anger, insecurity, melancholy, and desire for control, as well as his severe headaches and addiction to camphor) can perhaps be explained by the hormonal or chemical imbalance in one's body. In fact, Harmon notes, some of the depictions of Jason seem to come directly from the homeopathic manuals of the day.

All three of the Chopin essays deal with *The Awakening*, two with its text and one with its context. Donna J. Essner, in "Moving Beyond Acceptable Boundaries: Another Critical Awakening," critiques Chopin's famous novel in terms of its non-traditional content, but from a masculine rather than a feminine perspective. As Essner notes, just as Edna Pontellier's rebellion is set against Adele Ratignolle's characterization as society's ideal "mother-woman," so too does Robert Lebrun's portrayal challenge the notion of Leonce Pontellier as society's ideal man. Robert's rebellion is no more successful than Edna's, but, as Essner demonstrates, his actions evidence that men as well as women fell victim to the rigid codes of Victorian society.

Brian Howton's essay, "Music as a Motif in *The Awakening*," traces Chopin's extended use of musical allusions as a means of illuminating Edna's conflict with society. In examining four key scenes in the novel, Howton finds, in Mlle Reisz's accomplished renditions of selections by the Neoclassic Frédéric Chopin and the Romantic Richard Wagner, a parallel to Edna's emotional and psychological state. Unlike Mlle Reisz's music, however, Edna is not able to achieve a satisfactory balance of restraint and freedom in her life.

In the final essay, "Kate Chopin and 'Super-Spiritual Superior' Influences," Kathleen Butterly Nigro examines the backdrop of St. Louis society during the time that Chopin was writing. Nigro focuses particularly upon the popular Spiritualist movement and its opposition by those who linked it to female weakness, hysteria, and even insanity. Nigro's wide-ranging examination of case studies, medical texts, and public opinion thoroughly demonstrates the tremendous obstacles to freedom and equality encountered not just by Kate Chopin and her character Edna Pontellier but by all women of their day.

Storm Stories: Chopin and Faulkner in
New Orleans—and on the Gulf Coast

As many people know, often from personal experience, New Orleans has a way of changing people. The stories are familiar: an impromptu visit to Mardi Gras or Jazz Fest, a degree from Tulane or Loyola or Xavier, a visit to a college friend—and before you can say "sazerac" or "Louis Armstrong," you've terminated your lease in Toledo, packed your stuff, and moved into a shotgun double in the Lower Garden District; twenty years later, you've married a native, you have a closet full of purple, green, and gold clothes, and you can't quite remember where Ohio is. There are lots of stories like that. And as Hamilton Basso (like me, a native of Baton Rouge, who got down there as soon as he could) once explained, New Orleans has been a source of romance few writers have cared to resist—"a symbol of exotic alienness in the national mind" ["Introduction," *The World from Jackson Square* xi].

As it turns out, Kate Chopin and William Faulkner were no different. New Orleans proved critical both to their personal lives and to their careers as writers. For Kate Chopin, the effect of the city was a bit delayed. Chopin first visited New Orleans as a teenager in the spring of 1869, with her mother and cousins. Eighteen-year-old Katie O'Flaherty found the city an agreeable place: "N. Orleans," she wrote in her diary, "I liked immensely; it is so clean—so white and green. Although in April, we had profusions of flowers—strawberries and even black berries" [May 8, 1869] (*Private Papers* 85) . But it was of course her marriage to a native—or at least a resident—Oscar Chopin, the next year that really clinched her relationship to the city. Kate Chopin spent much of the first decade of her marriage in New Orleans and bore most of her six children there. More importantly, when she began to write in the late 1880s, years after her husband's untimely death and her return to St. Louis in 1884, it was New Orleans and the people and places of the Louisiana countryside that fired her imagination—and ultimately generated her best sales; her Louisiana stories, and especially her famous 1899 novel, *The Awakening*, eventually linked her name firmly with that city and state.

William Faulkner's first encounter with the city that he once described as one of the two largest cities in Mississippi (the other being Memphis) is not (as far as I know) recorded. But he had obviously visited the city often—and at least once he and his young friends (Phil Stone, Dot Wilcox, and Reno de Vaux) created enough havoc in the old Roosevelt Hotel that the police were summoned (Williamson 196). However, New Orleans assumed a more serious significance soon after his arrival in January 1925 with his friend Phil Stone. During the months that followed, Faulkner became a real writer—that is, he began to write continuously and even began to make a little money. Like so many others, Faulkner thought he was just passing through New Orleans that winter—on his way to Europe, about to make a two-year grand tour that would further his preparation as an artist: "*Je suis un poete*," he planned to say when he was introduced abroad—or so he confided to Dot Wilcox (Williamson 202). But while he was waiting around to catch the freighter on which he hoped to trade his labor for the price of his passage, he (like so many others) kept finding reasons to stay just a bit longer.

The first reason to linger was that he could earn a living—not a great living, but enough for a young man willing to bunk up with friends— first at the Sherwood Andersons and later with his new friend, the artist William Spratling, in a tiny apartment over Pirates Alley in the French Quarter. Although periodicals like the *Double-Dealer* and the *Times-Picayune* paid cash for his sketches and stories, Faulkner was also writing poetry, which he thought would be his métier, and, then, sometime that spring, he started "Mayday," which would become his first novel, *Soldiers' Pay* (Williamson 200).

But the second reason for staying in New Orleans was the more typical one: love. Among his new acquaintances that spring was James "Pete" Baird and his attractive twenty-one-year-old sister, Helen. The relationship (such as it was) actually developed a bit later on the Gulf Coast, where Phil Stone had arranged for Faulkner to stay during May and June. Stone's family had a summer house in Pascagoula on the Mississippi Gulf Coast—that pleasant stretch of sand that New Orleanians have always considered their private beach. Though Faulkner did a lot of writing that summer, he also spent some time with Helen Baird, whose family also had a beach house nearby; both—the beach and the woman—eventually became, like New Orleans, critical to Faulkner's imaginative life. Indeed, by July 7, the day Faulkner boarded the *West Ivis* with his traveling companion, William Spratling, bound for Genoa, Italy (*cf.* Williamson 202), several critical events had already occurred: he had mailed the manuscript of his first novel to a publisher, he had fallen in love (or at least—as Judith Sensibar argues—had found a focus for his infatuations [461]), and he had solidified his attachments to a city and a seacoast—all elements that would circulate powerfully throughout his literary life.

For both Kate Chopin and William Faulkner, in fact, the Gulf Coast and New Orleans occupy critical places in their fiction. The Coast, especially, is invested with a distinctively seductive power, one that is associated as much with loss as with passion. One reason might well be the literal paradoxes of the Gulf of Mexico: sensual and languorous, its warm waters generate fertility and leisure, even as they spawn sudden and destructive hurricanes, threatening the extinction of both. For those languid coast-dwellers among us who, just a few years ago, witnessed and survived Hurricanes Katrina and Rita, or more recently Ike and Gustav, that paradox has certainly been tangible enough.

Indeed, it was my own experience of the power of The Storm (as New Orleanians still refer to Katrina) to change everything that led me to think about the material of this essay: how hurricanes transform experience and also how they mirror such transformations, especially in writers like Chopin and Faulkner, who share—with me and so many others—an affection both for New Orleans and for the watery environs that make it such a splendid and evocative place. I began my research—rather unsurprisingly, given my scholarly past—with Kate Chopin, and found unexpected links between her experience of hurricanes and their effects on her fiction, particularly *The Awakening*. But there are also in Faulkner interesting traces of storms, both the literal ones that he un-doubtedly encountered in his days living along the Gulf Coast (a place to which he returned with some regularity throughout his life), as well as the subtle circulation of those storms in his novels, echoing that pivotal first summer's experiences of love and loss—and writing fiction.

Hurricanes were certainly not part of Kate Chopin's early conscious-ness. A native of St. Louis, she became a Louisiana resident only in the fall of 1870, following her marriage to Oscar Chopin. In fact, the first summer Chopin spent in Louisiana was unusually busy for both storms and floods. Just about the time her first child, Jean, was born, for example, in late May 1871, a crevasse (or break in the levee of the Mississippi River) opened at Bonnet Carre, fifteen miles upriver. The waters swelled Lake Pontchartrain, and the next week, when an early June hurricane struck, the lake overflowed its banks, making New Orleans appear, as the local papers reported, like a "submerged city."

As the *Daily Picayune* indignantly insisted, however, "only those dis-tricts lying in the rear of the city [we]re inconvenienced by the flood" (qtd. in Magill 38)—and, in fact, the Chopins' Magazine Street neigh-borhood has rarely flooded—even when the levees broke during Katrina—but the vulnerability of the city must have already been appar-ent. Indeed, less than a week later, another June hurricane made landfall on the Gulf Coast, causing still more flooding and damage in and around

New Orleans. Months later, in early October, high winds and "an unprecedented rainfall" of six to ten inches assaulted the city for four days, felling trees, unroofing houses, beaching and wrecking several pilot boats in the river, and killing at least four sailors (Roth 21). The perils of life in the lowlands of the Gulf Coast must have made an impression on a sensitive Midwesterner that first year.

In fact, Chopin need not have been alarmed: notable hurricanes were relatively sparse for the rest of the time she lived in Louisiana. A couple of strong hurricanes in September 1879 destroyed crops and buildings and sent a major storm surge into Cameron Parish (Roth 22-23)—similar to the ones generated by Hurricanes Rita and Ike—but by then the Chopins had moved inland to Cloutierville, where they lived until Oscar's untimely death four years later (1883). Chopin soon returned to St. Louis, although she stayed in close contact with her husband's family and often visited Louisiana over the next two decades.

St. Louis thus became Chopin's permanent residence, but Louisiana remained central to her imaginative life. Each visit down the river seemed to generate new ideas for fiction. For example, her first novel, *At Fault*, which involves a flooding river, was begun shortly after a visit in 1889, when she went to Cloutierville to retrieve Oscar's body for reburial in St. Louis; and following a winter trip in 1891, she wrote nine Louisiana stories in eight weeks (*Private Papers* 204). Obviously, Chopin's visits to her former home were inspirational.

Though Chopin wrote about Louisiana primarily because local color stories were marketable, she must also have found satisfaction in writing about places that had once been home—part of a past (with her husband and young children) that was now irretrievably lost, the kind of place to which we can only return in memory—and in fiction. Indeed, one impetus for writing is exactly to record what has been lost, what others, including ourselves, can only see—or hear—imaginatively—like the dark-haired spouse of our youth or the sandy beaches where our children first plunged into the sea. We can, at least in writing, thus go home again, and perhaps find a little comfort for our losses. Of course, current events often trigger such memories and writing, and one such event—a hurricane—had, it appears, a very powerful effect on Chopin's work.

The Great Storm of 1893 was a major Gulf Coast hurricane that destroyed several places that were important to Kate Chopin, namely, the resort communities of Grand Isle and Chenière Caminada, about ninety miles south of New Orleans. That event seems to have focused for Chopin the experience of loss: the loss of places saturated in memory, the total destruction that proscribes any hope of return or recovery. At the same time, that sense of loss generated a fictional current that produced some of Chopin's most powerful writing.

On Sunday night, October 1, 1893, as the *Daily Picayune* reported the next morning, the city of New Orleans had been "struck by a storm" ("City Struck"). As reports began to trickle in, it became apparent that this storm had been a monster, wreaking havoc on the coastal communities some ninety miles away ("Full Story"). Two thousand people were dead or missing, whole towns were flattened, cane and rice and orange crops had been obliterated. Exhausted survivors told terrible stories: children swept away, houses collapsed, animals dragged out to sea, heroic rescues, tragic suffering. The news was national: the storm had ravaged 500 miles of the coastline from Pensacola to Timbalier Bay in Texas, the worst in nearly forty years, with a tidal wave of fifteen feet and waves reaching over fifty feet (Roth 27). Of the two thousand dead, 779 (in a population of 1300) were from Chenière Caminada; the island would never be resettled. And neighboring Grand Isle had been devastated.

Donations poured in from around the country; the president of the Board of Trade in St. Louis was among those listed in the New Orleans papers as promising "to solicit contributions" ("Cities"). Like many fellow St. Louisans, Kate Chopin must have been shocked by the news. These were people and places she knew well: she and her children had spent many summers on Grand Isle; they had ridden the little steamer that now lay tossed on shore, a "total wreck." She had stayed at the Krantz Hotel, now just piles of rubble; she had attended masses at Our Lady of Lourdes on Chenière Caminada, whose bell had tolled throughout the night until the church itself collapsed ("Grand Isle").

For Kate Chopin, the news of the hurricane must have reinforced a profound sense of loss—of her life in Louisiana and New Orleans, of Oscar, of her children's childhood, of pleasant places drenched in memories.

On October 21, just a few weeks after the full impact of the storm had become clear, Chopin began writing her only short story set on Grand Isle. A reflection on passion and on loss, "At Chenière Caminada" recounts the story of a young fisherman, Tonie, and the death of his first love, Claire Duvigne. But the tale also introduces a number of characters and details that Chopin would use again (five years later) in *The Awakening*: Tonie and his plump mother, as well as the Lebrun family, who own the pension on Grand Isle and whose son Robert, who had "for two consecutive seasons" been the devoted attendant of Tonie's lost Mademoiselle Duvigne (*Complete Works* 53). The story of Edna Pontellier was perhaps already taking shape in Chopin's imagination—a story of losing not just a place, but one's self.

Though Chopin evidently did not return to Louisiana for several years after the 1893 hurricane, her next recorded visit—in late June 1897—seems to have stirred both memory and imagination. Shortly after her return to St. Louis, she began writing *The Awakening*. Opening and closing on Grand Isle, which would never really recover from the Caminada storm, the novel was Chopin's most daring examination of passion and social constraints, but it was also, as Emily Toth observes, "an elegy for a lost way of life" (139).

While critics have often commented on Chopin's use of Grand Isle as a compelling setting for Edna's awakening, not much attention has been paid to the way that the hurricane of 1893, which destroyed that evocative place, also shapes Edna's story. In situating her characters in a place whose destruction was imminent, Chopin must have recognized the poignancy she was adding to Edna's short-lived awakening—not unlike setting a tale about New Orleans in the spring of 2005—or, for that matter, one about Galveston in the summer of '08.

That Chopin deliberately set her novel the year before the hurricane is confirmed by several internal details. Mrs. Highcamp, one of Edna's acquaintances, for example, specifically notes her attendance at the New Orleans Folk-lore Society, which was only founded on February 8, 1892 (Jordan 33). The novel itself begins in mid-summer, perhaps July: the night Edna learns to swim is specifically noted by Robert as "the twenty-eighth of August" (*Complete Works* 909), and in the early scenes, Edna's pregnant friend, Adele, is barely showing, so that her baby, like Edna's self, is born less than nine months later, shortly after Edna's birthday dinner. Since Kate Chopin's own birthday was February 8, it probably isn't too far-fetched to suggest that she would allow Edna to share it.

Finally, Edna's last trip to Grand Isle clearly takes place in very early spring—February or March—when the actual waters of the Gulf were just beginning to warm. Barely seven months later in October of 1893, that same slow tropical heat had spawned a destructive storm, one that would sweep away the Creole community that had flourished on its shores. In linking Edna's final swim with the sea's awful power, Chopin signals how profoundly Edna's revolutionary will to possess her own soul challenges the social institutions of that traditional community, creating a personal storm that will, in the end, change everything.

Chopin plainly foregrounds the sea and the warmth of the Southern summer as a critical catalyst in Edna Pontellier's awakening to her self—learning to swim and falling in love, but also recognizing how unsatisfying and limiting her marriage has been. When Edna returns to New Orleans after that magical summer, everything is changed. From the veranda of her house on Esplanade, she sees nothing of her own: "the street, the children, the fruit vender, the flowers growing there under her eyes, were all part and parcel of an alien world which had suddenly become antagonistic" (*Complete Works* 935).

In truth, it is Edna who has changed, not the city nor her "home." Propelled by her inner dislocation to seek familiar ground, she tries to solace her restlessness with what she has lost, that vanished summer world of Grand Isle. She begins visiting the Ratignolles, seeks out Madame Lebrun, and then calls on Mademoiselle Reisz, who has letters and news from Robert in Mexico, hoping to reconstruct that time at "Grand Isle when strange new voices awoke in her" (*Complete Works* 946). But writing in 1898, Kate Chopin knew only too well that that world was gone forever, swept away by forces no less natural or irresistible than the simmering passions of her character.

Determined "never again to belong to another than herself" (*Complete Works* 963), Edna gradually discards the external trappings of her identity as Léonce's wife. In truth, what she seeks is already part of the past: when she and Robert are finally reunited in the city, they even describe their passion for each other in terms of a vanished place, a place of memory: "the waves and the white beach of Grand Isle; the quiet, grassy street of the *Chenière Caminada*; the old sunny fort at Grande Terre" (*Complete Works* 984).

As it turns out, Robert is profoundly shocked by Edna's new "place," her insistence that she will only "give myself where I choose" (*Complete Works* 992). He cannot live in the unconventional spaces she would now make "home." And when she returns from her visit to Adele, having her baby, there is only a scrawled note to explain Robert's absence: "I love you. Good-by—because I love you" (*Complete Works* 997). The only reality Robert can imagine is that of possession: to love a woman is to confine her, to build her a house. Simply to love her, without condition, would be saying "good-by" to the realities of nineteenth-century society; it would be to return to Grand Isle—that liminal place where desire is always promised, inhabitable in memory from Mexico and walking together on the darkened streets of New Orleans, but—as Chopin knew as she wrote his note for him—that place had already vanished.

Edna, of course, returns once more to just that place. But the changes wrought by the Gulf have now made her truly homeless. Unable to locate a home for her awakened self in New Orleans, when she returns to Grand Isle, she finds that it is no longer summer, no longer the place she remembers. Still searching for home, Edna finally swims into the sea, where her last recollections are of her first "home"—Kentucky.

She looked into the distance, and the old terror flamed up for an instant, then sank again. Edna heard her father's voice and her sister Margaret's. She heard the barking of an old dog that was chained to the sycamore tree. The spurs of the cavalry officer clanged as he walked across the porch. There was the hum of bees, and the musky odor of pinks filled the air. (*Complete Works* 1000)

As Edna swims out into the Gulf, Chopin, at least, knew that her character's longings for self-possession as well as for non-possessive love were already well beyond her grasp: the warming ocean was already brewing the storm that would sweep away any remnant of that possible world.

William Faulkner was just a newborn at the end of September 1897, when Kate Chopin must have been deep into the composition of her new novel. Growing up in northern Mississippi, Faulkner's acquaintance with hurricanes was a little more immediate than Chopin's. Gulf storms frequently empty their rain-soaked clouds onto the Upper South and wear out their winds on the inland forests. We often forget, for example, how severely central Mississippi was affected by Katrina; even in Oxford, winds reached 50 mph, the power was out for as much as twelve hours, and there were nearly five inches of rain.

Actually, the remnants of several major hurricanes passed near Lafayette and Union Counties during Faulkner's youth. Perhaps the most dramatic occurred when he was a teenager, still playing football in Oxford and starting to spend his summers hanging out with Yalie Phil Stone. The "Great Storm of 1915," as it was called, struck Grand Isle and then New Orleans in late September, with 100-mile-an-hour winds and the lowest barometric pressure ever recorded to that point in the U. S.; its blustery remnants then trailed north, passing only sixty miles east of Oxford ("1915 Hurricane of New Orleans"). The next summer saw five major hurricanes, one of which made landfall at Gulfport in early July and caused a good deal of damage, including four deaths, before sweeping across central Mississippi as a tropical storm, packing 70-mph winds as it moved south of Oxford ("Historical Hurricane Tracks"). The proximate thrill and distant danger of Gulf storms could not have escaped young Billy Falkner's attention.

Faulkner's summers in Pascagoula a few years later would have brought him into even closer contact with hurricanes. The early 1920s were not particularly active seasons, but the summer of 1926, which Faulkner spent in Pascagoula after his shortened European tour, did bring several major storms, including one whose powerful tail brushed the Mississippi Gulf Coast in late August 1926 ("Historical Hurricane Tracks")—just about the time Faulkner was writing one final love letter to Helen Baird, who had been ignoring his romantic attentions all summer (Blotner I:519)—and just weeks before he completed his second novel, *Mosquitoes* [1 September 1926] (Blotner I:523), which he later dedicated "To Helen." The links between lost, unrequited love, violent coastal hurricanes, and the processes of fiction were at least in place.

Unlike Chopin, whose fiction became identified with south Louisiana, for Faulkner, New Orleans and the Gulf Coast generally remained marginal to his true fictional territory—Yoknapatawpha and north Mississippi. But if New Orleans was not the center of Faulkner's fictional universe, it did define an alternate gravity: not just a complex counterpoint to the conservative values of the South in particular and of America in general (as it has for many writers), but cultural otherness itself—acting, as Carl Zender argues, as a scrim for Europe and its sophisticated perspectives, or, as John T. Matthews suggests, a fetishistic displacement of the Caribbean with its connotations of Africa.

Faulkner's early uses of New Orleans—as the primary setting of *Mosquitoes*, for example—only hint at the metaphoric power the city acquired in his later work, its resonance increased partly as a consequence of its offstage appearances: where Sutpen goes in *Absalom, Absalom!*, for example, to buy slaves and where the mystery of his past ultimately lies furled, or where the incompetent Percival Brownlee of *Go Down, Moses* finds "his true niche at last" as a preacher and later "proprietor of a select New Orleans brothel" (279-80). In two other novels, Faulkner did make New Orleans central: in *Pylon,* a dark and clotted narrative about aviators that he wrote in 1935 when he got stuck in the middle of writing *Absalom, Absalom!*, and in the novel that followed, *The Wild Palms.* In the latter, New Orleans and the Gulf Coast successfully take center stage, places whose watery physiology, subject to floods and hurricanes, aptly embody the stormy emotional struggles Faulkner himself was experiencing and trying to convey in fiction.

The Wild Palms (a title which Faulkner had originally applied to only one of the twin narratives of his manuscript, "If I Forget Thee, Jerusalem") has occupied a curious and somewhat vexed place in Faulkner's canon. Generally regarded as an imperfect work, it has won greater critical esteem in recent years, especially after Noel Polk's superbly reconstructed edition of 1996, which restored the text and title and reunited the narratives. A provocative and experimental text, *The Wild Palms* alternates two stories: that of Charlotte Rittenmeyer and Harry Wilbourne, whose chance meeting in New Orleans becomes a doomed and illicit affair that ultimately leads to Charlotte's death and Harry's imprisonment for her murder; and the tale of the otherwise unnamed "Tall Convict," whose compulsory mission to rescue victims of the Great Flood of 1927 becomes an episodic journey down the "Old Man" Mississippi River and back again to Parchman Penitentiary. Intricately and often subtly related, the two stories provide a disquieting meditation on love and passion, desire and loss, regret and grief—as well as two riveting dramas.

Like much of Faulkner's fiction, the power of *The Wild Palms* is covert, always implying more than its surfaces disclose—like the "black pitiless wind"(236) that threshes the invisible palm trees to make their "wild dry sound" (248) or the unnerving rumble, the "profound deep whisper" (61), of the flooding river. Though critics have explored various sources of the novel's impact, one of the most interesting is the complicated emotional circumstances of its composition—circumstances that, like the Great October Storm of 1893, seem to have pulled together powerful threads from Faulkner's past, particularly those critical months that he spent in New Orleans and Pascagoula as a young man.

Faulkner seems to have begun his eleventh novel some time in the fall of 1937. The previous couple of years had been personally rough. For much of that time, Faulkner had been in Hollywood, writing screenplays and finally making decent money, but it was work that he disliked in a place whose values and culture he disdained. One consolation of that time—if it might be called that—was his affair with a young script clerk, Meta Carpenter (formerly Doherty) (Minter 160). Faulkner's marriage with Estelle Oldham, his adolescent sweetheart from Oxford, whom he had married in 1929 after her divorce from Cornell Franklin, was always tumultuous. As Judith Sensibar has deftly explained, their relationship was a complex tangle of sexual, emotional, and creative exchanges, complicated by their shared alcoholic excess, their "sometimes not so private theater," and Faulkner's usually brief and "always long-distance affairs" with other women (252). But none of Faulkner's relationships with women was very mature. Both his enduring attachment to Estelle and his unrequited courtship of Helen Baird, for example, seemed based on fantasy rather than any clear appreciation of the complicated women they were. Like other men of his time, he tended to romanticize and idealize the women he desired, cherishing notions of "a sweet, tremulous girl" (Gray 71), a female whose virginity and innocence was central to her appeal—and, by definition, lost as soon as possessed.

Though Richard Gray suggests that Faulkner's affair with Meta Carpenter may have been "the most passionate sexual experience of Faulkner's life" (239), Meta herself quickly wearied of being treated like a "girl-child" by a man with no intentions of leaving his wife. In December, about a year after their meeting, she became engaged to a German pianist, whom she married a few months later in April 1937. The break-up, combined with Faulkner's general disillusionment with the movie business, took its toll; that summer, stiff drinking led to a six-week stay in a Los Angeles hospital (Parini 216). Fortunately, his work in Hollywood was pretty much over by that time, and he returned to Oxford that August. Before long, a new novel was underway.

Critics have long recognized "some kind of autobiographical or peculiarly personal significance" (qtd. in McHaney 21-22) in *The Wild Palms*. In fact, the best way to read its complicated and clotted emotionality is exactly as an intense, deliberate effort to explain to himself the break-up with Meta, or more truly, "the deep ambiguities inherent in his feelings about women, sexuality and love" (Gray 239). As in any such meditation, Faulkner necessarily reached back into his past—to other women he had loved and lost, like the elusive Helen Baird—and to places that once promised passionate love, like New Orleans and the Gulf Coast, where he had honeymooned with the even more elusive Estelle (Parini 238)—places that were now little more than vacation spots for his rather unhappy family.

While it isn't clear that the Faulkners actually visited the Gulf Coast on his return from California that year, they often spent time at the Stone family beach house (as they did the next August, in 1938 [Blotner II:1001]); but it is also tempting (for the sake of my thesis) to point out that at least two September storms had affected the Mississippi coast in 1937, the remnants of one passing just west of Oxford around September 1 ("Historical Hurricane Tracks"). Was this perhaps the same storm that, rather tantalizingly, Joseph Blotner reports—noting that shortly after Faulkner's return to Mississippi, a "fierce summer storm had sent an oak crashing down" (Blotner II:970) onto a brick wall at Rowan Oak, which he then tried to repair?

Although it would be pretty to think so, probably the more significant storms in the creation of his new novel were internal ones, stirred up the next month (October) when Faulkner visited New York. First, Faulkner saw Meta again for the first time since her marriage and departure for Europe back in April. She and her Jewish husband (Wolfgang Rebner) had had to flee the Nazi oppressions of Germany and were living in New York (Williamson 260). And if that wasn't enough, at a cocktail party, Faulkner ran into Sherwood Anderson, from whom he had been estranged since leaving New Orleans. The two were cordial—but shortly afterwards, when Faulkner had drunk himself sick, Anderson came to see him. Facing two failed relationships, one with a lover, the other with an influential friend and mentor, Faulkner had responded with serious drinking, passing out in the Algonquin Hotel and badly burning himself on a steam pipe. As McHaney has argued in some detail, these reunions, especially that with Anderson, clearly triggered a number of critical memories and associations: Faulkner's other abortive romance with Helen Baird (which was, as Sensibar notes, intensified by the simultaneous dissolution of Estelle's marriage to Cornell Franklin [461]); the composition of *Mosquitoes* (whose writing Anderson had encouraged, and which was itself a tribute to and evocation of that bohemian time—dedicated "to Helen" on the eve of her marriage to another man [McHaney 21-22]); and all those sensual, hopeful summers on the Gulf Coast.

When Faulkner finally returned to Oxford in November, he plunged himself into his new novel. At first the writing went well, but as he probed deeper, the task proved more difficult. Sometime in early January, he decided that "something was missing" from the compulsive story of the lovers, and he began composing a counterpoint, the tale of the "Old Man"[River], which he later described as "the story of a man who got his love and spent the rest of the book fleeing from it" (Blotner II: 980). The strategy worked, perhaps relieving some of the stress of writing so directly about his feelings, and the novel was finally mailed to Random House at the end of June 1938 (Blotner II: 995).

That Faulkner was drawing on a very painful and largely unconscious part of his emotional life is clear from his own accounts. In letters to his publisher that spring, he described his mental state as "a little mad . . . nerves frayed from three months' pretty constant pain and inability to sleep" (Blotner II: 987); later in July, he explained that

> I have lived for six months in such a peculiar state of family complications and back complications that I am not able to tell if the novel is all right or absolute drivel. To me, it was written just as if I had sat on the one side of a wall and the paper was on the other and my hand with the pen thrust through the wall and writing not only on invisible paper but in pitch darkness too, so that I could not even know if the pen still wrote on paper or not. (*Letters,* qtd. in Gray 239)[2]

For Faulkner, the storms of the Gulf Coast and the floodwaters of the Mississippi did not so much precipitate his meditations on the nature of loss and love (as the Great Storm of 1893 evidently did for Chopin), as they provided vehicles for the intense feelings that he was trying so hard to dramatize. That those feelings required one of his most experimental (and still not well understood) techniques—the counterpoint of the two tales as well as the oblique metaphorical structures of circular journeys, of escape and imprisonment, of wind and water—attest to their complexity and perhaps to how incompletely Faulkner himself understood his material.[3]

Like Edna, the primary characters of *The Wild Palms* are in pursuit of a dream, a particular construction of love and passion and identity that seems worth everything, every sacrifice. For Harry Wilbourne, love is something he has almost missed for twenty-seven years (Edna's age!)—and then, when it appears, first in Charlotte's invitation to have an affair, and then in the $1278 that allows them to pursue it, he hardly knows what to do—except to imitate (rather badly) the cultural fictions of romance—the belief that love and passion are guilty pleasures and that they are necessarily ended by marriage and commitment—notions that have also implicitly guided Edna's choices. For both Harry and Charlotte, the primary threat to passionate love is to act as if they were married— precisely the charade they have to engage in to secure hotel rooms and apartments and jobs. Caught in this paradox, they have to keep reinventing themselves as new lovers, fleeing their own histories:

> It's got to be all honeymoon, always. Forever and ever, until one of us dies. It cant be anything else. Either heaven, or hell: no comfortable safe peaceful purgatory between for you and me to wait in until good behavior or forbearance or shame or repentance overtakes us. *(71)*

For a while, they manage to avoid the engagement with reality and time that produces consequences and thus shatters their isolated duet. What draws them out is, in fact, the same reality that blocks Edna from her wish to "have everything": children. For women (and men) of the 1930s no less than for those of the 1890s, the absence of reliable birth control made pregnancy one of the potential costs of passionate sexuality—and for women, at least, one with (presumably deserved) painful physical and moral consequences. In language that echoes their related dilemmas, both Edna and Charlotte find that their children "hurt too much" (182). Neither woman wishes to "trample on the little lives" they have created; with Harry in Chicago, for example, Charlotte is clearly thinking of her daughters and buys them Christmas presents she can ill-afford. But neither is Charlotte—nor Edna—willing to renounce her own freedom and passionate selfhood for her children—borne without real consciousness or choice, but simply as the result of "arbitrary conditions," the failure of a douche-bag, the decoy of romantic love and marriage that turns women into mothers—willy-nilly.

Ultimately, both women choose to give up the "unessential," their physical lives, for what seems more important—their selfhood. If Edna dies trying to balance having her "own way" against the needs of her children (her living sons no less than those she might conceive with Robert or another lover), Charlotte's death results directly from her efforts to avoid the pain of another child, another contingency that would violate the isolation that seems to her, at least, an essential condition of passionate love.

In "Old Man," the problem of passion and its consequences are presented more obliquely and the alternatives for women appear less complicated. In this somewhat lighter, more comic narrative, the woman that the Tall Convict is sent to rescue from the flood is almost exclusively a child-bearer. Intent on delivering her baby, she is focused on fulfilling her destiny as a female body in this thoroughly patriarchal society—presided over by the Old Man himself. Unlike Edna and Charlotte, this woman is not only nameless but blank, given very little character in the novel. She has no self to protect or desire, beyond that which is decreed for her. Like Adele—perhaps even like Faulkner himself, given his creation of earth-mothers like Lena Grove or Addie Bundren—this woman would be completely non-plussed by the notion that "a woman . . . could do . . . [more than] give her life for her children" (97).

For the Tall Convict, the pregnant woman, all women, as it turns out, are a miserable burden, a source of desire that inevitably traps men into doing stupid things, like robbing banks or paddling small boats down a huge flooding river, or getting shot at when you're just trying to surrender. Even before the flood forces the Tall Convict into a thoroughly unwanted intimacy with the female body, his preference for the comfortable all-male prison or the asexual fidelity of his mule, John Henry, is clear. The Tall Convict already knows what Harry is only learning: how getting the woman—one's love, one's desire—just means losing it, losing everything: "Women, shit," he says, offering the novel's concluding, if not final, judgment (287).

Ultimately, both men—like Charlotte and Edna—have been seduced by contemporary notions of romantic love with its implicit opposition to marriage and responsibility—and, at least for Charlotte, even to joy. Many critics have, in fact, commented on the novel's critique of such notions of romance, often promulgated in popular fiction—and film (*cf.* King). Certainly, Faulkner, just back from Tinsel Town and always rather fearful that his own work would be judged shallow and sensational, was also reflecting in *The Wild Palms* on the real consequences of bad fiction. For Harry those consequences are quite painful: trapped in his own version of "female sex troubles," he ends up aborting the child that his passion for Charlotte has produced and, in the process, destroying her, his one true love, as well.

Though Harry, like the Tall Convict, ends up preferring the security of Parchman to the greater risks of living a passionate life, he is permitted some insight into his choices. As Faulkner writes, the "second time he almost got it" (265), Harry is awaiting trial in the Pascagoula prison for Charlotte's death, when

> just before dawn, in a driving squall, the tail of a hurricane struck. Not the hurricane, just the tail of it, a flick of the mane in passing, driving up the shore ten feet of roiled and yellow tide which did not fall for twenty hours and driving fiercely through the wild frenzied palm which still sounded dry. (264-65)

Still living at the edges of experience, as in the outer bands of the storm, Harry "almost gets it." What he eventually understands becomes the famous conclusion to *The Wild Palms*: "*Between grief and nothing I will take grief*" (273). Given a chance to escape to Mexico by Charlotte's husband or later to commit suicide rather than go to prison, Harry realizes that without his being alive to remember, in the flesh ("after all memory could live in the old wheezing entrails" [272]), the vital passion that he and Charlotte shared cannot exist at all. And so he will stay alive, bearing the remembrance of love in his grief. Better than no love at all, perhaps, but it's important to remember that in refusing the ticket to Mexico and the chance to love again, Harry also makes it clear that the living in memory is preferable to any re-involvement in life. Like the Tall Convict, Harry ultimately chooses to withdraw altogether from the messy possibilities of emotion and sex and women—shit.

Interestingly, the pursuit of this dream of romantic love, untouched by consequence, leaves the women, Charlotte and Edna, dead, while the men safely retreat to a place free from any further "female troubles." That that place is a prison suggests that Faulkner recognized at least dimly what Richard Gray calls the "highly charged, deeply contradictory notions of woman" (252) and passionate love that Faulkner was trying to sort out in the wake of his failed affair with Meta Carpenter and his emotionally ambivalent marriage. As Gray comments, Faulkner was "after all, writing out, and out of, his agony: mapping out territory the 'dim, indistinct iconography' of which he could never fully trace or understand" (248).

Like Kate Chopin, Faulkner had been forced to revisit the places of the past and was trying then to chart the links between love and loss—how desire and passion seemed to him, anyway, always accompanied by loss and grief—from Pascagoula and New Orleans to Helen Baird and Estelle and Meta. But while the emotional storms of his own life drove him inward—to write, "to think it into words" (272)—that sensual geography of his youth, saturated with hopeful possibilities, provided a rich metaphoric grid of meaning that gives both narratives of *The Wild Palms* a particular poignancy in Faulkner's canon. Both writers thus used the sensuality of the coast and the imagery of storms to track their characters' pursuit of a dream of love, but Chopin, at least, seemed to know what Faulkner evidently did not: that the dream they were charting was impossible.

Of course, to be fair, Chopin was not writing as close to her own life as Faulkner was, but neither was she as confined as he was in contemporary constructions of gender, especially those of women. And while she died just a few years after the publication of *The Awakening*, Faulkner lived to repeat his personal mistakes with women—several times. Chopin—if not Edna—at least had some appreciation of the destructive force of the hurricane she was unleashing; Faulkner, on the other hand, writing his novel "in the dark" seemed aware not of "the hurricane, but just the tail of it, a flick of the mane in passing." Both of them, however, gave us storm stories whose meanings we shall, with pleasure, continue to unfold.

Notes

1. A version of this material on Chopin appears in the Spring 2010 issue of *Southern Literary Journal*.

2. See also David Minter's account of the novel's labored composition (170-77), "written out of pain that was physical, marital and personal" (174–5).

3. "So if the reader is often confused about Harry and Charlotte and their affair, then this should come as no surprise, since Faulkner was just as confused himself. He was, after all, writing out, and out of, his agony: mapping out territory the 'dim, indistinct iconography' of which he could never fully trace or understand" (Gray 248).

4. Sensibar observes that Estelle herself had fallen for the same "romantic image" in marrying Cornell, "the southern gentleman cavalier," in part to escape the "unattainable Bill Faulkner" (357)—an observation that further complicates the reading of the novel.

Works Cited

"1915 New Orleans Hurricane." *Wikipedia, The Free Encyclopedia*. 5 Apr. 2010. Web. 22 Apr. 2010.

Basso, Hamilton. "Introduction." *The World from Jackson Square: A New Orleans Reader*, ed. Etolia S. Basso. New York: Farrar, Strauss & Co., 1948. xi-xvii.

Blotner, Joseph. *Faulkner: A Biography*. New York: Random House, 1974.

Chopin, Kate. *Kate Chopin's Private Papers*. Eds. Emily Toth, Per Seyersted, and Cheyenne Bonnell. Bloomington, Indiana: Indiana UP, 1998.

Chopin, Kate. *The Complete Works of Kate Chopin*. Ed. Per Seyersted. Baton Rouge: Louisiana State UP: 1969.

"Cities Send Generous Contributions to the Funds." [New Orleans] *Daily Picayune* 8 October 1893:2.

"City Struck by a Storm." [New Orleans] *Daily Picayune* 2 October 1893: 1.

Faulkner, William. *Go Down, Moses*. 1942. New York: Vintage, 1990.

———. *Selected Letters of William Faulkner*. Ed. Joseph Blotner. New York: Random House, 1977.

———. *The Wild Palms. [If I Forget Thee, Jerusalem.]* 1939. Ed. Noel Polk. New York: Vintage, 1995.

"The Full Story of Chenière Isle." [New Orleans] *Daily Picayune* 6 October 1893: 1.

"Grand Isle and Chenière." [New Orleans] *Daily Picayune* 18 October 1893: 12.

Gray, Richard. *The Life of William Faulkner.* Oxford, UK: Blackwell, 1994.

"Historical Hurricane Tracks." NOAA Coastal Services Center. [Charleston, SC] April 2007. Web. 22 Apr. 2010.

Jordan, Rosan Augusta, and Frank De Caro. "'In This Folk-Lore Land': Race, Class, Identity, and Folklore Studies in Louisiana." *Journal of American Folklore* 109. 431 (1996): 31-59.

King, Vincent Allan. "The Wages of Pulp: The Use and Abuse of Fiction in William Faulkner's *The Wild Palms.*" *Mississippi Quarterly* 51.3 (1998): 503–27.

Magill, John. "On Perilous Ground." *Louisiana Cultural Vistas* 16.4 (2005-06): 33-43.

Matthews, John T. "This Race Which Is Not One: The More 'Inextricable Compositeness' of William Faulkner's South." In *Look Away! The U.S. South in*

New World Studies. Ed. Jon Smith and Deborah Cohn. Durham: Duke UP, 2004. 201–26.

———. "Recalling the West Indies: From Yoknapatawpha to Haiti and Back." *American Literary History* 16.2 (2004): 238-62.

McHaney, Thomas L. *William Faulkner's "The Wild Palms": A Study*. Jackson: UP of Mississippi, 1975.

Millgate, Michael. *The Achievement of William Faulkner*. London: Constable, 1966.

Minter, David. *William Faulkner: His Life and Work*. Baltimore: Johns Hopkins UP, 1980.

Parini, Jay. *One Matchless Time: A Life of William Faulkner*. New York: Harper Collins, 2004.

Rhodes, Pamela, and Richard Godden. "*The Wild Palms*: Degraded Culture, Devalued Texts." In *Intertextuality in Faulkner*. Ed. Michel Gresset and Noel Polk. Jackson: UP of Mississsippi, 1985. 87-113.

Roth, David. "Louisiana Hurricane History." NOAA National Weather Service. 14 Jan. 2010. Web. 22 Apr. 2010.

Sensibar, Judith L. *Faulkner and Love: The Women Who Shaped His Art*. New Haven: Yale UP, 2009.

Toth, Emily. *Kate Chopin*. New York: Morrow, 1990.

Toth, Emily, Per Seyersted, and Cheyenne Bonnel, eds. *Kate Chopin's Private Papers*. Bloomington: Indiana UP, 1998.

Williamson, Joel. *William Faulkner and Southern History*. New York: Oxford UP, 1993.

Zender, Karl F. "William Faulkner, New Orleans, and Europe." In *Transatlantic Exchanges: The American South in Europe—Europe in the American South*. Ed. Richard Gray and Waldemar Zacharasiewicz. Vienna: Austrian Academy of Sciences Press, 2007. 419-436.

Miscegenation and the Mystique of New Orleans: Identity and Race Consciousness in *The Awakening* and *Absalom, Absalom!*

The distinct milieu of nineteenth-century New Orleans has long been a focal point of scholarship in discussing Kate Chopin's fiction. Regarding *The Awakening* in particular, critics such as Anne Rowe have rightly suggested that the city and its people play an important metaphorical role in Chopin's writing. The influence of New Orleans is far less obvious in the work of William Faulkner, yet the fact remains that Faulkner as a young man lived in the French Quarter for a short but formative period that enabled him to soak up the city's history at a time when much of its nineteenth-century elegance had fallen into disrepair; during Faulkner's residency, the mystique of Old New Orleans was still very much alive through memories and secondhand anecdotes. A very particular and complicated aspect of this history eventually finds its way into the plot and theme of his monumental novel *Absalom, Absalom!*.

In considering the relationship between New Orleans and what are arguably the respective masterworks of these two writers, I want to suggest that the city and its culture, as a historical setting in Chopin's work, and as a nostalgic revisionist history in Faulkner's novel, become coded into the thematic exploration of nineteenth-century race consciousness and its effect on social identity. This thematic concern with race and identity is evident in both the narrative design of *The Awakening* and *Absalom, Absalom!* and the writers' careful development of place and character. New Orleans and its various cultural types come to function almost as tropes in both these novels. Exploring such strategies allows readers, first of all, to fully contextualize the racial dynamics at the margins of—yet fundamental to—*The Awakening* by locating them within the city itself, and second, to illustrate how a full grasp of these racial dynamics may provide a better understanding of Faulkner's more explicit treatment of race in *Absalom, Absalom!*.

A significant body of scholarship has developed emphasizing the importance that Creole New Orleans's convoluted racial hierarchy plays in Chopin's construction of her novel's milieu, and in turn the role that race-consciousness plays in Edna Pontellier's awakening to her new identity. Joyce Dyer has pointed out the major influence that Toni Morrison, more than perhaps any other single contemporary critic, has held in recent readings of the novel's contextual influence. As Dyer writes, "The racial fuse lies just below the pages of *The Awakening*, and [...] it is lit" (142). What so greatly complicates the issue of race in the novel is Chopin's depiction of New Orleans's multitude of socially recognized, if not socially liberated, multiracial groups. The simmering fuse of race, and the city's elaborate racial hierarchy, is most evident in Chopin's treatment of her mixed-race female characters. The novel is full of women of color, mainly servants of Creole families, most of whom are at best vaguely characterized and identified only by racial distinctions—mulatto, quadroon, octoroon, and griffe. Though Chopin was writing at a time when notorious "one drop" laws were the legal standard throughout the South, her use of these terms alone invokes the unique racial hierarchy of the city and the gradations of color they indicate would have held great meaning to anyone familiar with New Orleans society. In the novel, these figures are depicted alternately as loyal yet bitter, maternal yet exotic, proper yet indignant. The Creole characters treat them, in turn, with reluctant gratitude and, alternately, a distrust that occasionally turns venomous.

One memorable scene in the novel occurs when Edna visits the Lebrun mansion in New Orleans, where she encounters Victor Lebrun and a female servant in a verbal altercation. The servant is not rebelling against her prescribed duties, the reader is told, but because she is not being allowed to carry out those duties. When Victor gives her an order, the narrator writes, "The woman grumbled a refusal to do part of her duty when she had not been permitted to do it all" (79). Victor immediately chastises the woman and explains apologetically to Edna that her behavior is due to "imperfect training, as he was not there to take her in hand" (79). In this instance, the servant figure is portrayed as decidedly black and willingly servile, wholly dependent on the Creole employer. Elsewhere female servants are portrayed as steadfastly loyal to their mistresses. Madame Ratignolle's nurse, for instance, described as a "griffe" (designating three-quarters of African blood), reacts with extreme indignation when her employer claims to have been "neglected" at a time of illness. "Neglected indeed," exclaims the nurse, who takes great pride in caring for this wealthy Creole woman who, in turn, takes that care for granted (131).

But perhaps the novel's most interesting servant figure is the Pontellier family's own quadroon nurse. At the most basic level, the quadroon stands in as a mother-figure to Edna's children, otherwise serving a peripheral role within the narrative and allowing Edna to pursue her artistic ambitions and sexual desires. Elizabeth Ammons goes so far as to suggest that the novel's memorable and tragic conclusion itself depends on the nurse, writing that "if Edna's children did not have a hired 'quadroon' to care for them night and day, it is extremely unlikely that she would swim off into the sunset" (75). Ammons finds Chopin comparatively liberal in her attitudes on race, yet unwilling to fully confront the issue in her work. However, critic Michelle Birnbaum suggests that the nurse serves as far more than just a convenient novelistic means of removing Edna's maternal responsibilities. She argues that while "Edna does not really want to know the experience of the people of color she sees dimly on the street; her new identity emerges only in the twilight of junctures, in the illicit coupling of her life to theirs" (306). According to Birnbaum, Edna comes to associate the novel's many women of color with, on the one hand, a marginalized social position not unlike the one she is pursuing, and, on the other hand, an eroticized potential grown out of existing nineteenth-century tropes (306). These women thus constantly maintain their own balancing act at the margins of the Creole order. Of the Pontelliers' nurse in particular, her own voice and identity silenced as she is relegated to chasing about with Edna's children, Birnbaum writes, "the quadroon . . . appears divested of subjectivity and, it would seem, of sexuality. And yet . . . Edna's sexuality is brought into relief by the quadroon's literary inheritance of sexual conventions" (307).

Along these lines, as Birnbaum points out, Chopin clearly made use of "mythic . . . historical racial types with which she was quite familiar" (303). To explore the influence of these racial types further and understand more fully why they carried such conflicting associations in the race consciousness of Creole society, it is necessary to understand the complicated historical context of race in nineteenth-century New Orleans. Though obviously a Southern city largely dependent on slave labor, antebellum New Orleans also was home to a large population of free blacks. In 1860, there were over 10,000 free people of color living in the city. John Blassingame, in *Black New Orleans*, notes that most of these freed individuals were the children of wealthy white men. Blassingame also estimates that, at one time, men comprised only one third of the free population (14). Thus, the culture of free people of color was dominated by women, many of whom possessed some measure of white blood. Blassingame suggests that this high population of light-skinned free women, along with what he regards as the socially accepted miscegenation that flourished in New Orleans at this time, led to one of the most decadent, highly sexualized, socially ambiguous, and romanticized institutions in the city's history. Throughout the nineteenth century, locations across the French Quarter—including, legend has it, the Orleans Ballroom—played regular host to what became known as the Quadroon Balls. These balls, operating at the fringe of Creole society, presented an opportunity for light-skinned free women, trained in the social arts and viewed as sexually desirable by aristocratic men, to assert tremendous power, if only within a marginalized role.

In describing the scene of these balls, Blassingame writes, "The wealthiest and most beautiful quadroons frequently chose from among several white suitors. After a period of courtship a wealthy white suitor met with the girl's parents and agreed to purchase her a house and to give a certain amount of money to each of the children which might result from the union" (18). These arrangements became known as plaçages, which existed beyond the legal system and operated somewhat like present-day common-law marriages. Such relationships reveal a unique power dynamic within New Orleans society—stripped of social acceptance and living as the exotic other on society's periphery, the quadroon women were nonetheless able to exert tremendous sexual power over their suitors; at the same time, such overtly sexualized behavior would have been entirely unacceptable for a Creole woman of proper breeding. This would seem to enrich Birnbaum's conclusion that for Edna Pontellier, "racial figuration is intimately involved in the warranty and production of her 'self.' To the extent such troping is in a sense 'productive' as well as repressive, race is constitutive of Edna's new identity" (317). Despite the illegality of interracial relationships, the Quadroon Balls lasted in one form or another throughout Reconstruction. More importantly, during her years in New Orleans, Chopin was positioned to internalize the greater scale of miscegenation in the city, observing the comparatively and surprisingly liberated population of multi-racial women who existed outside an outwardly strict hierarchy.

Of course, for the quadroon women themselves, the power they derived from the balls was not limitless. As Lyle Saxon writes, "The quadroon girl's future depended upon pleasing the man with whom she lived. Sometimes these liaisons lasted for years—occasionally for life. But more often than not they were broken off when the young man married" (181). Saxon's impressionistic history of the balls, published in 1928 in *Fabulous New Orleans*, presents the quadroon women and their octoroon offspring in a tragic and romanticized light. Because his account, although peppered with primary documents, is more personal than historical, and because of the time period in which he was writing, Saxon's depiction of the balls and the race-mixing they encouraged offers an excellent glimpse of the mystique that developed around this subculture as New Orleanians of the early twentieth century looked back on their city's perceived past glories. Among Saxon's many friends during the 1920s was William

Faulkner, who lived intermittently in the French Quarter between 1924 and 1926. New Orleans offered Faulkner not only avenues for literary apprenticeship, but also the opportunity to absorb the city's rapidly fading past. In reading his work, it is clear that the culture of the quadroons, if not the balls themselves, representative of the unique complications of race in Old New Orleans and filtered through the exotic, romanticized stories of his contemporaries, was part of this past that he absorbed.

Faulkner employed this subculture to great contextual effect in *Absalom, Absalom!*, which locates race and miscegenation at the very center of its complex narrative design. The complications of the novel's main plot are set in motion by the revelation that Charles Bon is married to a New Orleans octoroon, with whom he has a child. Miscegenation and issues of racial identity factor not only into the reader's understanding of Bon but the other characters as well. *Absalom, Absalom!* is notoriously fragmented, and its competing narratives often depend on conjecture and speculation as each narrator attempts to solve the mysteries surrounding Bon and his relationship to the Sutpen family. This makes for obvious difficulties in attempting to firmly establish particular plot points. However, the book's fragmentary and speculative nature actually works to emphasize the extreme race consciousness of its various narrators.

New Orleans makes its first appearance in a narrative strand told by Mr. Compson, who implicates the quadroons and their offspring, the octoroons, in the novel's subtext. He wonders at the incredibility of Henry's murdering Bon because of his involvement with the octoroon, describing "the existence of the eighth part negro mistress and the sixteenth part negro son, granted even the morganatic ceremony—a situation which was as much a part of the wealthy young New Orleanian's social and fashionable equipment as his dancing partners" (80). Thus, Compson immediately associates the city and the Creole society within which Bon has apparently been raised with the miscegenation reminiscent of the quadroon balls, his description of the "morganatic ceremony" suggesting that Bon's "marriage" to his mistress (which could not have occurred within the confines of the law) functioned as a plaçage arrangement. His description of Henry and Bon's imagined visit to New Orleans and the octoroon woman's house emphasizes the city's position as exotic and other, its social norms, and by extension its acceptance of race mixing, utterly foreign to those of Jefferson. Nearly everything about the experience is foreign to Henry, his "provincial soul" captivated and not a little disturbed by the "opulent, sensuous, sinful city," the rampart-like house to which Bon takes him, the French language, the Creole finery, and of course, Bon's mistress and light-skinned son (86-90). Henry at first reacts as the reader might expect of a young man of his upbringing—he calls the octoroon "a whore." Bon's response to this invokes the Creole gentlemen's attitude. "'Don't say that,'" he tells him. "'In fact, never refer to one of them by that name in New Orleans: otherwise you may be forced to purchase that privilege with some of your blood from probably a thousand men'" (91).

The complications of racial identity tolerated in Bon's New Orleans certainly are not equally tolerated in Henry's Mississippi. This point becomes quite clear in the contrast drawn by Compson's depiction of Bon's son, Charles Etienne, and his experiences at Sutpen's Hundred. The women of color in Chopin's work, as I indicated earlier, may be viewed as living a dual life between two worlds. However, considering the illicit sexual power with which they come to be associated as New Orleans "types," there is for them at least a liberatory impulse involved in the forging of their social identities. For Charles Etienne, however, transplanted to northern Mississippi, the prospect is far more grim. Charles is sent to live at Sutpen's Hundred after the octoroon's death, and as he grows into an adult and begins to understand the implications of his mixed-race ancestry, he comes to realize his subjugated social position. Rather than attempting to blend into the white culture of Jefferson (most of whose residents for years believe him to be white), Charles instead acts out with rage, leading to legal trouble and public "outing" as a person of mixed race.

A telling moment occurs when Mr. Compson describes the attempt of his own father, General Compson, to help Charles. Understanding that there is no place for the young man in Jefferson once his miscegenation is revealed, General Compson tells him, "'Whatever you are, once you are among strangers, people who don't know you, you can be whatever you will'" (165). The General gives him money and tells him to go away. He does not, it seems, suggest that Charles simply return to New Orleans, where there would have been a mixed culture into which he might have blended without concealing his racial origins. Rather, Mr. Compson seems to imply that his father, holding firm to provincial attitudes, intended for Charles to pass for either black or white, in either case concealing the truth and denying his racial identity. Charles's reaction to this advice is one of the most tragic and strangely poignant sections of the novel. Rather than accepting pre-defined racial notions and suppressing his own identity, he openly defies society's norms by marrying a full-blooded black woman, although doing so results in severe beatings at the hands of both whites and blacks unable to comprehend the relationship. In his choice, Charles is engaging in a practice that would have been at least marginally acceptable in New Orleans, but outside the almost mystically "other" culture in which he was born it is deemed repulsive. The description of his final return to Sutpen's Hundred is fitting, stressing, "returned (not home again; returned)" (166)—his home, as a man of mixed race, is New Orleans, not Yoknapatawpha County.

When Quentin Compson and his Harvard roommate, Shreve, seize control of the novel's narrative thrust, the story (now existing almost entirely of imaginative speculation) involves New Orleans far less, but issues of race consciousness and identity far more. Critic Ben Railton has described the transformation of Quentin into a "tormented old soul" at the novel's conclusion as motivated by "his understanding of the central role of miscegenation in Southern culture and of the guilt of the white South in denying its existence" (41). Quentin and Shreve are not only unable to deny the existence of miscegenation in Quentin's native region, but their narrative consciousness is, in fact, so consumed by it (no doubt, in part, because of the exotic and suggestive details in the stories Quentin has already heard from his father and Rosa Coldfield) that they begin, through their re-tellings, to take the slightest hints of possible race mixing and embrace them within the plot they are continually revising. Their final thesis is startling. They speculate that Henry Sutpen is ultimately willing to let Bon commit incest with his sister, but the one element that makes their marriage unacceptable is Bon's apparent mixed-race heritage.

One thing must here be duly noted and stressed—there is absolutely no direct evidence anywhere in the text that Bon's mother possessed African blood. There are, of course, any number of implications that what Sutpen found so "dishonorable" about Eulalia Bon's own heritage involved miscegenation, but many of those suggestions are generated by the various narrative speculations. Other explanations for Sutpen's abandonment of his apparent first wife might be possible, even if they don't seem likely to the novel's race-obsessed characters. Suspicions of adultery on the part of his wife, her family's reneging on financial agreements, or a mere streak of selfishness so evident in his character could have easily led someone like Sutpen to leave the West Indies, later allowing a romanticized version of his flight to be constructed around him. For Quentin and Shreve, however, the re-insertion of race into the story makes for an all-too-perfect explanation to the mystery of Sutpen and Bon. In their version, Henry's murder of Charles Bon is an attempt to preserve the racial status quo of the South and prevent miscegenation in the Sutpen family. However, in the end this is futile, as the last remaining Sutpen comes to be Jim Bond, mentally retarded, incomprehensible, and himself the product of miscegenation. As Shreve famously concludes, "'I think that in time the Jim Bonds are going to conquer the western hemisphere [...] and so in a few thousand years, I who regard you will also have sprung from the loins of African kings'" (302). Just as famous is the reaction of the now-shattered Quentin, who has grown up on stories of honor and purity in the Old South. It is not so much that he "hates" the South, as Shreve contends; rather, he no longer understands it in the face of such new, exotic complications.

Nineteenth-century New Orleans and its cultural associations regarding race are thus evident within—and fundamentally important to an understanding of—both these very different novels. Whether employing historical types to suggest a racially fused impulse toward female liberation, or using a subculture of miscegenation to re-read the history of the Old South, both Chopin and Faulkner invoke the city as exotic, progressive, mystical, and always transformative. Read together, *The Awakening* and *Absalom, Absalom!* provide intriguing and surprisingly compatible visions of race consciousness and identity construction in the nineteenth-century South. In *The Awakening*, these racial dynamics develop out of Chopin's attempt to realistically construct the contextual background of Edna's Creole society. In *Absalom, Absalom!*, they emerge out of what has been called, to invoke the title and spirit of W. Kenneth Holditch's essay on Faulkner in New Orleans, "the brooding air of the past," both in Faulkner's own attraction to the mystique of the city and in the narrative paranoia exhibited by his many characters (38). In both novels, conceptions of race play essential roles in characters' conflicted notions of self-identity within a social landscape they are constantly struggling to comprehend.

Works Cited

Ammons, Elizabeth. *Conflicting Stories*. New York: Oxford UP, 1991.

Birnbaum, Michelle A. "'Alien Hands': Kate Chopin and the Colonization of Race." *American Literature* 66.2 (1994): 301-23.

Blassingame, John W. *Black New Orleans: 1860-1880*. Chicago: U of Chicago P, 1973.

Chopin, Kate. *The Awakening*. 1899. Case Studies in Contemporary Criticism. Ed. Nancy A. Walker. Boston: Bedford/St. Martin's, 1993.

Dyer, Joyce. "Reading *The Awakening* with Toni Morrison." *Southern Literary Journal* 38.2 (2002): 138-54.

Faulkner, William. *Absalom, Absalom!*. 1936. New York: Vintage, 1990.
Holditch, W. Kenenth. "The Brooding Air of the Past: William Faulkner." In

Literary New Orleans: Essays and Meditations. ed. Richard S. Kennedy. Baton Rouge: Louisiana State UP, 1992. 38-50.

Railton, Ben. "'What Else Could a Southern Gentleman Do?': Quentin Compson, Rhett Butler, and Miscegenation." *Southern Literary Journal* 35.2 (2003): 41-63.

Rowe, Anne. "New Orleans as Metaphor: Kate Chopin." In *Literary New Orleans: Essays and Meditations*, ed. Kennedy. 29-37.

Saxon, Lyle. *Fabulous New Orleans*. 1928. Gretna, LA: Pelican, 1988.

Romances of the White Woman's Burden: Chopin's *At Fault*, Faulkner's *Light in August*, and the Legacies of U.S. Plantation Fiction

Since its earliest appearances in U.S. narrative fiction and nonfiction, the plantation has been depicted as a place of escape. In John Pendleton Kennedy's *Swallow Barn* (1832), the first U.S. novel to make plantation life its primary subject matter, it is portrayed as a place to escape *to*—a space for sojourning, one to which the novel's Yankee protagonist "steal[s] off quietly" in order to experience "the conviviality of country life" and "careless indolence" of the South's master class.[1] In the abolitionist literature that came into being soon afterward, the plantation is depicted as a space to escape *from*. "I was ever on the look-out for means of escape," writes Frederick Douglass in his 1845 *Narrative*.[2] His vigilance would soon be repeated in the figure of Cassy in Harriet Beecher Stowe's *Uncle Tom's Cabin* (1852): "Cassy had often revolved, for hours, all possible or probable means of escape. . . ."[3] Much twentieth-century criticism on plantation fiction and film discusses them as forms of popular-culture "escapism"—as texts into which audiences retreat in order to experience simpler worlds in which divisions of race, class, gender, and sexuality prove more salient. More recently, critics have taken such texts rather more seriously and explored how difficult it has been to move beyond the ways of thinking generated on the antebellum plantation and later popularized in U.S. mass culture. In their recent brilliant studies of the legacies of the plantation in contemporary culture, Jessica Adams and Elizabeth Christine Russ both identify escapability as a reason to continue studying works set on plantations. In Adams's view, "[T]he plantation, echoing with . . . historical revisions and haunted by them as by the dead, would come to exert a force difficult to escape" in U.S. culture despite the official death of slavery in 1865.[4] In Russ's analysis, there is reason to be hopeful that the haunting may one day end: "By looking at other factors, we not only guard against the danger of reasserting old hierarchies, but we allow ourselves to recognize that, however horrific, the plantation's reach is limited and we might one day escape from its grasp."[5]

The present essay examines writers who inclined toward Russ's optimism but who may in spite of themselves have substantiated Adams's claim that the plantation proves "difficult to escape." Its focus is on Kate

Chopin and William Faulkner, writers in whose works plantations figure often, sometimes prominently, other times peripherally. Its argument is that both writers inherit from postbellum plantation fiction a discourse of white paternalism that proves difficult to leave behind. Or to be more accurate, they inherit a discourse whose construction of race proves more enduring—indeed more dependable—than its construction of gender. Both write novels—Chopin's *At Fault* (1890) and Faulkner's *Light in August* (1932)—in which men have been displaced and women thrust into positions of authority in plantation societies before the action of either text even begins. Yet if men are thereby shown to be more incidental to plantation paternalism than southern tradition might have held, the form of whiteness the southern planter had come to symbolize by the late nineteenth century—a form expressed by the phrase "the white man's burden," whose genealogy I trace below—only proves more persistent. By attending to both writers' relationships to a discourse of burdened white manhood, we gain a different sense of Southern literary history and come to recognize how connected Chopin and Faulkner are to a cultural tradition they have long been thought of as breaking away from.

We glimpse the desire to leave behind a plantation tradition in Chopin's *The Awakening* (1899). In the first of the two dinner-party scenes that serve as turning points in the late chapters of the novel, Chopin surrounds Edna Pontellier with the three men most unnerved by her recent turns toward independent thought and action. These are her husband, Léonce, who complains in a previous chapter that his wife's "whole attitude— toward me and everybody and everything—has changed"; her doctor, Mandelet, whom Léonce has invited over to perform a covert diagnosis of Edna's new behavior; and her father, the Kentucky colonel, who reacts to his daughter's changed demeanor with less sensitivity, urging Léonce after the party to "[p]ut your foot down good and hard; the only way to manage a wife." The party itself goes surprisingly well, however, the result no doubt of everyone's drinking heavily. Late in the evening, and after what seems to be a fair indulgence all the way around in the colonel's toddies and the Pontellier's store of wine and champagne, the diners warm to each other and begin sharing stories. Léonce goes first. Growing "reminiscent," he recounts "some amusing plantation experiences, recollections of old Iberville and his youth, when he hunted 'possum in company with some friendly darky; thrashed the pecan trees, shot the grosbec, and roamed the woods and fields in mischievous idleness." Léonce is followed by the Colonel, who draws for his story from his experiences in the Civil War, "those dark and bitter days, in which he had acted a conspicuous part. . . ." He in turn is followed by Dr. Mandelet, who, unlike his predecessors, avoids autobiography in order to tell a cautionary tale of "a woman's love, seeking strange, new channels, only to return to its legitimate source. . . ." They are all superseded by Edna, who drifts even further from personal experience (though toward, as it turns out, prophecy) in order relate a story of "pure invention" in which "a woman . . . paddle[s] away with her lover one night in a pirogue and never c[omes] back. They were lost amid the Baratarian Islands. . . ."[6]

As is the case with most of the vignettes that compose *The Awakening*, there is much to be made of this tiny scene and the artful way in which Chopin has arranged it. The fact that Edna is outnumbered three to one gives some sense of how gender and power intersect at this stage in the novel.[7] The fact that Edna goes last, however, and gains in effect the final word in the scene, suggests that patriarchal power has its limits, even in bourgeois society in the southern city of New Orleans during the early 1890s. The sequence of speakers—from husband to father to doctor to Edna, or, alternatively, from man of business to man of war to man of science to Edna—replicates how Edna is introduced in relation to male authority figures at different stages in the novel. She is "wife" in the opening scene and throughout most of the early chapters. She becomes "daughter" in a middle chapter once her father arrives for the visit capped by the dinner party. She becomes "patient" in the penultimate chapter when Mandelet intervenes and urges her to seek his professional counsel, ostensibly to save her from herself. Yet she only really becomes "herself" in the novel's final chapter, "for the first time . . . naked in the open air . . . like some new-born creature, opening its eyes in a familiar world that it had never known" (301).

For the sake of this essay, though, it is a different reading of the first dinner-party scene and its dessert course of metanarrative that I wish to offer. My concern here is with Chopin's and Faulkner's relationships with the form of Southern fiction, the plantation romance, that proved most popular during both writers' careers. In keeping with my consideration thus far of how acts of storytelling can convey a subtle politics of positionality, I am interested specifically in a story critics have often told in order to locate Chopin and Faulkner in relation to their better-selling Southern literary predecessors and contemporaries. It is a story in which both writers are celebrated for their refusals to produce the sort of Southern fiction that might have won them more readers, namely the plantation fiction that had already gained a national following by 1890, the year Chopin published her first book, and that remained popular until at least 1962, the year Faulkner published his last. Whatever form this story takes—

whether Chopin is being named among the Southern realists "who consciously broke from the plantation-romance tradition," as she is in *The Companion to Southern Literature* (2001), or whether Faulkner is being likened to Frederick Douglass and Harriet Jacobs, "similarly react[ing] against the plantation myth by revealing the rapacious cruelty beneath its pleasant veneer," as he is in *A William Faulkner Encyclopedia* (1999)—it is a story that takes as its central metaphor the idea of *distance*.[8] Rather than writing within a plantation tradition, the story goes, Chopin and Faulkner wrote deliberately to revise it, critique it, subvert it, even transcend it—all forms of expression that place the two writers outside of Southern literary tradition by locating them in the above and beyond of great literary artistry and avant-gardism.

It is a way of thinking about their works that both writers encouraged, moreover—Faulkner, for example, when he claimed publicly not to have possessed the patience necessary to read *Gone with the Wind*, and Chopin (perhaps) when she intimates in *The Awakening* that Edna's story is the furthest thing possible from a plantation romance.[9] To reread the first dinner party with these considerations in mind is to recognize that Edna's story (which of course resembles *The Awakening* itself, watery ending and all) and Léonce's (which sounds like nothing so much as a plantation romance) come at opposite ends of the storytelling sequence. The gap that separates them—the fact that Léonce's story is long since over by the time Edna's begins—may symbolize how far apart husband and wife have grown by this stage of the novel. The gap in any event seems greater because of the differences in the kind of story each tells. Edna's is after all both innovative ("It was a pure invention") and apparently original ("She said that Madame Antoine had related it to her. That, also, was an invention") (183). Léonce's by contrast could not have been more derivative: his "amusing plantation experiences" involving "hunt[ing] 'possum" alongside "some friendly darky" could have been recollected from a newspaper or magazine story he had read earlier in the day just as easily as they may have come from "old Iberville and his youth."[10] The implication is thus that Edna has outdistanced Léonce and the other patriarchs of Southern society even in her relation to storytelling.[11] She outpaces them in her ability to "purely invent" stories whose settings may be localized ("amid the Baratarian Islands" off Louisiana's coast, for example) yet whose meanings prove much larger and more remote. And to the extent that, at least in this scene, Edna serves as a stand-in for Chopin herself, *The Awakening* may even be asking its readers to see it as an anti-plantation romance—as a novel that manages to escape the pull toward nostalgia characteristic of much Southern fiction of the turn of the century, hence a novel that leaves such spaces as "old Iberville" and the forms of patriarchal power they represent in a distant past.[12]

Does it? Does Chopin manage to move as far beyond the traditions of Southern fiction as the first dinner-party scene might suggest and as her critics have certainly long contended? Does Faulkner? The questions are worth pursuing since the study of both figures has so often depended on images of them as revolutionaries—as writers who wrote with a deep cognizance of the South's contentious past but were by no means bound by its literary history. Indeed Chopin sometimes appears as a pivotal figure in constructions of Southern literary history, her best works seeming in retrospect to have anticipated Faulkner's and her revisionary ambitions to have opened a breach in the edifice of Southern Letters through which the Bard of Oxford could later stride.[13] Yet whether either writer may be seen as transcending a tradition centered around a romantic image of the plantation depends on what else the tradition involves—whether it consists merely of happy clichés, the likes of which Léonce trots out in his tales of "old Iberville," or whether it involves something more. By the time Chopin published *The Awakening*, U.S. cultural discourse about the plantation centered around the idea of a "white man's burden," a concept that enabled the plantation South to be reinterpreted as uniquely *modern*. Taking multiraciality as a sign of modernity and imagining that the management of non-white races would prove the central challenge of the twentieth century, multiple writers advanced the idea that the plantation South had arrived at the modern era decades in advance of everyone else. They imagined Southern whiteness as a kind of national resource, even, and produced books, plays, and eventually films in which the plantation South's resurgence after Reconstruction was said to symbolize the rebirth of a nation. Most of these texts focused on men. A few, though, centered on women and wondered in effect what would happen if a woman were forced to take up the white man's burden and manage a plantation in the absence of a husband or father. (One of these—a novel in which a woman named Scarlett assumes control of a Georgia plantation after her father's death—would of course go on to become the bestselling work of U.S. fiction of the twentieth century.)

My focus here is on two women-centered novels, Chopin's *At Fault* and Faulkner's *Light in August* (1932), in which a plantation tradition conceptualized in terms of nationalist ideology registers powerfully. Published more than forty years apart, the two novels nevertheless have interesting things in common. Above all, they feature white women who inherit a sense of racial responsibility associated during their lifetimes with white men of the South's planter class. In the case of *At Fault*, she inherits an actual working plantation along with it. In *Light in August* she possesses merely the remains of an old plantation, though her overwhelming sense of duty toward former slaves and their descendents makes her an expression almost *ad absurdum* of the white man's burden as it had been envisioned in plantation fiction. Both women find the burden difficult to bear. More interesting is that both Chopin and Faulkner seem to have seen in it ways of moving beyond the South's patriarchal, plantation-centered past. What *At Fault* and *Light in August* reveal, however, is that any form of Southern whiteness conceptualized as a legacy will prove far more limiting than it ever will liberating, hence that the plantation romance may prove persistent even in stories that, like the one Edna tells in *The Awakening*, seem intended to break away from it.

To understand better what Chopin and Faulkner were reacting against requires that more be said about the plantation tradition as it developed during the late nineteenth century, the period during which Chopin wrote and at the end of which Faulkner was born. Popular during the antebellum era, plantation fiction of a sort existed prior to the publication of Kennedy's *Swallow Barn* in 1832.[14] It was Kennedy's novel, however, that marked "the first appearance of the plantation solely for its own picturesque qualities," as Francis Pendleton Gaines, the first literary historian to study plantation fiction, observed in 1924.[15] A lengthy work, *Swallow Barn* was nevertheless meticulous in its attention to physical detail and social custom. It needed to be, given the fact that the plantation was not overly familiar to U.S. readers as a literary locale. Yet while it sought to familiarize readers with the place (introducing them, according to Gaines, to details as peculiar as the "iced toddy," the likes of which Edna's father is still making decades later in *The Awakening*), the novel's primary purpose was to illustrate the plantation's *particularity*. Its cast of characters and settings ranging from the plantation's great hall to its corn and cotton fields to its humble slave quarters, all of which were destined to become clichés, were in *Swallow Barn* relatively novel elements intended to exhibit "the Old Dominion['s] . . . once peculiar, and . . . insulated cast of manners . . . [its] original distinctive habits and modes of life," as Kennedy records in a prefatory note appended to a later edition of the novel. Aiming absolutely to secure the plantation a place within a U.S. national imaginary, Kennedy's purpose was not to identify the plantation South as synonymous with "America." Indeed in the later preface he uses the term "nationalisms" in the plural to describe what he had hoped had been preserved in his novel: "The fruitfulness of modern invention in the arts of life, the general fusion of thought through the medium of an extra-territorial literature . . . all these, aided and diffused by our extraordinary facilities of travel and circulation, have made sad work, even in the present generation, with those old *nationalisms* that were so agreeable to the contemplation of an admirer of the picturesque in character and manners."[16]

A belief that the plantation South was unrepresentative of "America" persisted in U.S. fiction throughout the antebellum period and into the early years of Reconstruction. This is not to say that plantation fiction sought to be "unAmerican," a term Judith Fetterley has used to describe postbellum regionalist fiction that mounts a critique of U.S. nationalism by locating in the nation's rural districts alternate and often oppositional forms of political and social affiliation.[17] Rather, it is to suggest that plantation-fiction writers, including even those who wrote in hostile response to Harriet Beecher Stowe's *Uncle Tom's Cabin* (1852), sought up until secession to imagine an "America" that included their region as part of a decentralized national imaginary. The idea is intimated in an 1842 remark made by William Gilmore Simms, the leading Southern novelist of the antebellum period, when he called himself "an ultra-American, a born Southron, and a resolute loco-foco."[18] The goal was to imagine American-ness and Southern-ness (or "Southron-ness," as Simms might have termed it) as compatible with but not identical to one another.

Once questions over slavery and Southern independence were settled by the Civil War, however, a new kind of plantation fiction emerged. It almost immediately conceded that the South was better off with slavery eliminated but still sought to romanticize and indeed to preserve the old plantation as a set of *relations*, a social order whose racial hierarchies were said to be better for everyone since they promoted happiness and harmony and since, in any event, they were natural. In such writings Southern planters were remembered reverently for having confronted "the race problem" decades before anyone else—before the terms "race problem" or "negro problem" would become widely used, even. Thus, in an 1877 essay titled "The Old Plantation" Joel Chandler Harris, soon to become the leading plantation-fiction writer of the postbellum generation, celebrated the plantation South for having developed men of the character necessary to solve great problems:

> The scourge that swept slavery into the deep sea of the past gave the deathblow to one of the peculiar outgrowths of that institution. The results that made slavery impossible blotted from the Southern social system the patriarchal—we had almost written

feudal—establishment known as the old plantation. Nourished into life by slavery, it soon became one of the features of Southern civilization—a peculiar feature, indeed, and one which for many years exerted a powerful influence throughout the world. The genius of such men as Washington, Jefferson, Patrick Henry, Taney, Marshall, Calhoun, Stephens, Toombs, and all the greatest leaders of political thought and opinion from the days of the Revolution to the beginning of the Civil War, was the result and outgrowth of the civilization made possible by the old plantation. It was a cherished feature of Southern society, and it is not to be doubted that its demolition has been more deeply deplored by our people than all the other results of the war put together. The brave men and noble women who at the end found themselves confronting the dire confusion and desolation of an unsuccessful struggle have been compelled to set their faces toward the new future that is always ahead of the hopeful and truehearted; but how many times have they turned and sighed, endeavoring to get a glimpse of the ruins of the old plantation! Now that the problem of slavery, which even before the desperate cast of the die in 1861 had begun to perplex the more thoughtful of the Southern people, is successfully (but O how cruelly!) solved, even the bare suggestion of its reestablishment is unsavory; but the memory of the old plantation will remain green and gracious forever.[19]

The passage suggests the lineaments of a new way of viewing the old plantation. Locating the institution in a sealed-off past—an "almost . . . feudal" realm that, now that it lies in "ruins," may seem "green and gracious forever"—the passage nevertheless emphasizes how much the plantation meant "throughout the world" during its antebellum heyday as well as how much it continues to mean in a postbellum present. It produced the nation's founding fathers, Harris argues—a statement that by the turn of the century would have become a trope in writings about the plantation.[20] Yet even its less famous citizens were still involved in contemplating a problem, "the problem of slavery," that seems both "solved" and unsolved ("O how cruelly!") in the way Harris discusses it. The result is a portrait of the old plantation not quite accounted for by the term "nostalgia," for the passage both mourns the institution's passing and discovers its continued relevance. So long as "America" continues to live up to the promise of its founding, Harris intimates, the old plantation will in a sense endure.

This attitude becomes clearer in an essay Harris wrote a few years later focused on postbellum rather than antebellum Southern race relations.

What he had earlier regarded as a problem merely "cruelly" resolved he now confronted as a source of new tensions. Specifically, he worried that the South's former slaves had been granted rights as citizens they themselves were unprepared to exercise and their white counterparts to accept. Solutions to the problem were nevertheless being generated locally, he argued, and by the descendents of the founding fathers mentioned in the passage above: "[T]he duty of looking after the irresponsible blacks, was not only in the nature of unceasing drudgery, but involved the upbuilding and upholding of a patriarchal institution out of which grew new and grave responsibilities."[21] Harris's argument, which was espoused by many others, was that Reconstruction had failed primarily because it had offered black Southerners too much too soon. By unintended consequence, however, Reconstruction's failure had given white Southern men the opportunity to redeem themselves and prove once again their value to the nation. By "upbuilding . . . patriarchal institution[s]" from the "ruins" of the old plantation system, they could prove that their plantation upbringings had better equipped them to deal with the "looking after" of less developed races. They could reinvent the old plantation as a form of local knowledge—of racialized managerial expertise, even—whose "powerful influence," to quote again from the earlier essay, might once more be "exerted . . . throughout the world."

Thus, as the early post-Reconstruction period gave way to a new era characterized by economic and military expansion (which is to say, of U.S. global self-"exertion") as well as by increased immigration into the United States (which seemed to many the sudden relocation of "the world" to American shores), the plantation came to seem to many a model society, the planter a person uniquely capable of handling the challenges of a multiracial modernity. By the late 1880s, works of plantation fiction and nonfiction were staging this argument repeatedly, and by the turn of the century it was providing a narrative arc to lengthy novels. Thomas Nelson Page's *Red Rock* (1898), for example, follows the careers of several young men as they grow into the roles pioneered for them by their planter ancestors. Growing up hearing stories of their Indian-fighting and Revolutionary War-waging forefathers, they come to see in the opposition to Reconstruction their opportunity to continue a tradition of nation-building they conceptualize as virtually in their blood. Thomas Dixon, Jr.'s *The Leopard's Spots* (1902) tells a similar story on an even broader scale, opening "[o]n the field of Appomattox," proceeding from there to what it terms "the reign of terror" of Reconstruction, alluding in a late chapter to the Spanish-American War as proof that the South had risen once again to lead the nation, and ending at the turn of the century with the election of a white supremacist state government in North Carolina. Along the way it celebrates the rise of the Ku Klux Klan as proof that white Southern manhood was unconquerable—all of this in order to offer what its subtitle promises, *A Romance of the White Man's Burden, 1865-1900.*

That phrase—"the white man's burden"—was invented three years earlier by Rudyard Kipling in a poem addressing white Americans busy celebrating their successes in the war against Spain. Kipling's message to them was to continue forward with the civilizing mission of empire once the gleam of war had faded. By the time Dixon had appropriated it for the subtitle of *The Leopard's Spots*, however, numerous other white Southerners had claimed that bearing "the white man's burden" was something they and their ancestors had been doing for more than a century. Harris's reference in 1883 to the "grave responsibilities" involved in managing "irresponsible blacks" shows that white Southern men were thinking in terms similar to Kipling's well before he published "The White Man's Burden." For proof that the phrase crystallized a world-view, one need look no further than the proceedings from a conference held in Montgomery, Alabama, in 1900, mere months after the appearance of Kipling's poem, by the newly created Southern Society for the Promotion of the Study of Race Conditions and Problems in the South. Three separate speakers invoked Kipling's phrase in order to explain present conditions in the South. One called "the education and training of the Negro . . . 'the white man's burden' here, as it is elsewhere throughout the world." Another asserted that the race problem now provided the white South its sense of identity: "the war, with all its losses had so far solved nothing, and the white man's burden was still upon them and upon them alone." A third used the phrase to incite fears of "negro" rapists: "We speak of the white man's burden. It is but another name for the white man's duty. Nowhere does the burden of duty devolve so heavily or in so complicated and painful a form as it does here. . . . To the honor of the South it may be said, and men appreciate it everywhere, 'that the one great difficulty in dealing with the Negro question is the crime against women.'" Such formulations emphasized on the one hand the white South's uniqueness—the belief that the burden of civilizing ex-slaves fell "upon them and them alone," that "[n]owhere does the burden of duty devolve so heavily . . . as it does here." Yet on the other hand they insisted on the South's *universality*—the belief that the South's race problem was akin those "elsewhere in the world today" and that the sense of duty felt by white men toward their women was something "men can appreciate . . . everywhere."[22]

These claims parallel the sorts of assertions that had been made in such texts as Harris's "The Old Plantation" since the end of Reconstruction, namely that the plantation South was (paradoxically enough) a uniquely representative society. Its local color made possible claims about its universal significance. More to the point, it became routinely invoked as a symbol of a modernizing "America." If, from a white supremacist's perspective, the problem of the twentieth century promised to be not simply "the color line," as W.E.B. Du Bois would argue in 1903, but more specifically the challenge of *managing* across color lines and living up to the sense of racial duty outlined in the passages cited above, then the plantation South could be seen as a virtual nation-in-miniature, a space even in advance of the rest of the country in its having taken up the white man's burden.

Chopin's *At Fault* was published in 1890, almost a decade before Kipling's phrase could find its way into writings about the South but not before the plantation was being revived as a space whose history of race relations might have much to teach the world. Here is how Chopin introduces her protagonist, a thirty-year-old widow named Thérèse Lafirme, on the opening page of the novel. Upon the recent death of her husband, Thérèse became the sole inheritor of his Louisiana plantation and, with it, the responsibility of managing its labor force:

> For days she lived alone with her grief; shutting out the appeals that came to her from the demoralized 'hands,' and unmindful of the disorder that gathered about her. Till Uncle Hiram came one day with a respectful tender of sympathy, offered in the guise of a reckless misquoting of Scripture—and with a grievance.
> 'Mistuss,' he said, 'I 'lowed 'twar best to come to de house an' tell you; fur Massa he alluz did say 'Hi'urm, I counts on you to keep a eye open endurin' my appersunce;' you ricollic, marm?' addressing an expanse of black bordered cambric that veiled the features of his mistress. 'Things is a goin' wrong; dat dey is. I don't wants to name no names 'doubt I'se 'bleeged to; but dey done start a kiarrin' de cotton seed off de place, and dats how.'
> If Hiram's information had confined itself to the bare statement of things 'goin' wrong,' such intimation, of its nature vague and susceptible of uncertain interpretation, might have failed to rouse Thérèse from her lethargy of grief. But that wrong doing presented as a tangible abuse and defiance of authority, served to

move her to action. She felt at once the weight and sacredness of a trust, whose acceptance brought consolation and awakened unsuspected powers of doing.[23]

Readers who now know Chopin primarily through *The Awakening* might be surprised to see that the first character who speaks in *At Fault* is an ex-slave "Uncle" in the tradition of Stowe's Uncle Tom or Harris's Uncle Remus. That he speaks in dialect and that his first words come at the expense of his fellow ex-slaves and convey his loyalty to his mistress make the opening paragraphs of Chopin's first novel all the more unexpected. Yet her original readers may have been far less surprised by what they were encountering.[24] For one thing, soon after *At Fault* appeared, Chopin began to be successful at placing stories of Louisiana local color in newspapers and national magazines, some of these later to be collected and published in *Bayou Folk* (1893), her most popular publication during her lifetime. For another, she published *At Fault* at a time that Harris's Uncle Remus books (three of which were published during the 1880s) remained popular and Thomas Nelson Page's *In Ole Virginia* (1887) had shown only three years earlier that plantation fiction did not require Remus-like folktales to win large audiences. Page's ex-slave storytellers speak more straightforwardly than does Uncle Remus and make more frequent professions of their devotions to "ole marster" and "ole missis."[25]

Chopin's original readers may thus have "ricollicted" Page's and Harris's dialect writings when they opened *At Fault* and felt themselves immediately at home. They may have further recognized the novel's early central conflict—whether the old plantation can be perpetuated once its old master has died—as a problem around which Page was constructing short stories already. They may even have sensed what was fresh about Chopin's novel, namely that it was placing the old master's *wife* rather than his sons at the center of this conflict, making gender rather than generation the force that creates suspense in the text. Their responses may thus have been similar to those of Thérèse's neighbors, whom Chopin discusses in the novel's opening paragraph: "It was a matter of unusual interest to them that a plantation of four thousand acres had been left unincumbered to the disposal of a handsome, inconsolable, childless Creole widow of thirty. A *bêtise* of some sort might safely be looked for. But time passing, the anticipated folly failed to reveal itself; and the only wonder was that Thérèse Lafirme so successfully followed the methods of her departed husband" (5).

At Fault is thus from its outset a novel about inheritance. Unlike *The Awakening*, which proves most compelling when Edna aspires toward

"pure invention" and refuses to uphold tradition, *At Fault* involves its protagonist in a struggle to preserve what already exists. Thérèse's challenge
is to work *within* a social structure, not to move beyond it or overturn it;
and if her actions are in a sense rebellious, even "feminist" (her neighbors
after all expect her to act conventionally and either remarry or return
to her family), her rebellion takes place within the well-defined limits
of plantation power. She "successfully follow[s]" her late husband. She
soon proves herself as capable as any man (and more capable than her
nephews, who have lost their homestead due to mismanagement) at
making the kind of business decision that will allow the plantation to
remain in operation. When given the opportunity to convert a portion of
Place-du-Bois's wooded acreage to timberland, she does so; and though
her "beloved woods" are diminished as a result, she herself profits while
her plantation is preserved. Thérèse thus resembles the sort of young man
of the "New South" being celebrated by the late 1880s for his having
inherited from his planter forefathers not only a sense of grace but also
sound business instincts. She keeps the old plantation going not simply as a memory—a place worthy of celebration in story or song—but
rather as a functional economic institution. It can be adapted to changing
times and still remain Place-du-Bois, "place of the woods": a space that
sacrifices some of its trees in order to preserve a sense of space and set of
social arrangements that the unsentimental Thérèse professes nevertheless
to "belove."

What thus proves most remarkable about *At Fault*'s vision of the
plantation is what seems *unchanging*, namely the racialized power structure into which Thérèse steps when, only days after her husband's death,
she learns that her "disorder[ly]" black laborers are making off with the
cotton seed. Those laborers are barely permitted a voice within the novel.
Only Uncle Hiram and a few other ex-slaves similarly devoted to their
mistress are allowed to speak. When they do, it is usually to say the sort
of thing Uncle Hiram does on *At Fault*'s opening page: "'Massa he alluz
did say "Hi'urm, I counts on you to keep a eye open endurin' my apper-
sunce;" you ricollic, marm?'" Hiram is an agent of remembrance and, of
greater significance, a vehicle through which the old "massa" continues to
speak. Like the former slaves who populate Thomas Nelson Page's short
fiction, he is more resistant to change than the plantation's white owners
and operators. The words he speaks at the outset of *At Fault* ensure that,
if any changes are to take place at Place-Du-Bois, they will do so at its
mistress's behest, not because its black underclass manages any form of
initiative.

Thérèse of course responds to Hiram's invitation to take charge. She does so with an immediacy worth noting: "If Hiram's information had confined itself to the bare statement of things 'goin' wrong,' such intimation . . . might have failed to rouse Thérèse. . . . But that wrong doing presented as a tangible abuse and defiance of authority, served to move her to action. She felt at once the weight and sacredness of a trust, whose acceptance brought consolation and *awakened* unsuspected powers of doing." Almost a decade before *The Awakening*, then, Chopin wrote a novel in which a woman wakes up to feelings of power and a sense of command—sensations not unlike those Edna Pontellier experiences when she learns how to swim ("intoxicated with her newly conquered power, she swam out alone") and later asserts control over her body socially (when she refuses to wait at home for her Tuesday visitors, for example) and sexually (when she takes Alcée Arobin as a lover). What Thérèse awakens to, however, is much more explicitly a sense of racial prerogative. She is in fact moved to action because she senses that some form of "authority" latent in her has been "defi[ed]" and "abuse[d]." It might be allowed that this sense of authority is fundamentally proprietary: Thérèse now owns the plantation and all of the material goods on it, down to its cotton seeds. She is therefore reacting to having her rights as owner "abuse[d]"—in short, she is responding to what it feels like to be stolen from. Yet the language Chopin uses to characterize Thérèse's "awakening" suggests that something more is being violated than mere property rights, for what arouses in her "unsuspected powers of doing" and provides her a sense of "consolation" are feelings of *responsibility*, "the weight and sacredness of a trust. . . ." *At Fault* thus begins not only with a story of a woman's taking over a plantation but also with an image of her taking up the white man's burden. The consolation she experiences is analogous to the sense of resolution one encounters in stories by Page when a planter's son, his father dead and homeland devastated by the war, nevertheless gains a sense of purpose much larger than himself when he assumes control over the plantation and restores to its black labor force a proper sense of place. "[H]e was filled with a profound feeling which, perhaps, he himself could not have named": so muses the young male protagonist of Page's *Red Rock* the day after he returns from the battlefront to the plantation he now suddenly commands. "As he hobbled out to the front portico and gazed around on the wide fields spread out below him . . . he renewed his resolve to follow in his father's footsteps. He would keep the place at all sacrifices."[26] Thérèse's moment of renewal comes much later in postbellum history, and the events that precede it—the loss of a husband rather than father and the devolution of a plantation to her control by marital rather than filial right—are different. Yet both Thérèse Lafirme and the young white men who inherit plantations in *Red Rock* face "negro" problems immediately upon assuming control. The "weight and sacredness of trust" she feels replicates the "profound feeling[s]" Page describes in *Red Rock*. *At Fault* may even be said to borrow as heavily from plantation fiction as *The Awakening* strives later to repel it.

A plantation tradition manifests itself in other ways in Chopin's novel. When the novel seeks to convey how much Thérèse adores Place-du-Bois' beauty in its opening chapter, it includes a description of "negro quarters . . . scattered at wide intervals over the land, breaking with picturesque irregularity into the systematic division of field from field. . . . Thérèse loved to walk the length of the wide verandas, armed with her field-glass, and to view her surrounding possessions with comfortable satisfaction." Nothing in the novel ironizes the sense of pleasure-in-possession Thérèse feels as she contemplates what were once slave quarters via an aesthetics of the picturesque, transforming them into simply part of a landscape ("her gaze swept from cabin to cabin; from patch to patch; up to the pine-capped hills . . ."). Nor is there any irony a few chapters later when another character describes Thérèse in the midst of one of these surveys of her property and imagines her a sovereign: "Mrs. Lafirme is exceptional. Really, when she stands at the end of the veranda, giving orders to those darkies, her face a little flushed, she's positively a queen" (29). Thérèse possesses a mammy, who proves over the course of much of the novel the one person whom she can speak to more openly, less regally. While the relationship humanizes Thérèse, it also replicates a convention of plantation fiction, for like Uncle Hiram, Thérèse's *Grosse tante* ("or more properly, Marie Louise . . . Thérèse's nurse and attendant from infancy"; "a negress—coal black and so enormously fat that she moved about with evident difficulty") remains fixed in the past more firmly than her mistress. She refuses to move from the cabin in which she has lived for years even though it sits perilously close to an eroding river bank. She seems willing only to leave it when Thérèse falls sick and she arrives to nurse her, hence to repeat scenes from a past in which she was a slave and Thérèse literally her young mistress. Above all, she echoes Uncle Hiram in urging Thérèse to maintain the discipline of the old plantation. "'Make those niggers work more,' she tells Thérèse at one point. "You spoil them. I tell you if it was old mistress that had to deal with them, they would see something different" (90).

Such scenes compose the background in *At Fault*. The novel's central conflict is considerably more complex, even ahead of its time, for it concerns whether Thérèse can overcome her objections to divorce and allow herself to fall in love with and marry a divorcé named David Hosmer. A good match for her—he successfully manages the timber operation that allows her to preserve Place-du-Bois—he has nevertheless divorced his first wife because of her alcoholism. Her feelings toward him not withstanding, Thérèse insists that Hosmer remarry the woman, Fanny, and bring her to Place-du-Bois where Thérèse herself may supervise efforts to reform her. They fail. Fanny keeps drinking and the remarriage proves dreadful for everyone until, rather conveniently for the novel's two true lovers, Fanny drowns in a flood. The novel ends soon after Thérèse and Hosmer finally marry and Thérèse recognizes that she had been "at fault in following what had seemed the only right," which is to say, in her adherence to so rigid a sense of duty that she would deny certain realities—Fanny's alcoholism, Hosmer's lack of love toward the woman, Hosmer's deep love for her and hers for him, and so forth. As do other novels of the period, *At Fault* enacts the turn away from a romantic idealism and toward a realism that by the end of the 1890s would make possible such novels as *The Awakening*.

The turn toward realism that characterizes *At Fault*'s central story, however, makes all the more noteworthy the preservation of a romantic image of the plantation in the novel's background. Thérèse grows to recognize the limits of her ability to reform Fanny. She grows even to comprehend Fanny not as a "project" or "responsibility" but rather as a being who makes choices for herself, bad though they may be. She does not, however, grow to recognize in the "negroes" of Place-Du-Bois beings who do not necessarily require her supervision in order to subsist, nor does the novel ever intimate that she is "at fault" in thus failing to mature. Indeed in one of its final chapters Thérèse returns home after a short stay in New Orleans only to discover that "[t]hings had not gone well at Place-du-Bois during her absence, the impecunious old kinsman whom she had left in charge, having a decided preference for hunting the *Gros-Bec* and catching trout in the lake to supervising the methods of a troublesome body of blacks" (163). The mention of the grosbec, the same bird about which Léonce Pontellier will later wax nostalgic in the story he tells in *The Awakening*, suggests a link with a plantation romance tradition. The idea that any "body of blacks" will prove "troublesome" without proper "supervision" establishes it even more strongly. The link is solidified, however, by a passage that comes just before this one. On her way home from New Orleans, Thérèse recollects her plantation in a language that, if one were to substitute "Tara" for "Place-du-Bois" and "Rhett Butler" for "David Hosmer"—would fit comfortably in *Gone with the Wind*:

There was a full day's journey before her. She would not reach Place-du-Bois before dark, but she did not shrink from those hours that were to be passed alone. She rather welcomed the quiet of them after a visit to New Orleans full of pleasant disturbances. She was eager to be home again. She loved Place-du-Bois with a love that was real; that had grown deep since it was the one place in the world which she could connect with the presence of David Hosmer. She had often wondered—indeed was wondering now—if the memory of those happenings to which he belonged would ever grow strange and far away to her. It was a trick of memory with which she indulged herself on occasion, this one of retrospection. Beginning with that June day when she had sat in the hall and watched the course of a white sunshade over the tops of the bending corn. (162)

At Fault thus begins with a romantic image of the plantation in chapter one and, despite all of the changes that take place in the intervening chapters, offers essentially the same view in a late chapter. Place-du-Bois turns out to be for Thérèse a space very much like what Tara proves to be for Scarlett O'Hara on the final pages of *Gone with the Wind*: "a breathing space. . . . She thought of Tara and it was as if a gentle cool hand were stealing over her heart."[27] In fact *At Fault* offers its most startlingly traditional image of the plantation on its own final page. Finally married, Thérèse and Hosmer meet at the end of the novel on "the veranda, where the fading Western light came over their shoulders" (168). This is the same veranda from which a "queen[ly]" Thérèse "giv[es] orders to those darkies, her face a little flushed" during the day. On the final night of *At Fault*, however, Thérèse is much more the blushing Southern bride:

> 'Now, David, you are trying to mystify me. I believe there's a streak of perversity in you after all.'
> 'Of course there is; and here comes Mandy to say that "suppa's gittin' cole."'
> 'Aunt B'lindy 'low suppa on de table gittin' cole,' said Mandy, retreating at once from the fire of their merriment.
> Thérèse arose and held her two hands out to her husband.
> He took them but did not rise; only leaned further back on the scat and looked up at her.
> 'Oh, supper's a bore; don't you think so?' he asked.
> 'No, I don't,' she replied. 'I'm hungry, and so are you. Come, David.'

'But look, Thérèse, just when the moon has climbed over the top of that live-oak? We can't go now. . . .'

'Oh, surely not, David,' she said, drawing back.

'Then let me tell you something,' and he drew her head down and whispered something in her pink ear that he just brushed with his lips. It made Thérèse laugh and turn very rosy in the moonlight.

Can that be Hosmer? Is this Thérèse? Fie, fie. It is time we were leaving them. (170)

And so the novel ends. To readers who think of the final paragraph of *The Awakening* as among the most affecting in all of literature, this one likely disappoints. "Can that be Hosmer? Is this Thérèse? . . . *Can this be Chopin?*" one almost wishes to ask. If the conclusion of *At Fault* fails to live up to the levels of artistry Chopin achieves elsewhere in her fiction, though, it proves entirely consistent with the attitude toward the old plantation that otherwise characterizes her debut novel. The final word of its next-to-last paragraph is even "moonlight." If only the tree mentioned two paragraphs earlier were a magnolia rather than live-oak, *At Fault* would end quite literally in a land of moonlight-and-magnolia. It comes close enough as it is.

Chopin, of course, drew upon personal experience when she created Thérèse Lafirme and wrote a novel about a thirty-year-old woman's inheriting a plantation from a Creole husband recently deceased. She herself was thirty-two when Oscar Chopin, her husband of twelve years, died in 1882, leaving her a country store and several plantation proper-ties to manage (not to mention six children; the "childless" Thérèse is unlike her author in several respects, none more conspicuous than this). According to Emily Toth, Chopin's biographer, Chopin proved much more adept than her late husband at managing these operations.[28] The responsibilities she faced proved too taxing, however, for in addition to raising the six children, running the store, overseeing the plantations, and repaying the considerable debts her husband had left when he died, she was living in a portion of Louisiana, the north-central town of Cloutier-ville, that was far from the New Orleans where she and Oscar had lived at the beginning of their marriage and even farther from her native St. Louis. Having family there who could help her raise her children—and perhaps feeling the pull already to try her hand at writing—Chopin left Cloutierville in 1884 to return to St. Louis. Six years later she published *At Fault*.

In her first novel and in other writings, most notably of course *The*

Awakening, Chopin writes about women who discover that they possess far greater abilities (and far more complex subjectivities) than those around them are prepared to allow. They also however discover their limitations, some of them limitations in what they themselves may realistically hope to achieve (Thérèse must learn she cannot reform everyone), others limitations in what their societies will permit them to become (Edna comes to see marriage and motherhood as "the soul's slavery . . . they need not have thought that they could possess her, body and soul") (176). Examples once again of Chopin's attraction to the turn toward realism as a trope of narrative, these aspects of her fiction make all the more salient how relatively uncritical *At Fault* is toward the plantation myth. Michele Birnbaum and Sandra Gunning have explained Chopin's relative silencing of black voices in her fiction as a tendency comparable to colonialism: Chopin colonizes narratives of emancipation by imagining bourgeois white women as virtual slaves, Birnbaum argues, leading to what Gunning calls "a vision of white supremacy that both liberates and confines."[29] One might extend these analyses and observe that the colonizing whiteness that both enables and restricts her emancipatory visions reflects her investment in an idea of the Southern plantation—a space that was being reimagined via the colonialist trope of the white man's burden during the years in which Chopin wrote—as a place that permitted white women to rise above the limitations imposed by gender. She herself had proved a capable manager of plantations just before she resolved to become a producer of avant-garde fiction. The confidence brought about by the one may even have bolstered her determination to do the other. As *At Fault*'s strange return to a romanticized Place-du-Bois in its final chapter may reveal, however, the move away from Southern patriarchy may prove impossible when, in order to take place, it depends on its author's journey back to the old plantation, the most conventional of American plots during the late nineteenth century.

William Faulkner's debut as a novelist represented a decided turn away from a traditional Southern literary subject matter. *Soldier's Pay* (1926) centers around a World War I fighter pilot injured in combat, and while it follows him on his return to his hometown in Georgia, it is not a novel that tracks a journey back to an old plantation. Nor does Faulkner's second novel, *Mosquitoes* (1927), set in New Orleans, make the plantation its setting. Yet when it came time to follow Sherwood Anderson's legendary advice and write about "that little patch up there in Mississippi where you started from," the result was *Sartoris* (1929), a novel in which returns to an old plantation take place literally (in terms of the novel's geographic setting) and figuratively (in terms of its meditations on the relationship between a Southern present and Southern past). Plantation settings and plantation memories would then recur in several later novels, most notably in *Absalom, Absalom!* (1936) and *Go Down, Moses* (1942), both of which explore the ways in which the South's plantation past outlives itself. Even such novels as *The Hamlet* (1940) and *The Reivers* (1962), neither of which is primarily concerned with plantation legacies, manage to offer commentaries on the ways in which the institution persists. *The Hamlet*'s opening image of the Old Frenchman's place, "a tremendous pre-Civil War plantation . . . long since reverted to the cane-and-cypress jungle from which their first master had hewed them," may symbolize how durable the plantation has proved as a cornerstone of Southern culture. Its big house, though a bare "skeleton" of its former self, still stands; and the residents of Frenchman's Bend, though most lack the initiative that had allowed the Old Frenchman to build his plantation empire in the first place, still make use of his mansion, "pulling down and chopping up . . . the very clapboards themselves—for thirty years now for firewood."[30]

One of these later novels, *The Unvanquished* (1938), even explores what happens when a white woman assumes control over her son-in-law's plantation while he is away leading a Confederate regiment during the Civil War. The woman dies before the war's end and the man returns to his plantation soon afterward, however, making *The Unvanquished* a romance of the white woman's burden in only a limited fashion. The Faulkner novel that actually comes closest to *At Fault* thematically is *Light in August*.[31] Like Chopin's novel, it features a white woman who has inherited a plantation from a male relative, in this case her father, and it meditates at some length on what else devolves to her as a result. Also like *At Fault*, its female plantation legatee is depicted as possessing a reformer's instincts. The pressure to elevate those around her—already a defining feature of middle-class U.S. womanhood during the late nineteenth and early twentieth centuries—is made greater by her being implicated in a story about the plantation South and the responsibilities its leaders have inherited from their forefathers toward the descendents of its former slaves. *Light in August* even contains a sawmill and reflects (though much less deliberately than does *At Fault*) on the forms of change being occasioned by the growth of a Southern timber industry. Last, like *At Fault*, *Light in August* might be thought of as marking something of a debut for Faulkner as well. Faulkner's fifth Yoknapatawpha novel and his seventh overall, *Light in August* nevertheless marked for Faulkner what Eric Sundquist has termed "the extraordinary deepening of style and theme" that took place when he turned his attention more forcibly to the problem of race and its meanings to the South, nation, and world.[32] Not his first novel to confront race, *Light in August* may nevertheless be thought of as Faulkner's first to approach race as its principal territory for exploration—in a sense, as its setting. At the center of this story is the figure of Joe Christmas, a man rumored to be of mixed racial descent who has more or less accepted the rumor as fact. And at the center of Christmas's story is a white woman named Joanna Burden, *Light in August*'s analog to Thérèse Lafirme and a figure by way of whom Faulkner directly confronts the white man's burden as a concept that explicates the plantation South.[33]

Light in August and *At Fault* are of course very different novels, too. Faulkner's intertwines three major plots and several minor ones, while Chopin's focuses much more on the Thérèse-Hosmer relationship and relegates its other stories to subplots. *Light in August* taxes its reader with a great deal more interpretive work as well, unfolding in nonlinear fashion, featuring moments of stream-of-consciousness narration, and including several examples of the sort of opaque observation ("Memory believes before knowing remembers"; "Knowing not grieving remembers a thousand savage and lonely streets") that makes Faulkner's fiction seem so unlike that of a preceding generation of Southern novelists, including even such avant-gardists as Chopin. More relevant to the discussion at hand, *Light in August*'s central narrative is not so much a love story as it is a sex plot, and its participants are not differentiated by region (Hosmer is from St. Louis, Thérèse from Louisiana) but rather by race. Or, rather, the two are differentiated by a set of *fantasies* about race—Joe's, that even a rumor of "nigger blood" makes him "black"; Joanna's, that Joe's "race," which she no more *knows* to be "negro" than he, nevertheless makes him an object of conspicuous desire and an element of the fate assigned her by white male ancestors.

"'Remember this'," her father tells her on the (quite literally) fateful day that he first takes her to the graves of her grandfather and half-brother and explains to her how her whiteness condemns her to a life of metaphysical toil:

> Your grandfather and brother are lying there, murdered not only by one white man but by the curse which God put on the whole race before your grandfather or your brother or me or you were even thought of. A race doomed and cursed to be forever and ever a part of the white race's doom and curse for its sins. Remember that. His doom and his curse. Forever and ever. Mine.

Your mother's. Yours, even though you were a child. The curse of every white child that ever was born and that ever will be born. None can escape it." And I said, "Not even me?" and he said, "Not even you. Least of all you."[34]

The murders of Joanna's grandfather and half-brother form the pivotal episode in the "Skirmish at Sartoris" section of *The Unvanquished*. They are killed by John Sartoris, Yoknapatawpha County's Civil War hero and planter-sovereign *par excellence*, because they are trying to organize black voters on behalf of the Republican party during the very early years of Reconstruction. Sartoris's actions bring about the virtual end of radical Reconstruction in the county and signal an early local beginning of the era of Jim Crow. Yet Joanna seems barely to know any of this. What she recollects when she recounts her family's history to Joe Christmas is simply that her relatives were "killed . . . by an ex-slaveholder and Confederate soldier named Sartoris, over a question of negro voting" (248). She omits the additional historical details that might shed light on her ancestors' murders. On the contrary she discourses at length on the sense of white mission she possesses as a result of father's informing her of "the white race's doom and curse," a speech she seems to recall word for word despite having been only four years old the forty-plus years earlier she had heard it.

Joanna Burden thus differs from Thérèse Lafirme in an even more profound sense. Whereas Thérèse is descended from slaveowners, was once herself a young mistress destined to own slaves, and in any event seems content to preserve many of the relationships that had characterized the plantation during slavery, Joanna is the granddaughter of the staunchest abolitionist perhaps ever to set foot in Yoknapatawpha County and likely its only radical Republican. Her roots are in New England. Her reformism targets not white alcoholic women but rather "negroes," whose uplift she endeavors to assist by supporting "a dozen negro schools and colleges through the south" (233). She is committed in other words to seeing the South changed substantially, not to preserving its peculiar institution through forms of peonage, disenfranchisement, incarceration, intimidation, and violence.

Yet she is in the end no less committed than Thérèse to a vision of racial hierarchy. Indeed she would have little concept of herself without one. In advice he delivers to her after their visit to the graves of their murdered relatives, Joanna's father tells her that her mission in life will be to elevate "negroes" to a level short of which they will always fall:

I saw all the little babies that would ever be in the world, the ones not even yet born—a long line of them with their arms spread, on the black crosses. I couldn't tell then whether I saw it or dreamed it. But it was terrible to me. I cried at night. At last I told father, tried to tell him. What I wanted to tell him was that I must escape, get away from under the shadow, or I would die. "You cannot," he said. "You must struggle, rise. But in order to rise, you must raise the shadow with you. But you can never lift it to your level. I see that now, which I could not see until I came down here. But escape it you cannot. The curse of the black race is God's curse. But the curse of the white race is the black man who will be forever God's chosen own because He once cursed him." (252-3)

One gains an idea of what is happening in this passage simply by citing the first significant words of each sentence: "I . . . I . . . But . . . I . . . At last I . . . What I . . . 'You' . . . 'You' . . . But . . . But . . . I . . . But . . . The curse . . . But. . . ." The passage contains as many affirmations of what Joanna's "I" feels and desires as it does qualifications or negations: "But . . . But . . . But . . . But . . . But. . . ." It thus makes painfully evident the paradox at the heart of the white man's burden: that whites, by being bound by fate to elevate racial others, are bound also in a sense to keep them down. To preserve a sense of whiteness as a feeling of benevolence (as opposed to its inverse, a compulsion toward disciplinary violence, which *Light in August* also puts on display) requires that "the white race" hold steadfastly to the idea of the "negro" as a "problem" to be solved, a cross to bear, a "curse" to be endured.

 Light in August agonizes over this relationship in a way that *At Fault* does not. Indeed the passage just cited occupies the novel's actual middle, making possible the argument that what *At Fault* keeps offstage—a consideration of plantation racism and how it authorizes even a white woman's sense of power—*Light in August* places at its center.[35] Thérèse Lafirme's sense of self is underwritten by her belief that "negroes" need her. Whatever forms of uncertainty she may encounter as she adapts to her new roles as widow, plantation manager, businesswoman, counselor to an alcoholic, and finally wife of a divorcé-turned-widower, she can fall back on an essentially unchanging identity as "mistress," count on Uncle Hiram and Aunt Marie Louise to remain loyal to her, and expect always to have to rein in "a troublesome body of blacks." Joanna Burden is permitted no similar fall-back position. She does inhabit what is described first as "an old colonial plantation house two miles from town" and later as a "plantation . . . now broken by random negro cabins and garden patches," a depiction that uncannily repeats Chopin's opening description of Place-du-Bois: "The negro quarters were scattered at wide intervals over the land, breaking with picturesque irregularity into systematic division of field from field . . ." (*Light in August* 36, 424-5; *At Fault* 6). When away from her plantation, Joanna also professes to feel a sense of "homesickness for [its] sheer boards and nails, the earth and trees and shrubs" that parallels what Thérèse feels on her train ride homeward from New Orleans ("She loved Place-du-Bois with a love that was real; that had grown deep . . . [b]eginning with that June day when she had sat in the hall and watched the course of a white sunshade over the tops of the bending corn") (*Light in August* 240; *At Fault* 162).

Yet her role as communal matriarch produces in Joanna none of the sense of security and self-assuredness that it does in Thérèse. Instead it seems part of the same fantasy that compels her, when she discovers that Joe may be "part nigger," to stage sexual encounters in which she plays the role of rape victim and he the black beast—scenes ornamented with her exclamations of "'Negro! Negro! Negro!'" during intercourse (260). The fantasy also includes her visions of Joe's becoming a lawyer who might manage her family fortune for the good of black Southerners ("You would be helping them up out of the darkness and none could accuse or blame you even if they found out . . .") (276). Last, it includes her desire that Joe in effect convert to Christianity and kneel and pray with her, an act she eventually demands with gun in hand. It turns out to be her final act in both a literal and a theatrical sense of the phrase. Joe murders her immediately afterward, at which point he ceases to be the object of her civilizing mission and becomes instead the community's criminal responsibility (hence a white man's burden of the sort to which the speaker at the 1900 conference in Montgomery referred when he "sp[oke] of the white man's burden. It is but another name for the white man's duty. . . . [T]he one great difficulty in dealing with the Negro question is the crime against women"). If Joanna thus permits Faulkner to explore a range of potential meanings of the phrase "white man's burden," she also allows him to test its coherence—to reveal even that a concept of whiteness as a responsibility, genteel and perhaps even progressive though it may seem, may nevertheless lead more toward perversion, oppression, and death than to social harmony or racial uplift.

One might therefore expect Faulkner to have moved beyond the white man's burden in later writings, having exposed it so relatively early in his literary career as a sham belief system that serves more to perpetuate a set of race relations than to improve them. In many ways, though, he does not. It is beyond the scope of this essay to consider the ways in which Faulkner's later novels return repeatedly to an image of burdened white manhood, identify it as a peculiarly Southern racial subjectivity, yet manage not to defetishize it in the way that *Light in August* accomplishes. Placing it into the mind and onto the body of a white woman of Yankee heritage, Faulkner lays bare the white man's burden as a form of nonsense, a way of effecting change by trying to keep things the same. When it came time to write again about Quentin Compson in *Absalom, Absalom!* or to develop Ike McCaslin in *Go Down, Moses*, however—which is to say, when it came time to write about embodiments of the version of white Southern manhood most familiar to him—Faulkner found in the white man's burden a concept that seemed usefully expressive of a set of relations between black and white, men and women, and present and past. The novels do not reproduce the trope naively or uncritically, but nor are they marked by the same desire to move beyond it that characterizes *Light in August*. The later Faulkner works as much to preserve as to reject a sense of his own white subjectivity as a form of responsibility.

One might offer as evidence of Faulkner's peculiar commitment to the white man's burden the following passage, which derives not from a novel but rather from an address he delivered at the University of Virginia in 1958. "[T]he white race can never really know the Negro, because the white man has forced the Negro to be always a Negro rather than another human being in their dealings," Faulkner told the crowd gathered to hear his thoughts on Civil Rights. The statement echoes something Quentin Compson says in *The Sound and the Fury* (1929), namely that "a nigger is not a person so much as a form of behavior; a sort of obverse reflection of the white people he lives among," an observation that ranks among the keenest insights into race Faulkner's fiction offers.[36] Given its repetition at the outset of the Virginia address, one might have expected a speech that sought similarly to dismantle white Southern racial shibboleths and to disrupt complacent arguments. Instead one heard Faulkner address the race problem and "say to the North: All right, it is our problem, and we will solve it." Then came this, Faulkner's solution:

> For the sake of argument, let us agree that as yet the Negro is incapable of equality for the reason that he could not hold and keep it even if it were forced on him with bayonets; that once the bayonets were removed, the first smart and ruthless man black or white who came along would take it away from him, because he,

the Negro, is not yet capable of, or refuses to accept, the responsibilities of equality.

So we, the white man, must take him in and teach him that responsibility. . . . Let us teach him that, in order to be free and equal, he must first be worthy of it, and then forever afterward work to hold and keep and defend it. He must learn to cease forever more thinking like a Negro and acting like a Negro. This will not be easy for him. *His burden will be that*, because of his race and his color, it will not suffice for him to think and act just like any white man: he must think and act like the best among white men. . . .

So we alone can teach the negro the responsibility of personal morality and rectitude. . . .[37]

The white man's burden may have seemed strangely reassuring to Faulkner in 1958, more than a quarter century after the publication of *Light in August* and at a moment that black Southerners were making increasingly apparent their capacity to advance toward equality without the forms of paternalistic tutelage Faulkner calls for here. Despite these changes, Faulkner's words in his 1958 speech move backward toward the 1880s and '90s, decades that saw numerous figures claim that the uplift of black Americans was a peculiarly Southern responsibility, a challenge that, as Faulkner repeats here, "we alone" can undertake. He foists the burden also upon African-Americans—"*His burden will be that*"—and requires of them a peculiar performance. Yet if "the Negro" were essentially a performative category to begin with—"a sort of obverse reflection of the white people he lives among"—then what would it have meant for him then to "act like the best among white men"? Had not his own example of Joe Christmas, for example, made clear the deep risks involved when "the Negro" acts white?

The white man's burden would prove no less paradoxical in 1958 than it had in 1932. It seems, though, to have proved equally persuasive, too—a way of imagining race relations that proved almost as compelling during the final years of Jim Crow as it had at the beginning. It proved at any rate difficult to leave behind. One may therefore wonder whether Kate Chopin, whose *The Awakening* moves so far beyond *At Fault* though it was published only nine years later, would have reproduced an image of the white woman's burden in the fiction she might have published had her best novel been received differently and had in any event she lived past 1904. One cannot of course know whether, like Faulkner, she would have kept returning to an idea inherited from plantation fiction and expressive of white Southern racial superiority as well as guilt. One may note, however, that *The Awakening* ends with one of the most remarkable images of a plantation in all of American literature. Its first dinner party scene signals Edna's desire to move beyond the romantic plantation narratives of Léonce and Old Iberville. Its final image, however, involves the remembrance of an old plantation. Early in the novel, when Edna is being introduced as "an American woman" not entirely at home in the company of Louisiana Creoles, she "talk[s] about her father's Mississippi plantation and her girlhood home in the old Kentucky blue-grass country" (9). Later she recollects both homes as places where her sexuality began to dawn upon her. In Kentucky she had one been "passionately enamored of a dignified and sad-eyed cavalry officer who visited her father. . . ." In Mississippi "her affections were deeply engaged by a young gentleman who visited a lady on a neighboring plantation" (44-45). Both memories, which could well be described as plantation romances, nevertheless teach her about the contingencies of desire and transience of ardor; they do not produce the sort of timeless wisdom that plantations were otherwise supposed to be generating during the late nineteenth and early twentieth centuries, and they certainly do not seem to her places from which she has inherited the burden of uplifting ex-slaves. Yet the plantation proves persistent, too, in *The Awakening*, for it is there in its memorable final paragraph. As Edna swims out to sea, her thoughts turning from her children to Dr. Mandelet to her ambitions as an artist to her present predicament, an image of her girlhood home in Kentucky intrudes finally into her mind:

> She looked into the distance, and the old terror flamed up for an instant, then sank again. Edna heard her father's voice and her sister Margaret's. She heard the barking of an old dog that was chained to the sycamore tree. The spurs of the cavalry officer clanged as he walked across the porch. There was the hum of bees, and the musky odor of pinks filled the air. (303)

Edna's final moments represent a return to her old Kentucky home, a journey through memory complete with a Confederate officer, a father's voice, and a final image of fecundity and reproduction. Yet the memory is involuntary and, in the end, insignificant: it is composed of elements that cannot be reassembled into a vision that would instruct such descendants as Edna what they are tasked with doing for the remainders of their lives.

As a vision of the plantation it is singular. As a sign of what Chopin might have written when next she returned to the old plantation as a site of literary exploration—hence of what Faulkner and others would have had to build upon had Chopin arrived at her place in a Southern canon much earlier than she did—it can only make us wonder what we may have missed.

Notes

1. Kennedy, *Swallow Barn*, 13, 95, 162.

2. Douglass, *Narrative of the Life*, 139.

3. Stowe, *Uncle Tom's Cabin*, 345.

4. Adams, *Wounds of Returning*, 4.

5. Russ, *The Plantation in the Postslavery Imagination*, 19.

6. Chopin, *The Awakening*, 170, 182-3, 186. Subsequent references are cited parenthetically.

7. At the next dinner party, by which point Edna has moved into her own domicile and taken Alcée Arobin as a lover, the ratio is an even five to five. Had not Adele Ratignolle and Madam Lebrun cancelled at the last minute, moreover, the ratio of women to men at the later affair would have been seven to five.

8. Gingher, "Realism," 723; Makowsky, "Southern Literature," 369.

9. "[N]o story takes 1,037 pages to tell," Faulkner reportedly said about Mitchell's novel. See Porter, "*Gone with the Wind*," 705.

10. Léonce is in fact depicted as reading a newspaper in the opening scene of the novel. Had it been any of the papers served by the McClure syndicate, Léonce might have come across Joel Chandler Harris's fictionalized autobiography, which was being serialized by McClure in 1891. Later published in book form and titled *On the Plantation* (1892), the narrative includes extended scenes in which a stand-in for a young Harris hunts "'possum" and "'coon" alongside exuberant plantation slaves.

11. One might go further with this analysis. Following Léonce's plantation romance comes the Colonel's story exemplifying a darker Realism, the literary mode thought by many to have displaced Romanticism and taken hold in the United States precisely because of what the Colonel is talking about, the Civil War. Following him comes Mandelet's story, which seems to aspire to a Realism of a different sort, one grounded more in psychology than in history. The story at least acknowledges a woman's wayward, no doubt extramarital desires before "channel[ing]" them back to their "legitimate source," making Mandelet's a story

that seems to flirt with a sexual Realism before turning didactic and returning to a more conventional moral footing. The fact that Edna supersedes all of these with her Awakening-like tale of "pure invention" may indicate Chopin's belief that her novel was not contained by any of the major genres then being practiced by U.S. fiction writers.

12. For proof that the plantation remained popular in 1899, the year *The Awakening* was published, one need look no further than some of the other titles that appeared that very year, among them Joel Chandler Harris's *Plantation Pageants*, J. Campbell Phillips's *Plantation Sketches*, William E. Barton's *Old Plantation Hymns*, an anonymous memoir titled *The Old Plantation Home*, Charles Chesnutt's *The Conjure Woman*, Francis Hopkinson Smith's *Colonel Carter of Cartersville*, Victoria V. Clayton's *White and Black under the Old Regime*, and Maria Howard Weeden's *Bandanna Ballads*. Thomas Nelson Page's *Red Rock* was among the many plantation titles published the year before.

13. Though it hails from a different discipline, Moral Philosophy, one might cite as evidence here the following observation from Judith N. Shklar's *Ordinary Vices* (1984): "One of the most enduring themes of Southern fiction, from Kate Chopin to William Faulkner, is racial betrayal. In Chopin's "Désirée's Baby" a white father discovers that his newborn child has negroid features. . . . Far more compelling is Faulkner's telling of this basic myth in *Absalom, Absalom!*" (150-1).

14. See Davis, "The Virginia Novel before *Swallow Barn*."

15. Gaines, *The Southern Plantation*, 22.

16. Kennedy, *Swallow Barn*, 8-10. Emphasis in original.

17. Fetterley, "'Not in the Least American,'" 15-16.

18. Qtd. in Horsman, *Race and Manifest Destiny*, 165.

19. Harris, "The Old Plantation," 90.

20. In his 1897 study of *Social Life in Old Virginia before the War,* for example, Thomas Nelson Page asserts that "the Old South . . . largely contributed to produce this nation; it led its armies and its navies; it established this government so firmly that not even it could overthrow it; it opened up the great West; it added Louisiana and Texas, and more than trebled our territory; it christianized the negro race in a little over two centuries. . . ." James Battle Avirett's *The Old Plantation* (1901) would amplify these statements four years later: "Numerically inferior to the North for the first sixty-four years of the republic, the South furnished the President for fifty-two years. . . . Who commanded our armies at the battle of New Orleans? General Andrew Jackson, a Carolinian. Who were in the lead, when Louisiana, with more than one million square miles of territory, was acquired? Do we not owe the acquisition of Florida to the same source? Who opposed the war with Mexico, by which the vast empire of Texas and New Mexico, together with

California, were added to our country? Northern statesmen. . . . We of the old South cannot be blamed (for we are not wrong) in saying that, as there was no hurry among us in those days, no need of haste, men took time to be truly conservative and fastened the taproot of their every-day life deep down into the soil which was pressed by the foot-prints of George Washington, Jefferson, Madison, Monroe, Henry, and such others as gave dignity and honor to American citizenship." Page, *Social Life in Old Virginia before the War*, 184-185; Avirett, *The Old Plantation*, 17-20.

21. Harris, "Observations from New England," 165. Describing Yankee "school-ma'ams" who came southward during Reconstruction with idealistic notions of how to reconstruct the South, Harris argues that the women came to recognize how much more effective a home-grown paternalism was than their alien and idealistic reform measures.

22. *Race Problems of the South*, 129, 183, 176.

23. Chopin, *At Fault*, 5-6. Subsequent references are cited parenthetically.

24. Her original readership was likely small. Rejected by magazine publishers, Chopin herself paid for *At Fault* to be published and likely lost money on the deal. See Toth, *Unveiling Kate Chopin*, 115-16.

25. Chopin may well have been relying on Page rather than Harris for her dialect. The word "obliged" appears in *Uncle Remus, His Songs and His Sayings* (1880) as "bleedzd," for example. In *In Ole Virginia* it appears as it does in *At Fault*: as "bleeged."

26. Page, *Red Rock*, 68.

27. Mitchell, *Gone with the Wind*, 1036.

28. Toth, *Unveiling Kate Chopin*, 93-4.

29. Birnbaum, "'Alien Hands,'" 303; Gunning, *Race, Rape, and Lynching*, 135. See also Menke, "The Catalyst of Color and Women's Regional Writing."

30. Faulkner, *The Hamlet*, 3-4.

31. An expanded version of the following discussion of *Light in August* will appear in *Romances of the White Man's Burden: Race, Empire, and the Plantation in American Literature, 1880-1936*, forthcoming from Vanderbilt University Press.

32. Sundquist, *Faulkner*, 67.

33. *At Fault* even includes a figure of mixed racial descent, a man named Joçint, whose propensity toward violence parallels Joe Christmas's. As Gunning argues, however, *At Fault* directs Joçint's violent tendencies toward white men, not white women, removing from the novel the threat of "black" rape that *Light in August* makes its central concern. Gunning, *Race, Rape, and Lynching*, 120-1.

34. Faulkner, *Light in August*, 252-3. Subsequent references are cited parenthetically.

35. Of the 505 pages that compose the Vintage International edition of the novel, the passages in which Joanna's father imparts to her her sense of mission span pages 252-3. In terms of the novel's twenty-one chapters, the passages come at the end of chapter eleven. Ten chapters precede and ten follow.

36. Faulkner, *The Sound and the Fury*, 86.

37. Faulkner, "To the Raven, Jefferson, and ODK Societies of the University of Virginia, 1958," 157-8. Emphasis added.

Works Cited

Adams, Jessica. *Wounds of Returning: Race, Memory, and Property on the Postslavery Plantation*. Chapel Hill: U of North Carolina P, 2007.

Avirett, James Battle. *The Old Plantation: How We Lived in the Great House and Cabin before the War*. New York: F. Tennyson Neely, 1901.

Birnbaum, Michele A. "'Alien Hands': Kate Chopin and the Colonization of Race." *American Literature* 66.2 (1994): 301-23.

Chopin, Kate. *At Fault*. 1890. New York: Penguin, 2002.

———. *The Awakening*. Chicago: Herbert S. Stone, 1899.

Davis, Richard Beale. "The Virginia Novel before *Swallow Barn*." *The Virginia Magazine of History and Biography* 71 (1963): 278-93.

Dixon, Thomas, Jr. *The Leopard's Spots: A Romance of the White Man's Burden*. New York: Doubleday, Page and Company, 1902.

Douglass, Frederick. *Narrative of the Life of Frederick Douglass, an American Slave*. 1845. New York: Penguin, 1982.

Faulkner, William. *The Hamlet*. 1940. New York: Vintage International, 1991.

———. "To the Raven, Jefferson, and ODK Societies of the University of Virginia, 1958." In *Essays, Speeches, and Public Letters*, ed. James B. Meriwether. New York: Modern Library, 2004. 155-159.

———. *Light in August*. 1932. New York: Vintage International, 1985.

———. *The Unvanquished*. 1934. New York: Vintage International, 1991.

Fetterley, Judith. "'Not in the Least American': Nineteenth-Century Literary Regionalism as UnAmerican Literature." *College English* 56 (1994): 877-95.

Gaines, Francis Pendleton. *The Southern Plantation: A Study in the Development and the Accuracy of Tradition*. New York: Columbia UP, 1924.

Gingher, Robert. "Realism." In *The Companion to Southern Literature: Themes, Genres, Places, People, Movements, and Motifs*, eds. Joseph M. Flora and Lucinda H. MacKethan. Baton Rouge: Louisiana State UP, 2002. 723-725.

Gunning, Sandra. *Race, Rape, and Lynching: The Red Record of American Literature*, 1890-1912. New York: Oxford UP, 1996.

Harris, Joel Chandler. "Observations from New England." In *Joel Chandler Harris: Editor and Essayist*, ed. Julia Collier Harris. Chapel Hill: U of North Carolina P, 1931. 159-76.

———. "The Old Plantation." In *Joel Chandler Harris: Editor and Essayist*, 89-92.

———. *On the Plantation: A Story of a Georgia Boy's Adventures during the War*. New York: D. Appleton and Company, 1892.

———. *Uncle Remus, His Songs and His Sayings*. New York: D. Appleton and Company, 1880.

Horsman, Reginald. *Race and Manifest Destiny: The Origins of American Racial Anglo-Saxonism*. Cambridge: Harvard UP, 1981.

Kennedy, John Pendleton. *Swallow Barn; or, A Sojourn in the Old Dominion*. 1832. Baton Rouge: Louisiana State UP, 1986.

Makowsky, Veronica. "Southern Literature." In *A William Faulkner Encyclopedia*, eds. Robert W. Hamblin and Charles A. Peek. Westport, Connecticut: Greenwood Press, 1999. 368-72.

Menke, Pamela Glenn. "The Catalyst of Color and Women's Regional Writing: *At Fault, Pembroke*, and *The Awakening*." *Southern Quarterly* 37.3-4 (1999): 9-20.

Mitchell, Margaret. *Gone with the Wind*. 1936. New York: Warner Books, 1999.

Page, Thomas Nelson. *In Ole Virginia; or, Marse Chan and Other Stories*. New York: Charles Scribner's Sons, 1887.

———. *Red Rock: A Chronicle of Reconstruction*. New York: Charles Scribner's Sons, 1898.

———. *Social Life in Old Virginia before the War*. New York: Charles Scribner's Sons, 1897.

Porter, Carolyn. "1936, *Gone with the Wind* and *Absalom, Absalom!*" In *A New Literary History of America*, eds. Greil Marcus and Werner Sollors. Cambridge: Harvard UP, 2009. 705-10.

Russ, Elizabeth Christine. *The Plantation in the Postslavery Imagination*. New York: Oxford UP, 2009.

Shklar, Judith N. *Ordinary Vices*. Cambridge: Harvard UP, 1984.

Southern Society for the Promotion of the Study of Race Conditions and Problems in the South. *Race Problems of the South*. Montgomery: B.F. Johnson, 1900.

Stowe, Harriet Beecher. *Uncle Tom's Cabin; or, Life among the Lowly*. 1852. Ed. Elizabeth Ammons. New York: W.W. Norton, 1994.

Sundquist, Eric J. *Faulkner: The House Divided*. Baltimore: Johns Hopkins UP, 1983.

Toth, Emily. *Unveiling Kate Chopin*. Jackson: UP of Mississippi, 1999.

The Green Breast of the Southern Plantation: Equating Women and Property in Faulkner's *Go Down, Moses* and Chopin's "A No-Account Creole"

This essay examines how Faulkner and Chopin both inherit and revise the plantation traditions of Southern literature with a focus on the differences between the two, specifically in their equation of women and the plantation land itself. While many of Chopin's works undoubtedly are feminist and progressive, I want to examine one of her well known short stories that, in my interpretation, is much less so, more aligned with the Old South plantation school depictions of women.[1] "A No-Account Creole," the first story in Chopin's 1894 collection *Bayou Folk*, shares many striking similarities to Ike McCaslin's story in Faulkner's 1942 novel *Go Down, Moses*, and both of these stories have some important connections with the plantation literature tradition of the South. Their similarities make for an opportunity to compare these two authors' appropriation and revision of the pastoral traditions.

The basics of Ike McCaslin's story are well known: he renounces his inheritance of the family plantation after a lengthy debate in "The Bear" with his cousin Cass about the ethics of owning both people and land. Most readers and critics see Ike's disavowal of the McCaslin family land and its legacy of slavery as admirable to a point, but as ineffectual as far as actually bringing any changes to the institutions and principles he rejects. Chopin's "A No-Account Creole" may not be as familiar, so a bit of a recap of that story is in order. In the beginning of Chopin's tale, Wallace Offdean has just inherited $25,000 at age 26 (as opposed to Ike's being 21 at the time of his inheritance) and is looking to establish himself in the world. Chopin also tells us that Offdean is, like Ike, full of metaphysical concerns about sin and morality: "Above all, he would keep clear of the maelstroms of sordid work and senseless pleasure in which the average American business man may be said alternately to exist, and which reduce him, naturally, to a rather ragged condition of the soul" (3). Again, Chopin's words could easily be describing Ike when she writes a page later that Offdean's inheritance brings "what he felt to be the turning-point in his life." Turning down a risky investment offer, Offdean decides to be the "land inspector" of "a troublesome piece of land on the Red River," upstate in Louisiana, a former slave plantation foreclosed on by the company he works for (4).

Chopin describes the plantation, the old Santien place, as "[a] shadowy, ill-defined piece of land in an unfamiliar part of his native state, [which] might, he hoped, prove a sort of closet into which he could retire and take counsel with his inner and better self" (4). It is a chance for a classic pastoral retreat from the big city of New Orleans to the countryside, a journey that usually (in both the pastoral and Southern pastoral traditions) results in the revelation of a moral or ethical shortcoming in the society that has been left behind, exposed by the contrast with the ostensibly simpler, purer, and more authentic rural setting. The plantation school fiction of writers like Thomas Nelson Page and Joel Chandler Harris, for instance, is a variety of pastoral in which the imagined simplicities and superiorities of the past are juxtaposed with the problems and chaos of the present (often including overt justifications of slavery and/or racial subjugation).

Faulkner's and Chopin's versions of pastoral both grapple with another element of the plantation school: the association of women with nature. As "A No-Account Creole" continues, the connection of the plantation land with the female body becomes clear. The "No-Account Creole" of the title is Placide Santien, the only one of three sons left who inherited the plantation from their father only to have it taken over by creditors (Offdean's New Orleans employers). Placide, a carpenter like Ike McCaslin, intends to marry Euphrasie, the daughter of the caretaker of his family's former plantation. He has been fixing up a little house in the nearby town to bring her to as his wife, establishing a connection between woman and property. But Euphrasie is linked strongest to the Old Santien place, as the plantation is still called.

Chopin tells us that Placide once held Euphrasie as a baby "and he straightaway believed she had been sent to him as a birthday gift" (11-12). His desire for possession of his family's ancestral land is similar, but he bitterly proclaims the land is nothing to him (19), substituting his desire for possession of Euphrasie for that of the land. In a bit of foreshadowing, Chopin details the "foreboding of ill" Placide feels "when he found that Euphrasie began to interest herself in the condition of the plantation" (9). Euphrasie is also taking interest in her own internal condition, and her groping toward self-determination is a threat to Placide's intentions for possession of a future wife: "It made him very fierce to think of the possibility of her not being entirely his own" (29). Offdean comes to visit the plantation and becomes a rival of Placide's for both possession of the land and Euphrasie. Staying with Euphrasie and her father as he assesses the property, Offdean feels after just two weeks "very much at home" there, learning about the land until "he came to know it as if it had been his own" (20).

Euphrasie is his guide around the property much of the time, and he is learning about her as much as he is the land. In fact, when Offdean returns to New Orleans for business, the connection of woman and land in the story is abundantly clear in his pining for both:

> The interest which he felt in the improvement of this planta-
> tion was of so deep a nature . . . that he found himself thinking
> of it constantly. He wondered if the timber had all been felled,
> and how the fencing was coming on. So great was his desire
> to know such things that much correspondence was required
> between himself and Euhprasie, and he watched eagerly for [her]
> letters. . . . But in the midst of it, Offdean suddenly lost interest
> in the progress of work on the plantation. Singularly enough,
> it happened simultaneously with the arrival of a letter from
> Euhprasie which announced . . . that she was going down to the
> city . . . for Mardi Gras. (26)

Placide accompanies her on the trip, but pointedly refuses his host's attempts to teach him more about the city, shunning New Orleans as if it were another woman. Here in the city where legal ownership of the plantation resides, Placide and Offdean duel for Euphrasie's affections while she struggles internally with her attraction to both men.

When Offdean later returns north to the old Santien place, the conflation of woman and land continues, culminating in Offdean's plantation fantasy of himself as a gentleman planter: "In the space of a moment he saw the whole delicious future which a kind fate had mapped out for him: those rich acres upon the Red River his own, bought and embellished with his inheritance; and Euphrasie, whom he loved, his wife and companion throughout a life such as he knew now he had craved for,—a life that, imposing bodily activity, admits the intellectual repose in which thought unfolds" (38). Offdean's plans barely regard Euphrasie's thoughts and feelings, and the fact that they have not actually discussed their feelings (much less marriage) is dismissed with the thought that "had they not spoken over and over to each other the mute and subtile [*sic*] language of reciprocal love—out under the forest trees, and in the quiet nighttime on the plantation when the stars shone" (38-9). "Surely no other speech was needed," Offdean thinks, as he now can hardly wait "to tell her that he wanted her for his very own" (39), which he soon does by saying, "The plantation is mine, Euphrasie—or it will be when you say that you will be my wife" (41).

Of course, Placide has his own designs on Euphrasie (or is it Euphrasie's land? It gets hard to tell.), and unbeknownst to Offdean when he delivers his declaration, she is engaged to be married to Placide in two days. Also, unknown to both Euphrasie and Offdean is that Placide (who is hiding on the porch) happens to overhear Offdean's confession of love and Euphrasie's subsequent rejection. Despite hearing her tell her suitor to leave, Placide assumes that she in fact secretly loves Offdean: "He had heard Euphrasie tell the man she did not love him, but what of that? Had he not heard her sobs, and guessed what her distress was?" (44). Both men completely ignore Euphrasie's words, projecting their own desires and feelings onto her, even when her words contain the opposite meaning. The problem, however, is that the story proves them right, in the end, and is not at all critical of their silencing of Euphrasie's voice, turning her into little more than another piece of the plantation property they are battling to own.

Placide breaks off the engagement, telling everyone that Euphrasie has dumped him, as she apparently is in love with Offdean, despite her saying the opposite. Euphrasie is relieved to have the wedding called off, but when Offdean asks her permission to return to court her soon, Euphrasie refuses to speak. Again, her silence is all Offdean needs to somehow divine that she does want him: "She still made him no reply, but she did not tell him no" (50). Offdean returns to New Orleans at the story's end confident of his possession of both woman and land, regardless of what the woman has or has not said. Rather than showing the wrongs or consequences of ignoring the woman, as we might expect from a feminist writer, Chopin seems to endorse the imposition of male desire on a passive female landscape and woman by suggesting the men are *correct* to ignore what she says, that Euphrasie either must not know what she wants (and so needs a man to tell her) or that she is playing coy and no really means yes.

While Offdean converts his inheritance into possession of land and a woman, Ike McCaslin, in *Go Down, Moses*, rejects his inheritance of the family plantation and thereby rejects the wife whose body has been equated with the land. Ike remembers his last visit to the Big Woods, before "the lumber company moved in and began to cut the timber," in a flashback that comes just after the scene in which his wife offers her body in exchange for the McCaslin farm (Faulkner 301). Essentially she tells Ike that he will not have her body again if he rejects his family land. Louise Westling argues that this "anachronistic juxtaposition" of scenes suggests that "feminine sexuality seems to lead to destruction of the Delta Eden" and disguises the blame of Major de Spain, who actually sells the land to the lumber company. This same formula, where "men are the agents of sin . . . but women . . . are to blame" (Westling 122) applies to the story of Sam Fathers, who was sold into slavery by his father, yet, we are told by Cass Edmonds, was "betrayed through the black blood which his mother gave him . . . not willfully betrayed by his mother, but betrayed by her all the same" (Faulkner 162). Westling identifies this pattern as a "cultural habit of gendering the landscape as female" which she traces through a long line of male, American writers who "disguise and evade the responsibility of white men for the displacement of another people on the land and the ravishing of an existing ecosystem for their own gain" (Westling 5). However, Faulkner breaks with this tradition, according to Westling, as he "writes his way towards an understanding of this process in *Go Down, Moses*, and he comes very close to exposing it totally" (16).

What Westling is referring to are moments when Faulkner reveals and exposes how the feminizing of nature helps to justify its exploitation. Ike nostalgically remembers the beginning of his marriage as a time of unity and mutual understanding with his unnamed wife: "they were married and it was the new country, his heritage too as it was the heritage of all . . . and in the sharing they become one: for that while, one: for that little while at least, one: indivisible" (297). But open association of her body and sexual gratification with the land of the plantation makes "the chaste woman, the wife" seem different, her naked body "changed, altered" into what Faulkner calls "the composite of all woman-flesh," which Ike associates with mystical knowledge beyond his relational capacity: "*She already knows more than I with all the man-listening in camps . . . They are born already bored with what a boy approaches only at fourteen and fifteen with blundering and aghast trembling . . . She is lost. She was born lost. We were all born lost*" (299-300). Ike's desire for absolution from guilt for his family's and culture's sins becomes a wish for a return to original innocence through rejection of the female body, but the futility of this desire is revealed in the destruction of Ike's revered woods, his Delta Eden.

Thus although we see here, as in Chopin's story, the equation of the female body with the land of the plantation, Faulkner suggests that this formula is highly problematic, as it results in the loss of the woods, the family land, and the marriage. In a sense, Faulkner is deploying the same symbolism as Chopin but in order to critique the very symbolism he uses. Because Ike accepts the plantation school formulation of the land as woman's body, he loses everything. Ike sees the land as already fallen, tainted, or corrupted by human sin, and he extends that notion to the "woman-flesh" of his wife. She too must be rejected, leaving an extremely barren view of the future that I do not think Faulkner condones. Ike, in contrast, is identified as "uncle to half a county, father to no one" (3), signaling the impotence that results from his linking the female body to the land he rejects.

While men are revealed as the agents of destruction, women are the agents of (potential) salvation. The key trait in the struggle for future survival is endurance, a trait Faulkner identifies in three offspring of mixed heritage: the son of Roth and his cousin, the expected child of Natalie and George Wilkins, and the fyce that Ike saves from Old Ben. Faulkner says that the little dog represents "the indomitable spirit of man," and he calls it the antithesis of the bear in a later interview, saying: "the fyce represents the creature who has coped with his environment and is still on top of it, you might say. That he has—instead of sticking with his breeding and becoming a decadent, degenerate creature, he has mixed himself up with the good stock where he picked and chose" (Gwynn and Blotner 280, 37). Running counter to Ike's fears of miscegenation, then, is Faulkner's belief that heterogeneous elements increase adaptability, which is essential for survival. The children of the Beauchamp line of the family, including Roth's illegitimate son, are most like the admirable fyce and offer the possibility of change and revitalization in the midst of a "treeless," "denuded and derivered" Southern wasteland (Faulkner 347).

So Faulkner has taken the plantation school tradition (replicated by Chopin) of equating women and land, but challenged and revised it. Rather than portraying men as saviors of the land and its women, Faulkner shows them to be responsible for the destruction of nature. Faulkner's women are not passively aligned with a domesticated version of nature, but made active agents of change and adaptability, more like a wilderness ecosystem than an orderly plantation. I wouldn't necessarily call Faulkner in this case more of a feminist writer than Chopin. Rather I would argue that the differences in these stories are attributable to the nature side of the equation, specifically Faulkner's attitudes towards the environment. I think Faulkner is more of an accidental feminist because he is more in tune with the natural environment which is linked to women in the pastoral formulation.

The decades leading up to the composition and publication of *Go Down, Moses* were a time of growing environmental awareness in the U.S. and the South in particular. Chopin is writing at the beginning of the cut-and-get-out phase of lumbering in the South, while Faulkner witnesses the end results of an ecologically devastating fifty-year boom. The Mississippi of Faulkner's lifetime was an overwhelmingly rural state where most people's lives were concretely and significantly affected by natural processes, primarily through the agricultural and timber industries. The activities of these industries also permanently altered the landscape, often with disastrous results for those who depended on Mississippi's air, land, and water for their livelihood, as Faulkner would have witnessed. As Don H. Doyle remarks in *Faulkner's County: The Historical Roots of Yoknapatawpha*,

> By the time Faulkner began writing about his native land in the 1920s, the evidence of destruction was everywhere to be seen. He grew up in a land torn apart by gullies that ran down the hillsides, with creeks and rivers clogged by quicksand sludge, a landscape also of denuded fields pocked with stumps left by the lumbermen who had cut their way through the woods like locusts. (300)

In *The Hamlet* (published in 1940, two years before *Go Down, Moses*), Faulkner provides his own description of the desecrated landscape that anticipates Doyle's:

> after the Indians it had been cleared where possible for cultivation, and after the Civil War, forgotten save by small peripatetic sawmills which had vanished too now, their sites marked only by the mounds of rotting sawdust which were not only their gravestones but the monuments of people's heedless greed. Now it was a region of scrubby second-growth pine and oak among which dogwood bloomed until it too was cut to make cotton spindles, and old fields . . . gutted and gullied by forty years of rain and frost and heat into plateaus choked with rank sedge . . . and crumbling ravines striated red and white with alternate sand and clay. (190)

The gullies and ravines referred to in this passage (which are also called "Mississippi canyons") are created when fields that are left bare form a hard surface that sloughs off water in torrents which carry away huge amounts of topsoil, leaving gullies ten to twenty feet deep resembling "bleeding sores" that drain "the lifeblood of the land" (Doyle 297-8). Even as far back as the 1870s, state geologist and University of Mississippi professor Eugene Hilgard found "a wasteland of eroded fields, deep gullies, and silt-filled creeks" in the north central region of the state that includes Lafayette County, and he blamed the "rapacious, short-sighted strategy of its migratory inhabitants" who stripped the land of vegetation, wore out the soil and exposed it to erosion by planting only cotton and corn year after year, before moving on to the next frontier (297).

Even more dramatic and startling were the changes to the landscape and the environment produced by a virtual explosion in the lumber industry of Mississippi between 1880 and 1920. An 1876 bill legalizing private sales of public lands with no limits on purchase size opened the door for lumbermen and speculators who, for the next twelve years, bought over 2.6 million acres of federal pineland in Mississippi at bargain rates as low as $1.25 per acre (Hickman 71-84).[2] In 1890 there were 338 mills statewide with a total capital investment of $3 million. Not even 20 years later, in 1909, the totals had leaped to 1,647 mills and almost $40 million of investment capital (155).[3] Combined with increasing saw speeds and the construction of "tramroads," usually standard gauge rail lines, into previously inaccessible areas, the vast number of mills and their workers (many of whom were displaced tenant farmers eager for the steady wages) led to the near total destruction of the state's virgin pine forests.

A more dramatic example of the consequences of this profit-driven approach is the wide use of "skidders" after 1900 in order to decrease costs. These steam-powered skidders used steel-wire cables 1,000 feet or more in length, which were unwound from drums on the tramroads and attached to logs in the woods. As the revolving drums reeled in the cables, five to fifteen logs were dragged to the track on each pull-in, but these devices also destroyed everything in their path as they dragged trees across the ground. Nollie Hickman describes the devastating results:

> No trees or vegetation of any kind except coarse wire grass remained on the skidder-logged hill and ridges. For miles and miles the landscape presented a picture of bare open land that graphically illustrated the work of destruction wrought by the economic activities of man. . . . Nor was the work of destruction a temporary condition, for twenty-five years later the boundaries between skidder-logged areas and those where other methods prevailed were apparent even to the untutored eye. (165-6)

This barren wasteland is precisely the type of scenery that Ike would have viewed during trips from Jefferson to the hunting grounds: "the land across which there came now no scream of panther but instead the long hooting of locomotives" (Faulkner 325). Indeed, James E. Fickle's *Mississippi Forests and Forestry* shows "the symbiotic relationship between

Mississippi's lumber industry and railroads." The devastation of the landscape by the skidders, "which virtually destroyed any prospects for natural reseeding of the cutover lands," leads Fickle to conclude that "[t]here has never been a more short-sighted or destructive method of logging" (77, 98, 66).

It is within this context of wanton environmental destruction that Faulkner composed *Go Down, Moses* and in which the novel's action takes place. Consequently, Faulkner subverts the woman-as-Southern-garden metaphor of the plantation tradition not necessarily out of any feminist impulses but rather because of his environmental consciousness. Faulkner understood at the time what has become a central insight of ecocriticism and ecofeminism: the linking of minorities and women with nature helps justify their subordination to men. Thus, Faulkner's revision of the traditional linkage of passive women and passive nature derives from the ecological destruction he witnessed around him, but it also produces female characters in *Go Down, Moses* who are markedly different from the heroine of Chopin's short story: the difference between a fighting fyce and a fallow field.

Notes

1. At the Faulkner and Chopin conference, this paper followed Jeremy Wells's presentation on women and the plantation tradition (also included in this volume), allowing me to "piggy-back" on some of his analysis.

2. Other states were selling similar land at the time for $19 per acre (Hickman 97), perhaps suggesting why Mississippi's forests fell into the hands of a few large syndicates which then could level hundreds of thousands of forest acres in a relatively short period.

3. In 1908, when Faulkner was 11 years old, a report compiled by U.S. government foresters concluded that "more than half of the longleaf pineland of Mississippi had already been converted into stumps" (Hickman 261).

Works Cited

Chopin, Kate. "A No-Account Creole." In *Bayou Folk*. 1894. Americans in Fiction Series reprint. Ridgewood, NJ: The Gregg Press, 1967: 1-50.

Doyle, Don H. *Faulkner's County: The Historical Roots of Yoknapatawpha*. Chapel Hill: U of North Carolina P, 2001.

Faulkner, William. *Go Down, Moses*. 1942. New York: Vintage, 1990.

————. *The Hamlet*. 1940. New York: Vintage, 1990.

Fickle, James E. *Mississippi Forests and Forestry*. Jackson: U of Mississippi P, 2001.

Gwynn, Frederick L., and Joseph L. Blotner, eds. *Faulkner in the University*. Charlottesville: University of Virginia Press, 1959.

Hickman, Nollie. *Mississippi Harvest: Lumbering in the Longleaf Pine Belt 1840-1915*. Montgomery, AL: Paragon, 1962.

Westling, Louise. *The Green Breast of the New World: Landscape, Gender, and American Fiction*. Athens: U of Georgia P, 1996.

How Merry Are the Widows in Chopin's *At Fault* and Faulkner's "There Was a Queen"?

The female characters in William Faulkner's oeuvre represent the gamut of female archetypal roles: mother, sister, daughter, whore, virgin, object, and other.[1] Within the framework of these categories, the character development is often limited to a one-dimensional glimpse of the woman, often as a reflection of her men. In fact, many of Faulkner's female characters seemingly exist only as a means to provide further access to the internal functions of the male characters. Certainly early criticism of Faulkner points to such misogynistic tendencies in his works.[2] Similarly, feminist criticism of Faulkner's works has focused on the restrictions that the author has placed on his women and the gender encoding, implicit or otherwise, exhibited and reinforced by such depictions. However, more recent scholarship has approached Faulkner less through accusations of sexism and misogyny and more from the standpoint of objectively studying how Faulkner may be interacting with his women. For example, Deborah Clarke and Minrose Gwin both espouse remaining open to the possibilities for feminist studies within Faulkner's works in their respective *Robbing the Mother* and *The Feminine and Faulkner*.[3] Although not everyone would agree with Harold Bloom's assessment that "No feminist critic will ever be happy with Faulkner. His brooding conviction that female sexuality is closely allied with death seems essential to all of his strongest fiction" (1), feminist criticism continues to approach Faulkner from the standpoint that he is guilty until proven innocent.

On the other hand, Kate Chopin's critics have celebrated the female empowerment witnessed through such characters as Edna Pontellier in *The Awakening*. Chopin has long been cast as a "woman's writer" from the standpoint that her fiction revolutionized the portrayal and consideration of women in fiction. Whether we believe that Chopin was operating from a feminist perspective or whether she was responding to the circumstances of her time, she definitely presents women who break with precedent. According to Anna Shannon Elfenbein, "Kate Chopin's *The Awakening* (1899) shocked its nineteenth-century readers by presenting without comment the adultery of Edna Pontellier, a wealthy, white American wife and mother adrift in Creole society. The shock was so great that the novel went unread for almost sixty years" (304). Although the novel may have been largely shunned for a number of years, its impact on feminist understandings of late nineteenth-century literature has been profound. Feminist scholars have considered the novel from aspects of sexual identity, gender isolation, female independence, feminine power (over both men and other women), and the racially constructed female.[4] Elizabeth Fox-Genovese classifies the novel as a female *bildungsroman* with a twist, indicating that the novel is much more nuanced than this classification would allow. Chopin is simultaneously exploring feminine identity as reflective of natural or social law, the male-female power dynamic, the female-female power dynamic, and the "institutional context of female life" (257). Although Chopin's works often consider her female characters' quest for identity. That being said, the complicated web of influence impacting that conception of self exceeds the parameters of the traditional *bildungsroman*. Variances in focus aside, we can agree that the majority of feminist criticism has emphasized how Chopin functions as a progressive writer of women's fiction. Despite the fact that she and her works may not always be categorized within a feminist framework, she is nearly always interpreted as innovative and provocative.

Considering these authors' divergent approaches to the portrayal of women and the respective reception, it is interesting to consider where the female narratives of these two authors might converge. For example, is there any common ground between a nineteenth-century, widowed, Creole plantation mistress and the post-World War I widow of the last member of an old Southern family? How might these two women share similar experiences based on their shared experience of widowhood? Could their status as widow elevate them from the marginalized role to which society relegates them as women? I propose to examine these questions through a consideration of Chopin's Thérèse Lafirme, the protagonist of *At Fault*, and Faulkner's Narcissa Sartoris, the central character of "There Was a Queen."

The possibility to transcend the gender boundaries enforced upon them as young unmarried women and matrons exists within the framework of widowhood. During the nineteenth century, widows were considered to be "free and legally independent women" (Wood 4), an assessment which would naturally extend into the twentieth century. What this meant for these women was that they were responsible for paying taxes and other debts, they could enter into contracts and be sued, and they were required to survive on their dower[5] and what they could earn. Despite the fact that widows were often portrayed as objects of pity who would become burdens on their male relations, they did possess the capability to assert their independence, particularly in cases where the husband had been wealthy and influential. The connection between Thérèse Lafirme of *At Fault* and Narcissa Sartoris of "There Was a Queen" can be located through their status as the widows of influential and/or wealthy men. From that position, the widows have the unique opportunity to function as their own people, legally and economically (Wood 4). Unfortunately, while these widows' budding autonomy is asserted, their identities are ultimately profoundly influenced by the traditional female roles defined by their society.

Both Thérèse and Narcissa are initially presented as women of substance who are capable of doing what must be done. They appear to function beyond the boundaries of traditional female roles. They exert control over their lives and, to a lesser extent, the lives of those around them. In both narratives, we see these women acting in ways that exhibit a certain determination and practicality, traits which are at first glance unusual and admirable. What we come to realize, however, is that what drives these women is not strength of character but fear. Their fears may not manifest themselves in the same ways, but their actions are definitely influenced by an anxiety sparked by societal pressures. Far from operating beyond societal influence, they are very firmly entrenched within the codes of Southern society. Rather than empowering them, their widowhood serves only to reinforce their conventional female roles. In the end they are both reliant upon their men—Thérèse on her husband David, and Narcissa on her son Bory.

Let me first assert as a baseline the idea that feminine identity within Southern culture is immersed in the façade of "pure" womanhood. The Southern lady in her perfection has been elevated to her statuesque position not just by her men but by an entire society. The reality of the Southern woman's experience is eclipsed by the pedestal on which she stands; there is no room for the subjective portrayal of the woman— the three-dimensional depiction of an actual person with flaws and deficiencies—because the constructed persona must embody all of the desired virtues of her culture. Although Southern culture as an entity may be fallible, the Southern woman represents only the positive aspects of the South. She exists as the embodiment of everything that is good within the culture. Anne Goodwyn Jones describes the Southern woman and her place within her society as follows: "…the image of the Southern lady represents her culture's idea of religious, moral, sexual, racial, and social perfection" (9). As an object, the Southern woman has become synonymous with innocence, grace, kindness, and charity. Within her cloistered experience, this woman is disconnected from concerns of sexuality, power, and material wealth.

Encoded within the iconography of the Southern woman is the political agenda of Southern hegemony. The construction of this icon rests upon an ideology that removes women from any real participation in their culture. As long as they are placed upon a pedestal, women function in a particular manner, allowing the men within this culture to exercise control over their existence. The foundation of Southern patriarchal culture rests upon the ability to convince women that the male is the unchallenged ruler of the society. Thus women are restricted to a very narrow role within Southern society. Under the influence of their husbands, they are not allowed to voice opinion, dissent, or desire. They are expected to avoid any passion whatsoever, remaining in a state of childlike innocence that keeps forever buried their unrealized sensuality. Such scholars as Wyatt Bertram-Brown, Kenneth O'Brien, Anne Goodwyn Jones, and Betina Entzminger have considered the motivation behind the men's subjugation of their women.[6] Whether this control stems from attempts to render the men more admirable by association, feelings of inadequacy, fear of women's competence and independence, or even a need to preserve the purity of the race, Southern men hold their women firmly in hand. Having defined the traditional role of Southern woman, we can better assess how the characters of Thérèse Lafirme and Narcissa Sartoris initially move beyond those parameters but how they are eventually returned to patriarchal Southern society.

At Fault opens just after the death of Thérèse Lafirme's husband, and the fate of the 4,000-acre Cane River plantation has not been determined. The speculation of friends and neighbors is centered on whether the new widow will be able to overcome her grief before her crops, property, and home have gone to ruin and her fortune has been lost. Despite the fact that the majority of landowners in Louisiana, and the rest of the South, suffered severe financial setbacks during and immediately following the Civil War, the Lafirmes have managed to hold on to their land and to succeed, if not thrive, in the post-war economy. Fortunately, for Thérèse and everyone at Place-Du-Bois, the widow is thrust out of her grief-induced catatonia and into the running of the plantation. A seemingly insignificant occurrence, the theft of cotton seed from the plantation, fires Thérèse's indignation and her sense of duty. From that point forward, she assumes responsibility not only for the running and upkeep of the plantation but the moral stability of her plantation community.

While such a role does not fit the standard for nineteenth-century Southern womanhood, the idea that a widow would seize control of the business as well as the domestic aspects of the plantation is not without precedent. As indicated, widowhood was perhaps the one instance when a woman could assert herself into the male-dominated public sphere. This presence was still frowned upon, but the possibility that a widow could involve herself in business matters was not rejected out of hand. In *The Plantation Mistress*, Catherine Clinton explains that while most widows did not fare well, some rose to the occasion and overcame financial hardships left by mismanagement, disorder, and limited liquid assets. Chopin builds Thérèse's credentials as a business woman, capable of functioning within the masculine landscape of industry. At one point, Chopin even depicts Thérèse in a decidedly manly fashion:

> Thérèse loved to walk the length of the wide verandas, armed with her field-glass, and to view her surrounding possessions with comfortable satisfaction. Then her gaze swept from cabin to cabin; from patch to patch; up to the pine-capped hills, and down to the station which squatted a brown and ugly intruder within her fair domain. (6)

Her initial resistance to the progress represented by the railroad and lumber companies is soon overcome. When David Hosmer first approaches her with the notion of logging her beloved woods, she cannot imagine an unlikelier proposition. Allowing pragmatism to overcome sentiment, however, she takes one last walk through the wooded hills to say goodbye and agrees to Hosmer's cultivation proposal.

Thérèse's authority extends beyond the affairs of business, for she functions also as the moral compass for her community. She has a very defined sense of right and wrong, exercising that sense on those around her. When she learns that her nephew Gregoire is "goin' to the devil" (18), she sends for him. She has not had contact with her brother or his family for many years due to a falling out over how Jules Santien was raising his boys. However, she does not let that stop her from saving Gregoire from ruin, financially and morally, exhibiting her strong sense of conscience. She is obligated to sanction Jules' parenting of his children, but she also feels a duty to help her nephew. She goes so far as to give Gregoire much of the operational charge of the plantation, but no one has any misunderstanding as to who is actually in charge of Place-Du-Bois or its inhabitants. In fact, Gregoire tells Mellicent Hosmer, "Oh, they ain't no betta woman in the worl' then Aunt Thérèse, w'en you do like she wants" (18), indicating his affection for his aunt but also his intimidation.

Gregoire is not the only man in her life who is affected by Thérèse's well-developed sense of morality. The fact that her potential lover, David

Hosmer, is divorced comes as a great shock to Thérèse. Of course, her Catholicism factors into her views on divorce, but she emphasizes the notion that each person is responsible for his/her views on this issue. Thérèse's views are surprising, given that the Catholic Church still does not sanction divorce and only allows for the dissolution of marriage through annulment. Notwithstanding her Catholic upbringing, Thérèse's views fit within what James Barnett characterizes as a small but growing splinter group that supported divorce. According to Barnett:

> It is probable that the shift in attitude towards the institution of marriage and, consequently, towards divorce, began in the early decades of the [nineteenth] century and slowly diffused throughout the whole structure of American society. Conservative opinions and institutional judgments were in the saddle, but there was a small, then a larger body of opinion that sanctioned divorce and contributed to the radically altered conception of marriage which prevails today. (44)

Thérèse's views on marriage and divorce are far more progressive than her situation and background would suggest. In presenting Thérèse as tolerant on this very controversial issue, Chopin further opens the gate for Thérèse to develop her personhood free from the constraints of a societally established female identity. Through her widowhood, she can exist as not only legally and economically independent but within a framework that allows for some flexibility within the recognized moral code.

Interestingly, rather than David's divorce, what Thérèse really objects to is the fact that David has abandoned his wife in a time of crisis. Instead of helping her overcome her addiction to alcohol, he leaves her in a position wherein her condition will only worsen. She is left alone to drink. Therefore, David's failed obligation to his wife is more worrisome than any societal view on the immorality of divorce. Apprised of all of the details of the situation, Thérèse implores David to undo his cowardly actions and return to his wife. Thérèse's extreme influence over David is nowhere more evident than in the following resultant exchange:

> "What would you have me do, Mrs. Lafirme?"
> "I would have you do what is right," she said, eagerly approaching him.
> "O, don't present me any questions of right and wrong; can't you see that I'm blind?" he said, self accusingly. "What ever I do, must be because you want it; because I love you." (40)

Thérèse's sense of right and wrong has become the guiding force for not only her actions but David's as well. He does not subscribe to her beliefs and values, but he is willing to embrace them to please her. Thérèse's will encompasses and overtakes that of David's, thereby exhibiting just how much control she has over him.

Although Narcissa Sartoris may not exercise as grand a control over her circumstances as Thérèse Lafirme, she does manage to build a position of authority within her small sphere. Elnora's protestations to the contrary, Narcissa has established herself as the mistress of the Sartoris household. Miss Jenny is one of the last surviving members of the Sartoris family, having watched "her brother die and then her nephew and then her great-nephew and then her two great-great-nephews, and now she lived in the unmanned house with her great-great-nephew's wife and his son, Benbow" (728). Despite her obvious position as the matriarch of the family, Miss Jenny does not control the household. One might argue that Elnora, the housekeeper, actually exerts her influence over the happenings in that house, but even she grudgingly acquiesces to the dictates of young Bayard's widow. When the stranger comes to dinner and is revealed as both Jewish and a Yankee, Miss Jenny's only recourse is to go to her room and remain there, refusing her supper. She does not have the authority to tell the man to leave or even to request that Narcissa do so; instead, she can only remove herself from the situation.

It is significant that Narcissa holds sway in a household that is not technically her own, but it is even more extraordinary that she takes matters into her own hands to save her reputation. When the federal agent contacts her about the "love letters" that were sent to her years before, she knows that she must do whatever it takes to get them back. Before her marriage to Bayard Sartoris, Narcissa received several "anonymous" letters from Byron Snopes, the former bookkeeper in Colonel Sartoris' bank. When the letters begin to arrive, Narcissa reveals their existence to Aunt Jenny, who counsels her to let Colonel Sartoris handle the situation for her. When Narcissa objects to the public airing that this would involve, Aunt Jenny advises her to destroy the letters. Not following any of Aunt Jenny's recommendations, Narcissa keeps the original letter along with ten more that she subsequently receives. Only after they have been stolen does Narcissa worry about their existence and their being "out in the world" (739).

In a strange series of events, the FBI ends up with the letters, which were either dropped or thrown away by the fleeing clerk-turned-thief. The night that the letters were stolen, the clerk also robbed the bank where he was employed. Still working the case twelve years later, the FBI agent contacts Narcissa to question her about her association with the bookkeeper. The agent believes that she must have information about the bookkeeper because of the personal nature of the letters. The appearance of the FBI agent represents Narcissa's fear of discovery, both in terms of having kept the letters and having enjoyed reading them. Arising from those fears are considerations of the sensuality of her nature and its concomitant dismissal of Southern womanhood. Michael Lahey asserts that this story explores "the balance between possibility and failure in the area of privately imagined identity" (161). In Narcissa's case, her imagined identity can become realized through the reemergence of the letters and the options that she has as a woman and widow in re-obtaining them.

Despite her success at moving the fact of their existence to the back of her mind, Narcissa has always been panicked at the notion that someone might possess such an intimate piece of her life. That being said, however, the lengths that she is willing to go to are surprising given the way that she is depicted in *Sanctuary*. In juxtaposition to the sexualized character of Temple Drake, Narcissa functions as the meter for morality, particularly in terms of sexuality. She distrusts anyone who is ruled by his passions, and she puts all men and some women in that category. As David Minter indicates,

> Narcissa . . . epitomizes the cult of respectability. Since she regards all expression of sexuality as both offensive and danger-ous, she speaks consistently for repression. . . . In this judgement we see not only Narcissa's commitment to repression but also her deepest assumptions: that society depends upon repression, par-ticularly of sexual energy; that men can never be depended upon to exercise adequate restraint; and that women must therefore bear the burden of civilization. (125)

In some ways her later actions are consistent with these views. In "There Was a Queen," she reiterates her opinion that men behave in only one manner. She knows that she cannot pay to get the letters back, so she barters herself, confident in the fact that this form of payment will be ac-cepted. She is not terribly upset by the choice she has made; she views it as expedient. In telling Miss Jenny about the encounter, she explains she went to Memphis only in consideration of Miss Jenny and Bory. She did not go away to hide what she was doing but rather to save her family any kind of worry or embarrassment.

One could argue that Narcissa is forced into her actions by the threat of exposure, but she views her behavior as consensual. She made the decision to go to Memphis to get the letters back. She took control of the situation. Melvin Bradford goes so far as to assert that Narcissa takes advantage of the FBI agent and coerces him into betraying his oath of office by promising herself to him in exchange for the letters. Although this interpretation seems extreme, Narcissa does assert herself in this situation and provide her own solution. Just as she did not let Colonel Sartoris handle the situation for her so many years before, she does not let anyone else resolve the difficulty for her now. Of course, her status as widow affords her some protection from the consequences of her actions. Unlike an unmarried girl, she is not cast out of the house or married off in a hurry. She does not suffer the untimely fate of Stephen Crane's Maggie, for example. She is not the unfortunate victim of a cautionary tale. In fact, it is unlikely that anyone will know what she has done or that it will matter to her daily existence. Miss Jenny's response to the news is to ask for her hat, a request she makes when she is very upset. She puts on her hat and sits looking out the window. Of course, Miss Jenny's death could easily be viewed as a consequence of Narcissa's actions, but the direct effect of that event on Narcissa may not be catastrophic. While Narcissa's behavior may be questionable, she does not necessarily suffer because of it, and she is able to exert her will over Miss Jenny and the federal agent to achieve her ends.

While both Thérèse and Narcissa appear to be in control of their environments and the people in them, the question arises as to whether they are comfortable in their non-traditional female roles. Certainly it does not seem unusual for Chopin to incorporate such a character as Thérèse Lafirme into her novel, given her predilection for creating women characters who consistently transcend the established boundaries of womanhood, and particularly Southern womanhood. What is interesting to note is that both Chopin and her fictional character, Thérèse, are widowed at age 32 and undergo something of what Sharon O'Brien terms as an emancipation after their husbands' deaths. In a review of Emily Toth's Chopin biography, O'Brien explains that "when she [Chopin] began to write her stories of bored wives and jubilant widows, Chopin's husband and mother could not figure among her readers and she was no longer defined by the roles of wife and daughter" (O'Brien 10). What is more surprising is that she would create a character who forfeits her newly won freedom for the strictures of married life. Having settled into a position of autonomy, why would Thérèse Lafirme be so eager to abandon it?

Less surprising is the possibility that Faulkner would create a female character who might appear to assert her independence but would eventually seek solace in her female role. Faulkner's characters, both male and female, are more often flawed than not, and the majority of them do not exhibit tremendous strength of character. Narcissa's brother, Horace, is an excellent example of this. While he has good qualities, Horace's attraction for his step-daughter, Belle, is at once inappropriate and destructive. Even more unsettling is the notion that Horace's obsession with Belle replaces the one that he formerly maintained for his sister. Faulkner's characters very often struggle with the notion of sexuality and its expression, and the fact that Narcissa might take comfort in the image of Southern womanhood, in all its purity, is not astonishing, especially as we understand her perspective on sexuality.

Ultimately neither woman maintains the independence presented through her status as widow; both women re-embrace their traditional female identity of wife and mother. While Thérèse literally forfeits her widowhood, Narcissa figuratively gives it up when she makes Bory the focus of her existence. The question that reasserts itself here, though, is why? What prompts this reaffirmation of traditional womanhood? The answer that resonates throughout both stories is that both women are so afraid of the unknown, the precipice, that they cling to the identity that is most familiar to them and, thus, offers the greatest security. Throughout *At Fault*, Thérèse does exercise control over her small community, but this is a known quantity. Her plantation and its environs are at once close and material. When she is forced to consider the abstract, she becomes overwhelmed and frightened. The night of the fire, when Gregoire kills Jocint, Thérèse shies away from the larger question of what Gregoire's actions mean and allows the men to take care of the situation.

After seeing the condition of Fanny and David's relationship first-hand, Thérèse begins to question her view of right and wrong. Has she counseled David well in returning to Fanny and subjecting himself to a life of misery? Instead of wrestling with this question, she convinces herself that her selfish heart is merely sympathizing with David's position. She cannot handle these larger questions on her own; they threaten her understanding of herself and her environment. Her need for her eventual husband to help her with these larger issues is best expressed by David: "'Thérèse, the truth in its entirety isn't given to man to know—such knowledge, no doubt, would be beyond human endurance. I have not cared to stop in this struggle of life to question. You, perhaps, wouldn't dare to alone. Together, dear one, we will work it out'" (165). As David's wife, she will be able to face such philosophical crises; David, perhaps through his alter ego Homeyer, will be able to explain it to her. Homeyer is presented as a friend of David's, who is much more sophisticated in his views of politics, religion, and ethics. At one point, when Thérèse asserts that she is beginning to think that Homeyer is not real, David replies, "Indeed he is no myth; but a friend who is fond of going into such things and allows me the benefit of his deeper perceptions" (11). Throughout the novel, Homeyer functions as the outlet for the philosophical and ideological stances that David cannot express, and it is he who objects to Thérèse's suggestion that David return to St. Louis to remarry Fanny.

Narcissa, on the other hand, seeks solace and protection through her role as mother, because only in that role can she allay her fears of the unknown. Narcissa's fear stems from the latent sexuality that emerges when she receives the letters. When the first letter arrives, she approaches Miss Jenny to ask for her advice and is told to allow Colonel Sartoris to investigate and find the man responsible. Narcissa's reluctance to do this appears to stem from a natural embarrassment at the situation. She indicates that she would rather burn them and forget them than to let anyone know what has happened. We later find out that Narcissa has not only kept the first letter but that there are additional letters. Narcissa's continued possession of these letters, until they are stolen during a burglary, reflects a morbid fascination with their sexual content. She is somehow drawn to the statements of "love" and to her representation as a sexual being. All of a sudden, she has much more in common with Temple Drake than she would care to admit. Narcissa cannot face what this might imply, and this is the reason for her worry about the letters being "out in the world" (739). The unknown for Narcissa is what her fascination with the letters says about her own sexuality, and so she must wipe the letters out of existence to remove the threat of that unknown. She realizes that being Bory's mother makes her feel protected from the awfulness of the letters and their significance. After she has returned from Memphis and destroyed the letters, she takes her son to the creek so that they might bathe themselves in the waters of the "Jordan." In that act, she at once baptizes and purifies herself, removing all traces of the "sins" she has just committed. She is ready, then, to reassume the role of "mother." As evidence of this, she pleads with Bory to ensure that they are never separated again. She will not allow him to exert his independence, as is expected of children, but instead will use him to permanently and unequivocally define herself as mother.

As startling as this realization may be, Chopin and Faulkner have created characters in Thérèse Lafirme and Narcissa Sartoris who have a great deal in common despite differences in the historical periods and circumstances of their experience. Bearing in mind Chopin's reputation as a writer of women, we approach *At Fault* with the expectation that we will encounter another strong female in the form of Thérèse Lafirme. We likely do not have similar hopes for Faulkner's Narcissa Sartoris, knowing that Faulkner's women have often been classified as two-dimensional characters who live only in relation to their male counterparts. Much to our surprise, however, we find that Thérèse and Narcissa not only share the experience of widowhood but also the struggle between independence and familiarity. Both women allow their fear of the unknown to cripple them and prevent them from assuming the autonomy that their position as widows affords them. They have a very real opportunity to take control of their own lives, but they forfeit this chance in favor of the known world of their given society. In doing so, they are permanently folded into a patriarchal society that will ignore their individual identities as women in order to maintain the ideal of Southern womanhood. Thérèse and Narcissa will be subsumed by their society, and their status as widows will matter not at all.

Notes

1. In "William Faulkner: Life and Art," Joseph Blotner identifies five types of female characters in Faulkner's works: "the admirable little girl (e. g. Caddy Compson as child), the slim and virginal young woman (Pat Robyn in *Mosquitoes*), the voluptuous young woman (Eula Varner), the mature temptress (Belle Mitchell in *Sartoris*), the matron (respectable: Maggie Mallison [Gavin Stevens's sister] and disreputable: Reba Rivers in *Sanctuary*), and the venerable matriarch (Granny Millard)" (11). In *Faulkner and Southern Womanhood*, Diane Roberts explores Faulkner's use of the stock characters of Southern womanhood—the Confederate Woman, Mammy, the Tragic Mulatta, the New Belle, the Night Sister, and Mothers and Motherhood—to show how he conflates the distinctions between these stereotypes and destabilizes the Southern hegemony's hold on its society.

2. According to Doreen Fowler, ". . . some critics, including such well-known authorities as Leslie Fiedler, Irving Howe, and Albert Guerard, have even charged Faulkner with harboring a deep-seated and thinly veiled hatred of women" (144). Echoing this sentiment in a 1975 address given at the annual Faulkner Conference held at the University of Mississippi, Ellen Douglas concluded her remarks with these words: "In this sense, woman is wilderness, is South, is lost innocence, is failed and sinful humanity. Of course, Faulkner hates women. Of course, Quentin hates the South" (166). For all four scholars, Faulkner presents a patriarchal society that at best leaves little, if any, room for its women to present themselves or to make an impact and, more likely, creates an openly hostile environment for its women to navigate. For more information, see Leslie Fiedler, *Love and Death in the American Novel* (New York: Criterion, 1960); Irving Howe, *Faulkner: A Critical Study*, 2nd ed. (New York: Vintage, 1962); Albert J. Guerard, "Forbidden Games (III): Faulkner's Misogyny," in the *Triumph of the Novel: Dickens, Dostoevesky, Faulkner* (New York: Oxford UP, 1976); and Ellen Douglas, "Faulkner's

Women," in "*A Cosmos of My Own": Faulkner and Yoknapatawpha, 1980,* ed. Doreen Fowler and Ann J. Abadie (Jackson: UP of Mississippi, 1981): 166.

3. Other examples include *Faulkner and Women*, a collection of essays from the 1985 Faulkner and Yoknapatawpha Conference, which contains several essays that explore the ways in which Faulkner's obsession with the father, masculinity, and sexuality impact his female characters and their ability to be heard and seen. Similarly the collection of essays representing the 1994 Faulkner and Yoknapatawpha Conference on "Faulkner and Gender" explore exactly where and how Faulkner comes down on the "gender line." In "William Faulkner as a Lesbian Author," Frann Michel considers the possibility that Faulkner has constructed a work that empowers women through female creativity; however, she does ultimately decide that "[f]aced with the impossibility of identifying themselves as masculine, Faulkner, as writer, and a number of his male characters act to assert a masculinity by more or less violently disempowering female and feminine figures" (143). The very fact that Michel looks at how Faulkner might positively impact a female audience and transform a male audience is indicative of a progressive approach to Faulkner studies. For further reading, see Doreen Fowler and Ann J. Abadie, eds., *Faulkner and Women: Faulkner and Yoknapatawpha, 1985* (Jackson: UP of Mississippi, 1986); Donald Kartiganer and Ann J. Abadie, eds., *Faulkner and Gender: Faulkner and Yoknapatawpha, 1994* (Jackson, UP of Mississippi, 1996); and Frann Michel, "William Faulkner as a Lesbian Author" in *Men Writing the Feminine: Literature, Theory, and the Question of Genders*, ed. Thaïs E. Morgan (Albany, NY: State U of New York P, 1994.) 139-54.

4. For further reading, see the following: Nancy Walker, "Feminist or Naturalist: The Social Context of Kate Chopin's *The Awakening,*" *Southern Quarterly* 17 (1979): 95-103; Elizabeth Fox-Genovese, "Kate Chopin's *The Awakening,*" *Southern Studies* 18 (1979): 261-90; Sandra M. Gilbert, "The Second Coming of Aphrodite: Kate Chopin's Fantasy of Desire," *Kenyon Review* 5 (Summer 1983): 42-66; Anna Shannon Elfenbein, *Women on the Color Line: Evolving Stereotypes and the Writings of George Washington Cable, Grace King, and Kate Chopin* (Charlottesville: UP of Virginia, 1989); Cynthia Griffin Wolff, "Un-utterable Longing: The Discourse of Feminine Sexuality in *The Awakening,*" *Studies in American Fiction* 24 (1996): 3-22; and Helen Taylor, *Gender, Race, and Region in the Writings of Grace King, Ruth McEnery Stuart, and Kate Chopin* (Baton Rouge: Louisiana State UP, 1989).

5. In most instances, the dower consisted of one-third of the husband's real-estate assets upon his death. If the dower did not meet their needs, they were forced to find some kind of work to support themselves. Because the dower very often was not sufficient, widows required additional support from their friends, family, and charitable organizations.

6. For further reading, consult Bertram Wyatt-Brown, *Hearts of Darkness: Wellsprings of a Southern Literary Tradition* (Baton Rouge: Louisiana State UP, 2003); Kenneth O'Brien, "Race, Romance, and the Southern Literary Tradition," in *Recasting:* Gone With the Wind *in American Culture,* ed. Darden Asbury

Pyron (Miami: UP of Florida, 1983): 153-166; Anne Goodwyn Jones, *Tomorrow Is Another Day: The Woman Writer in the South, 1859-1936* (Baton Rouge: Louisiana State UP, 1981); and Betina Entzminger, *The Belle Gone Bad: White Southern Women Writers and the Dark Seductress* (Baton Rouge: Louisiana State UP, 2002).

Works Cited

Barnett, James Harwood. *Divorce and the American Divorce Novel, 1858-1937*. New York: Russell & Russell, 1968.

Bloom, Harold. "Introduction." *William Faulkner*. New Edition. Ed. Bloom. New York: Bloom's Literary Criticism, 2008: 1-5.

Blotner, Joseph. "William Faulkner: Art and Life." In *Faulkner and Women: Faulkner and Yoknapatawpha, 1985*, ed. Doreen Fowler and Ann J. Abadie. Jackson: UP of Mississippi, 1986. 3-20.

Bradford, Melvin. "Certain Ladies of Quality: Faulkner's View of Women and the Evidence of 'There Was a Queen.'" *Arlington Quarterly* 1 (1967): 133.

Chopin, Kate. *At Fault*. 1890. New York: Penguin Books, 2002.

Clarke, Deborah. *Robbing the Mother: Women in Faulkner*. Jackson: UP of Mississippi, 1994.

Clinton, Catherine. *The Plantation Mistress*. New York: Pantheon Books, 1982.

Elfenbein, Anna Shannon. "Kate Chopin's *The Awakening*: An Assault on American Racial and Sexual Mythology." *Southern Studies* 26.4 (Winter 1987): 304-12.

Faulkner, William. *Flags in the Dust*. New York: Random House, 1973.

———. *Sanctuary*. 1932. New York: Vintage Books, 1993.

———. "There Was a Queen." *Collected Short Stories of William Faulkner*. New York: Vintage Books, 1955. 727-44.

Fowler, Doreen. "Joe Christmas and 'Womanshenegro.'" In *Faulkner and Women: Faulkner and Yoknapatawpha, 1985*, ed. Doreen Fowler and Ann J. Abadie. Jackson: UP of Mississippi, 1986. 144-161.

Fox-Genovese, Elizabeth. "Kate Chopin's *The Awakening*." *Southern Studies* 110.18 (1979): 261-90.

Gwin, Minrose. *The Feminine and Faulkner: Reading (Beyond) Sexual Difference*. Knoxville: U of Tennessee P, 1990.

Jones, Anne Goodwyn. *Tomorrow Is Another Day.* Baton Rouge: Louisiana State UP, 1981.

Lahey, Michael. "Narcisssa's Love Letters: Illicit Space and the Writing of Female Identity in 'There Was a Queen.'" In *Faulkner and Gender: Faulkner and Yoknapatawpha, 1994,* ed. Donald M. Kartiganer and Ann J. Abadie. Jackson: UP of Mississippi, 1996. 160-180.

Michel, Frann. "William Faulkner as a Lesbian Author." In *Men Writing the Feminine: Literature, Theory, and the Question of Genders*, ed. Thaïs E. Morgan. Albany, NY: State U of New York P, 1994. 139-154.

Minter, David. *William Faulkner: His Life and Work.* Baltimore: Johns Hopkins UP, 1980.

O'Brien, Sharon. "Bored Wives and Jubilant Widows." Rev. of *Kate Chopin* by Emily Toth. *New York Times* 30 Dec. 1990: BR 10. 2 Oct. 2008.

Roberts, Diane. *Faulkner and Southern Womanhood.* Athens: U of Georgia P, 1994.

Wood, Kirsten. *Masterful Women: Slaveholding Widows from the American Revolution through the Civil War.* Chapel Hill: U of North Carolina P, 2004.

Empowering the Pedestal: Unvanquishable Grannies in Faulkner and Chopin

Throughout the antebellum period, the Southern planter class responded to the growing national tension regarding the institution of slavery by promoting the image of Southern society as an ideal social arrangement governed by an aristocracy committed to the principle of *noblesse oblige*. The antebellum, pro-slavery, plantation school of literature, intent on shifting the view of slavery from the notion of a "necessary evil" to a "positive good," further honed the regional version of the national ideal of femininity and exaggerated the requisites of "True Womanhood," which included piety, purity, submissiveness, and domesticity (Welter 152). In this patriarchal society, the plantation mistress became an important symbol of gentility, refinement, and gracious living. Yet the reality of plantation mistresses' daily lives was vastly different from the "magnolia myth"; indeed, the endless responsibilities of these women equipped them with the tools necessary to maneuver within the severe restrictions of the Old South's caste system, particularly for older women. In this essay I demonstrate the ways in which Granny Millard in William Faulkner's *The Unvanquished* and Madame Valmondé in Kate Chopin's "Désirée's Baby" further empower themselves by strategically negotiating a legal and social system predicated on their powerlessness, thus epitomizing the highest ideal of maternal commitment.

Many scholars of Faulkner's tenth novel, *The Unvanquished*, have examined the character Rosa Millard, most often within the specific cultural/historical context of the Civil War; by contrast, only peripheral attention has been paid to Chopin's character Madame Valmondé. Yet these characters share much in common, particularly in their roles as experienced plantation mistresses and the power both derive from their commitment to the family. Most scholarly analyses of Rosa Millard regard her strength, however, as the result of a transformation brought on by the Civil War. Diane Roberts, for example, identifies Granny as a representative "Confederate Woman," defining the term as a combination of "the images of belle and warrior, Spartan woman and Roman matron ... embodying the romantic, religious and political discourses of the Civil War" (233). June Dwyer takes a similar approach, contending that Granny "is transformed by the War" (58). Such transformation requires, according to Roberts, a "near-unbearable tension in *The Unvanquished* between the masculine and feminine spheres of Granny's life. Her masculine annexation of power as the plantation master leads her to steal and lie while her role as feminine moralist forces her to condemn her own actions. She moves between male and female roles" (239). However, as the comments of Bayard and Ringo demonstrate throughout the first four sections of the novel, Granny does not *become* empowered; she has always been empowered; yet during the war, she additionally shows herself to be a master of adaptation.

The position Granny occupies in the role of a Southern lady was a crucially important symbol in plantation culture, but as Southern girls grew into women, they often became entangled in the contradictions between their actual lives and the expectations of the Southern chivalric ideal of womanhood. A particularly paradoxical aspect of the social system that antebellum women often complained about in journals, letters, and diaries was the contradictory attitude regarding labor juxtaposed to the reality of daily life. Anne Goodwyn Jones notes:

> Southern settlers brought with them from England a belief in patriarchal values . . . these values made the man the source of family authority, the family the source of societal order and stability, and the planter class the source of authority within society. Then, as early as the seventeenth century, a native southern aristocracy developed an "ethos of leisure and consumption" that "stipulated that women should perform an essentially ornamental function in society." (11)

Yet in spite of the cultural ideal of privileged indulgence, "the practical needs of plantation life cast her in quite a different role. The clash of myth and reality was monumental. . . . First and foremost, manual labor and physical work were disdained" (Clinton 17). Indeed, manual labor operated as an index of the class system in the Old South and signified yeoman and working class status. Juxtaposed to its binary image of leisure as a sign of elite status, the extensive labor upper-class women performed operated in direct opposition to their real life experiences.

The reality of daily life for upper-class women was indeed a constant contradiction to the leisure ethic, yet due to the size of plantations, the distance between other plantations and farms, and the difficulties of travel throughout the antebellum period, the labor elite women performed was obscured from view, typically visible only to members of the household. Moreover, the duties these women performed were considerable. Plantation mistresses customarily functioned as domestic plantation managers.

While overseers worked in the fields, making agricultural decisions, maintaining discipline, and organizing the daily tasks of the slaves,

> the planter's wife was in charge not merely of the mansion but of the entire spectrum of domestic operations throughout the estate, from food and clothing to the physical and spiritual care of both her white family and her husband's slaves. The borders of her domain might extend from the mansion's locked pantry to the slave-quarter hospital and the slaughtering pen for the hogs. (Clinton 18)

Because this role was so crucial to the viability of a working plantation, planters who lost wives due to death or disability typically turned to an unmarried female relative to take over the enormous responsibilities of the plantation mistress. Moreover, because "southern women were more likely to die as a result of childbirth . . . twice the maternal mortality rate in the New England and Middle Atlantic states," the practice was a common one (McMillen 81). Faulkner's Rosa Millard, for example, illustrates the custom, assuming the role of plantation mistress for John Sartoris after her daughter, as Bayard notes, "died when I was born" (17).

The narrative events of the novel begin during the second year of the war, but glimpses of life before the war for this family are referenced by Bayard and Ringo. Furthermore, while the number of slaves owned by John Sartoris is unclear, textual evidence suggests that Sartoris ran an extensive plantation before the war, enabling him, as Uncle Buck explains, to raise "'the first damn regiment in Mississippi out of his own pocket and took 'em to Ferginny and whipped Yankees right and left with 'em before he found out that what he had bought and paid for wasn't a regiment of soldiers but a congress of politicians and fools'" (58). After his demotion, Sartoris finances another outfit to form "his irregular cavalry" (56). References to the physical layout of the Sartoris domain also contribute to evidence that suggests a large working plantation. For example, after a day confined inside due to rain, when the weather clears, the boys flee the house and run past the "smokehouse, stables, and the cabins" (22). A map of Yoknapatawpha County, included in the novel *Absalom, Absalom!*, indicates that the Sartoris plantation also featured a cotton gin. Granny's duties before the war were thus extensive.

In addition to raising her grandson, as well as demonstrating a substantial role in raising Ringo, Granny manages the household and assumes the role of moral authority and disciplinarian. Bayard notes that "Granny had never whipped us for anything in our lives except lying, and that even when it wasn't even a told lie, but just keeping quiet, how she would whip us first and then make us kneel down and kneel down with us herself to ask the Lord to forgive us" (32). Granny demonstrates other responsibilities typically required of plantation mistresses, such as those identified by Sally McMillen: "[to] garden, nurse her children, supervise slaves and household members, sew, cook, clean, or tend to the thousands of duties associated with nineteenth-century households" (41). Granny is featured engaged in a wide range of these types of duties, often indicating that these were routine events, such as the weekly task "each Tuesday afternoon" of Granny, Louvinia, and Philadelphy polishing the silver (16). Another common practice is evident by several references to sewing, which, as Catherine Clinton points out, was a plantation mistress's "most demanding task" (26). For example, as Bayard and Ringo wait for Colonel Sartoris to begin telling stories of the war, "Granny sewed beside the lamp on the table" (19), and on a rainy day, the boys approach Granny who then "put the sewing away" (21). Another common task in Granny's life is keeping the boys occupied, which she does by drawing on her domestic role and reading recipes from the cookbook. Her question, "What shall we read about today?" (21), indicates that this is a familiar practice.

Granny's role and experience as a plantation mistress reveals a competent, intelligent, and strong woman. Indeed, Ringo's confidence in Granny's mettle not only provides evidence of her strength but her courage and conduct further show that Ringo is indeed smarter than Bayard (91). When John Sartoris expresses his concern for Granny: "'Lord, Marse John,' Ringo said, 'is you still worrying about Granny? I been knowed her all my life; I ain't worried'" (74). And as they prepare to travel to Memphis, Ringo tells Bayard: "'I bet if she stayed here wouldn't no Yankee nor nothing else bother that trunk, nor Marse John neither, if he knowed it'" (44). On another occasion, after the mules are stolen and Ringo and Bayard are separated from Granny, they return to the plantation to find Granny back home. Ringo tells Bayard confidently, "'I tole you they wasn't no Yankees gonter stop Granny'" (71).

Ringo's relationship shows his unique appreciation for her abilities, and his faith in Granny is duly rewarded after he and Bayard shoot at the Yankee soldier and kill the company's prized racehorse. When the soldiers storm the house in search of the boys, Granny's quick thinking, by concealing them under her skirt, shows her sharp intellect and bold courage. Granny successfully fools the first officer to question her, but she is aware that she has not been successful with Colonel Dick. Granny quickly shifts her strategy and draws on her role as Southern lady by reading the gesture of Colonel Dick, "who looked at Granny sitting in the chair with her hand at her breast, and took off his hat" (34). When he begins to question her, "Granny gave him look for look while she lied" (35). Granny's quick assessment of Colonel Dick is a bold but brilliant move and highly effective. When the soldiers complain about their orders to leave the house, the Colonel is compelled to operate according to Granny's status, which won't permit him to challenge her claim. He tells the men: "'Didn't you just hear this lady say there are no children here'" (35). As the textual events unfold, Ringo is shown to be an accurate and savvy judge of character. Indeed, it is little wonder that Granny chooses Ringo as her strategic partner.

As Granny and Ringo embark on their schemes to swindle the federal government, Granny draws on her role as Southern lady on numerous occasions, which allows them, for example, to travel together under the guise of a typical Southern mistress accompanied by her servant. In addition to the interdependence between the two, they are depicted as intellectual equals and are often featured together engaged in discussions of strategy. As they plan their next move, Bayard notes that "they sounded like two people playing a guessing game in code" (141). The game they are playing, however, is revealed to be Granny fulfilling the promises that had been used to justify privileged class status in a society theoretically founded on the principle of *noblesse oblige*, which was an image of slaves and other dependents viewed "as inferior members of their extended households from whom they expected work and obedience but to whom they owed guidance and protection" (Kolchin 112). Granny's sense of obligation, not simply to her own family but to those of her community who need her help, is evident when "Granny sent for them, sent out word back into the hills where they lived in dirt-floored cabins, on the little poor farms without slaves . . . men, women, and children and the dozen niggers that had got free" (153). As the needy arrive in church, Granny confesses her sins and asks: "'I want you all to pray for me'" (156). Granny and Ringo then open "a big blank account book" and begin to call out the names, distribute money, loan mules, and ask what "they intended to do with the money" (157).

Granny ultimately misjudges only once, but that single mistake is deadly. She errs in assuming that her code of honor is more extensive that it proves to be. Ringo expresses his concern about the plan Ab Snopes sets up, but Granny responds, "'They won't hurt a woman'" (173). This miscalculation costs Granny her life. Yet during her funeral, the community's regard for her is evident by the massive turnout, including "most of the Jefferson people" as well as:

the old men and the women and the children, and the niggers . . .
the hundred more who had returned to the country since, who had
followed the Yankees away and then returned, to find their families
and owners gone, to scatter into the hills and live in caves and hollow trees like animals I suppose, not only with no one to depend on
but with no one depending on them, caring whether they returned
or not or lived or died or not. (177-78)

The turnout suggests that the mourners are not simply those who
knew Granny personally but the many whose lives she touched. Ringo's
repeated assessment of Granny's personal power proves to be profoundly
accurate and deeply insightful, verifying not just a woman empowered
by the war, but a woman empowered by a lifetime of responsibility and
competence, requiring adaptation to suit the circumstances of war and
deprivation.

Kate Chopin's short story, "Désirée's Baby," depicts a woman similarly
empowered by, or perhaps in spite of, her role as Southern lady. Because
her involvement in the narrative events is brief and often peripheral, little
scholarly attention has been given to this character, yet her actions function as a powerful form of cultural critique and social scrutiny. Published
in 1893, "Désirée's Baby" is set in antebellum Louisiana and opens on the
day Madame Valmondé travels from her plantation to visit her daughter, Désirée. Désirée, as a new mother, is beginning to fulfill one of the
most important components of the duty of Southern womanhood. For
Southern women, the role of motherhood was the most crucial of the
Old South's shibboleths. Sally McMillen notes that "southern men glorified the maternal role and criticized as masculine northern women who
stepped beyond it. . . . A positive attitude toward having large numbers
of children reflected the vigor of the patriarchy, the importance of the
southern family, and the prosperity of the region" (3). However, in spite of
the glorified image of Southern motherhood,

the realties surrounding childbirth for an antebellum southern
woman were a far cry from the mythical image of her gliding
through days of leisure. . . . More likely the typical privileged
southern woman bore and reared several children, suffered poor
health, exhaustion, and a variety of physical ailments, grieved
over the death of at least one child, and was either pregnant or
nursing a newborn in every year until her midforties. Married
women in the Old South found their lives defined by their
duties. (3)

Furthermore, regardless of class, in a predominantly agrarian culture, these duties were numerous and required physical and emotional stamina, yet Southern women have typically been viewed as weak and dependent, and thus seen as contributors to their own oppression.

Numerous historians have noted that women in the South largely failed to participate in the nineteenth-century's reform movements, particularly regarding the issues of abolition and women's rights. Indeed, the most well known exceptions to this regional rule, Sarah and Angelina Grimké, felt compelled to leave the South in order to participate publicly in antislavery and feminist social reform protest. However, more recent feminist scholars have introduced new ideas regarding women's roles and their involvement in their culture, suggesting a different kind of feminism, rather than total lack of feminist commitment. Susan Stanford Friedman challenges the notion of an all-encompassing, universal feminism and instead proposes a theory of feminism that addresses shifting historical factors and geographical specificities. Thus, a locational feminism recognizes

> how different times and places produce different and chang-
> ing gender systems as these intersect with other different and
> changing societal stratifications and movements for social justice.
> Locational feminisms thus encourages the study of difference in
> all its manifestations without being limited to it, without estab-
> lishing impermeable borders that inhibit the production and
> visibility of ongoing intercultural exchange and hybridity. (5)

In this respect, actions within the context of time, place, and location can thus be viewed as challenging oppression from within rather than without or not at all.

Madame Valmondé's brief but important role throughout the short story suggests a challenge from within evident by Chopin's strategic use of various narrative devices. As such, it is important to point out the distinction between story and plot because the narrative techniques Chopin employs function to distribute information strategically. While story is defined as a specific narrative event, the organization of events combines to create the narrative plot. Chopin utilizes third person throughout the narrative but alternates between internal and external focalization, and within the first five paragraphs, there are four temporal shifts which provide distinct stories. The account opens with Madame Valmondé traveling to L'Abri to visit her daughter and new grandchild. Chopin then uses the technique of analepsis to provide the history of Désirée's adoption by the childless Valmondés, internally focalized through Madame Valmondé's perspective using free indirect discourse, which maintains the third person point of view while "a character's thoughts (as opposed to utterances) are represented" (Prince 36). In the following paragraph, Chopin provides a more detached history of the union of Désirée and Armand and then shifts the narrative directly to an external depiction of Madame Valmondé bending over Désirée.

Chopin continues to use external focalization to demonstrate Madame Valmondé's reaction to the sight of Desiree's baby. Her comment indicates surprise and additionally functions as a foreshadowing device: "'This is not the baby!' she exclaimed, in startled tones" (141). Her scrutiny of the baby indicates that Madame Valmondé notices an unexpected aspect regarding her grandchild, but her behavior and subsequent comment also demonstrate that this is not the first time she has seen the baby. She "had never removed her eyes from the child. She lifted it and walked with it over to the window that was lightest. She scanned the baby narrowly, then looked as searchingly at Zandrine" (142). As Madame Valmondé returns the baby to his mother, she remarks to her daughter: "'Yes, the child has grown, has changed'" (142). Her comment indicates that the baby has changed from the physical ambiguities typical of newborns to a baby developing the distinct features Madame Valmondé recognizes as indicators of mixed racial identity. While many scholars have noted that racial categories of "white" and "black" are the "product of history, not of nature," as Evelyn Brooks Higginbotham points out, "to argue that race is a myth and that it is an ideological rather than a biological fact does not deny that ideology has real effects on people's lives," a point clearly not lost on Chopin (225). Chopin then ends Madame Valmondé's involvement in the story abruptly, and thus the sense of concern regarding the baby's appearance resonates into the following section.

The narrative pace of the story then jumps forward three months, depicting a troubled Désirée on the bed with her baby pondering the disturbing changes in Armand over the last three months while "one of LaBlance's little quadroon boys—half naked too—stood fanning the child slowly" (143). This scene functions as a parallel to the earlier scene in which Madame Valmondé gazes on the child, specifically the similar reaction of startled comprehension. Désirée looks "from her child to the boy who stood beside him, and back again, over and over. 'Ah!' It was a cry that she could not help" (144). Désirée thus discovers what her mother has already suspected. Armand confirms her fears and banishes her and their child from L'Abri for bringing shame "on his home and his name" (146). Distraught, Désirée writes her mother: "'My mother, they tell me I am not white. Armand has told me I am not white. For God's sake tell them it is not true. You must know it is not true. I shall die. I must die. I cannot be so unhappy, and live'" (145). Madame Valmondé has had three months to contemplate the inevitable revelation of the grandchild's racial identity, and her response to Désirée is a powerful challenge to the social, legal, and ideological foundation of the society in which she lives. She writes: "My own Désirée: Come home to Valmondé; back to your mother who loves you. Come with your child" (145). The letter is brief but every word is a bold and courageous challenge to the Southern caste system. Using the pronoun "my" followed by the adjective "own" reaffirms the maternal connection between mother and daughter. Referring to Valmondé as "home" establishes the plantation as a safe domestic haven. Use of the word "mother" indicates that there is no change to the nature of the relationship between Madame Valmondé and Désirée regardless of other circumstantial changes, and finally, asking Désirée to bring her child also acknowledges the baby as a recognized member of the Valmondé family as well. The letter is direct, unequivocal, and conveys no sign of doubt or hesitation.

Within the cultural and historical context of the text, Madame Valmondé's brief note is a profound rejection of the Southern social order. Margaret Bauer notes that "no woman with even a trace of African blood in evidence would be allowed by the slaveholding South to be the mistress of L'Abri, the plantation of a white man. Indeed, their marriage would have been illegal in antebellum Louisiana" (163). Madame Valmondé thus invites not only her rejected daughter back but one who is now legally and socially a fallen woman by virtue of giving birth to an illegitimate child. Furthermore, Bauer argues persuasively that readers have missed the most important point in Chopin's story, which is "that Armand Aubigny has been aware *all along* of his own racial heritage" (161). Yet regardless of which parent Madame Valmondé believes to be responsible for the child's non-white racial identity, Barbara J. Fields points out "the well-known anomaly of American racial convention that considers a white woman capable of giving birth to a black child but denies that a black woman can give birth to a white child" (9). Thus, whether Madame Valmondé invites her white daughter who has given birth to a black child or her black daughter who has given birth to a black child, the inclusion of her grandchild adds depth to the unconditional love evident by the eighteen powerful words of her brief but profound note.

In his novel *The Blithedale Romance*, Nathanial Hawthorne's character Zenobia complains that "women possess no rights, . . . or, at all events, only little girls and grandmothers would have the force to exercise them" (59). This character's complaint suggests that formidable grandmothers were not limited to Southern examples, yet regional, class, and historical factors demonstrate that the power exercised by Southern Grannies was very different from the traditional New England matriarch. Often compelled to negotiate a Southern system in which their role was viewed as ornamental, yet living a contradiction through the demands of their daily lives, Southern women developed a savvy ability to maneuver within an oppressive and often physically isolating social system. As the characters Madame Valmondé and Rosa Millard suggest, Southern women, particularly those with age and experience, negotiated a complex system with remarkable skill and thus epitomize the highest ideal of "True Womanhood."

Works Cited

Bauer, Margaret D. "Armand Aubigny, Still Passing After All These Years: The Narrative Voice and Historical Context of 'Désirée's Baby.'" In *Critical Essays On Kate Chopin*, ed. Alice Hall Petry. New York: Hall, 1996. 161-83.

Chopin, Kate. "Désirée's Baby." *Bayou Folk*. 1894. Amherst: Prometheus Books, 2002.

Clinton, Catherine. *The Plantation Mistress: Woman's World in the Old South*. New York: Pantheon Books, 1982.

Dwyer, June. "Feminization, Masculinization, and the Role of the Woman Patriot." *Faulkner Journal* 6.2 (1991): 55-64.

Faulkner, William. *The Unvanquished*. 1938. New York: Vintage, 1966.

Friedman, Susan Stanford. *Mappings: Feminism and the Cultural Geographies of Encounter*. Princeton: Princeton UP, 1998.

Fields, Barbara J. "Race, Slavery, and Ideology in the United States of America." *New Left Review* 181 (1990): 95-118.

Hawthorne, Nathaniel. *The Blithedale Romance*. 1852. New York: Norton, 1958.

Higginbotham, Evelyn Brooks. "African-American Women's History and the Metalanguage of Race." *Signs* 17 (1992): 251-74.

Jones, Anne Goodwyn. *Tomorrow Is Another Day: The Woman Writer in the South, 1859-1936*. Baton Rouge: Louisiana State UP, 1981.

Kolchin, Peter. *American Slavery 1619-1877*. New York: Hill & Wang, 1993.

McMillen, Sally G. *Motherhood in the Old South: Pregnancy, Childbirth, and Infant Rearing.* Baton Rouge: Louisiana State UP, 1990.

Prince, Gerald. *Dictionary of Narratology.* Lincoln: U of Nebraska P, 1987.

Roberts, Diane. "A Precarious Pedestal: The Confederate Woman in Faulkner's *Unvanquished." Journal of American Studies* 26.2 (1992): 233-46.

Welter, Barbara. "The Cult of True Womanhood: 1820-1860." *American Quarterly* 18 (1966): 151-74.

In Search of Agency:
Edna Pontellier and Charlotte Rittenmeyer Find Independence, and Death,
in *The Awakening* and *The Wild Palms*

To appreciate this discussion of Edna Pontellier's and Charlotte Rittenmeyer's "agency," it is necessary to first understand the approach that is being employed. Toward this end, consider Lara M. Ahearn's "Language and Agency" from the *Annual Review of Anthropology* in which she states: "Agency refers to the socioculturally mediated capacity to act." In other words, "all action is socioculturally mediated, both in its production and in its interpretation" (112). Discussions of agency often remain focused merely upon "free will" and "resistance," but the definition cannot stop there. Ahearn cautions against using these oversimplified concepts and argues, instead, that the definition of action theorists and philosophers be employed to explain human agency. Ahearn explains their theory "requires some sort of concomitant mental state, such as 'intention'…, 'presence of self'…, a 'rational point of view,' and a 'domain of intentional control'…, or [in simpler terms,] 'motivation, responsibility, and expectation of recognition or reward'" (114).[1] Ahearn continues by referencing Anthony Giddens' "structuration theory." She explains:

> Unlike scholars who treat agency as a synonym for free will or resistance, Giddens consistently links agency to structure through his discussion of rules and resources. Central to Giddens' theory of structuration is the understanding that people's actions are shaped (*in both constraining and enabling ways*) [my emphasis] by the very social structures that those actions then serve to reinforce or reconfigure. (117)

These aspects of Ahearn's discussion of agency allow relevant, useful terms for the analysis of agency in Edna Pontellier, from Kate Chopin's *The Awakening*, and Charlotte Rittenmeyer, from the "Wild Palms" section of William Faulkner's *The Wild Palms*.[2]

Despite the overriding patriarchal social constructs within which women in the late 1800s were forced to operate, first-wave feminists had slowly been making progress. Women were beginning to view themselves as more than property and were demanding their right to vote, own property, and control money and their own bodies. Chopin experiences these changes as she rejects social norms and chooses independence and self-sufficiency after her husband's death, perhaps even before, and incorporates them into the character of Edna Pontellier whose powerful "awakening" allows her to gain independence and a life of her own choosing as she gains agency and acts according to her own beliefs instead of those constructed by society. Edna represents first-wave feminists who gain agency and the freedom to control their lives. These women move beyond their roles as their husbands' property—another piece of furniture to be arranged or a servant to be commanded. While Edna's story does not end happily, it represents progress for women in the patriarchal controlled society of the late 1800s. Within *The Awakening*, only Edna and Mademoiselle Reisz have taken, or are ready to take, steps toward agency and being the women they want to be instead of conforming to society's expectations. As Southern patriarchy and its social structure attempt to shape Edna, she reconfigures these social structures by defying their limitations and rebelling from their efforts to confine her, as a feminist model for the "New Woman."

Consequently, the groundwork has been laid for *The Wild Palms'* Charlotte Rittenmeyer to take the next steps toward further independence for women in the decades that follow. Living in the late 1930s, Charlotte represents the continued progress, along with aspects of women's lives that need further reform, within first-wave feminism, as women continue to rebel against the patriarchal social constructs that seek to confine, shape, and define their roles in society. Edna and Charlotte both possess the three components required to fulfill the aforementioned definition of human agency: they are motivated to find a different way of life, they are responsible for their decisions, and they expect to find real love as their reward. Consequently, a more complex, nuanced interpretation of agency becomes integral in their analysis because it allows for an examination that goes beyond the original critical view, which designates Edna and Charlotte as tragic figures of patriarchal oppression who become dissatisfied with their marriages, abandon their children and husbands, commit adultery, and, consequently, must die as punishment for their adulterous sins. This oversimplification leaves many unanswered questions, for it fails to examine the nuances of these characters as independent women who have agency: motivation, responsibility, and expectation of recognition.

Viewed "as one looks at a valuable piece of personal property" (Chopin 2), Edna is a portrait of the wealthy Southern woman in the late 1800s. However, her vacation on Grand Isle and her time with Robert Lebrun spark an "awakening" in her that begins with "[a]n indescribable oppression, which seemed to generate in some unfamiliar part of her unconscious, [and] filled her whole being with a vague anguish" (6). Soon after this, Chopin characterizes Edna: "Mrs. Pontellier was not a mother-woman" because she was not one of the "women who idolized their children, worshiped their husbands, and esteemed it a holy privilege to efface themselves as individuals" (8). Edna recognizes that "[a] certain light was beginning to dawn dimly within"; however, "it served but to bewilder her. It moved her to dreams, to thoughtfulness, to shadowy anguish." Chopin articulates Edna's feelings as she is "beginning to realize her position in the universe as a human being, and to recognize her relations as an individual to the world within and about her" (13). Katherine Kearns argues that Edna's "discovery of the 'I' is the first, necessary realization of self, and Edna's movement toward 'mastery' must further suggest a positive capacity for and (partial) realization of *Bildung* [growth]" (64). The self-discovery and growth Edna experiences allow her artwork to become the catalyst for her attainment of both agency and independence.

Learning to swim creates a shift from Edna's dream-like thoughts of herself as an individual into someone who acts independently in ways that were previously unknown to her. While swimming, "[a] feeling of exultation overtook her, as if some power of significant import had been given her to control the working of her body and her soul" (27), which had previously been under the control of her husband and patriarchal society. The sense of accomplishment that swimming brings becomes a turning point for Edna's agency in the novel. As Edna and Robert sit in silence, the air is "pregnant with the first-felt throbbings of desire" (30). These "first-felt throbbings" provide Edna the necessary motivation and an offer of the potential reward of a passionate, satisfying love, when she gains agency over her life. When Léonce returns from the Klein's hotel, Edna immediately acts on her newfound understanding that she must act in order to gain agency and independence. She refuses to yield to Léonce's repeated demands to go inside: "Another time she would have gone in at his request. She would, through habit, have yielded to his desire; not with any sense of submission or obedience to his compelling wishes, but unthinkingly." This time Edna meets Léonce's demand with an outright refusal: "Léonce, go to bed . . . I mean to stay out here. I don't wish to go in, and I don't intend to.

Don't speak to me like that again; I shall not answer you'" (31). This initial test of wills signals the change their marriage will undergo as Edna's newly realized agency continues to develop upon their return to New Orleans.

In New Orleans, Edna abandons her expected duties during the Tuesday afternoon reception days without any explanation or excuse. Léonce, who follows social expectations and acts according to prescribed social norms, becomes exasperated by Edna's behavior and lack of concern: "'we've got to observe *les convenances* if we ever expect to get on and keep up with the procession'" (51). Edna questions his concern for these societal expectations: "'Why are you taking the thing so seriously and making such a fuss over it?'" Léonce insists, "'it's just such seeming trifles that we've got to take seriously; such things count'" (51). However, Edna no longer feels obligated to follow these "trifles"; she acts on her own behalf with an eye toward finding the happiness and fulfillment she felt on Grand Isle. Toward that end, Edna renews her interest in art and visits Mademoiselle Reisz to tell her: "'I am becoming an artist'" (63). Mademoiselle Reisz accuses Edna of having "pretensions" and warns her: "'To be an artist includes much; one must possess many gifts—absolute gifts—which have not been acquired by one's own effort. And, moreover, to succeed, the artist must possess the courageous soul. . . . The soul that dares and defies'" (63). Edna's courageous soul continues to develop as she "dares and defies" Léonce until he seeks advice from Doctor Mandelet because he "can't make her out." In attempting to explain Edna's action, Léonce reports "[s]he lets the housekeeping go to the dickens," which he views as a symbol of the fact that "[s]he's got some sort of notion in her head concerning the eternal rights of women" (65). Léonce presents the dominant, oppressive, patriarchal position and acts as its mouthpiece, pushing Edna farther away and adding to her desire for Robert.

In Léonce's absence, Edna sends the children to her mother-in-law's, which frees her from her limited, maternal duties and allows her to take a critical step in gaining independence by cutting her ties, figuratively anyway, to Léonce when she moves out of the house on Esplanade Street. Edna uses her art proceeds, her trust from her mother's estate, and her race winnings to leave Léonce and rent a "little four room house around the corner." She tells Mademoiselle Reisz: "'I am tired looking after that big house. It never seemed like mine, anyway. . . . The house, the money that provides for it, are not mine'" (79). Once Edna settles into her "pigeon-house" its "intimate character of a home" gives her the "feeling of having descended in social scale, with the corresponding sense of having risen in the spiritual" (94). Fleeing from the confined, prescribed social roles her husband demands of her, Edna feels "[e]very step which she took toward relieving herself from obligations added to her strength and expansion as an individual" (94). Her art reflects this developing individuality. Consequently, her sketches, which sell because they represent the realistic portrayals of objects that the public market desires at the time, are not necessarily artistically significant, nor do they attest to Edna's exceptional skill level; however, Laidmore "says [her skill] grows in force and individuality" (79). This growth mirrors the developing force of her agency.

Edna's marriage to Léonce "was purely an accident" and the result of Léonce's love and absolute devotion for Edna. However, to Edna, "the violent opposition of her father and sister . . . to her marriage with a Catholic" helped convince her that "she would take her place with a certain dignity in the world of reality" by playing the role of "devoted wife" and leaving behind her ideas of "romance and dreams" (18). Edna's dalliance with Alcée Arobin provides her with experience to which she can compare both her married life with Léonce and the feelings she has for Robert. Edna recognizes that her relationship with Arobin is nothing like what she felt during her time on Grand Isle with Robert. This is evident by her reaction when he suddenly returns and finds Edna at Mademoiselle Reisz's. Seeing him, Edna feels "the same tender caress . . . the same glance which had penetrated to the sleeping places of her soul and awakened them." In Robert's absence, Edna was changing and becoming more independent; she imagined he would visit her immediately upon his return, and she "always fancied him expressing or betraying in some way his love for her" (98). In part, these thoughts contribute to Edna's motivation for gaining agency and independence because her feelings for Robert were responsible for "awakening" her recognition of the potential for a more satisfying relationship with a man than the one she shared with Léonce.

Ultimately, in response to Robert's evasive behavior after returning from Mexico, Edna confronts Robert, asking: "'Why have you kept away from me?'" (106). Robert, uncomfortable with her "personal" inquiry, begs Edna to accept any of a number of excuses. However, Edna, no longer the obedient woman he remembers from Grand Isle, will not be assuaged. She criticizes him: "'You are the embodiment of selfishness. . . . You save yourself something . . . [and] in sparing yourself you never consider for a moment what I think, or how I feel your neglect and indifference'" (106). As a representative of the conventional male role that supports, or at least dares not question, the status quo, Robert explains that he thinks Edna is "cruel," and he admonishes her: "'you seem to be forcing me into disclosures which can result in nothing: as if you would have me bare a wound for the pleasure of looking at it, without the intention or power of healing it'" (106). Later at the "pigeon-house," Robert confesses that he has been "fighting against" (107) his feelings; he admits:

> There in Mexico I was thinking of you all the time, and long-ing for you. . . . Something put into my head that you cared for me; and I lost my senses. I forgot everything but a wild dream of your some way becoming my wife [because] . . . [r]eligion, loyalty, everything would give way if only you cared. . . .Oh! I was de-mented, dreaming of wild, impossible things, recalling men who set their wives free. . . . [However] I realized what a cur I was to dream of such a thing, even if you had been willing (108).

Edna's response indicates the extent of her growth and her conviction in her newfound independence; she tells Robert: "'You have been a . . . fool-ish boy, wasting your time . . . when you speak of Mr. Pontellier setting me free! I am no longer one of Mr. Pontellier's possessions to dispose of or not. I give myself where I choose'" (108). Robert "[k]issed her with a degree of passion which had not before entered into his caress," and be-fore leaving to help Mrs. Ratignolle, Edna tells him: "'I love you . . . only you; no one but you. It was you who awoke me last summer out of a life-long, stupid dream'" (108, 109). Despite Robert's plea that she stay with him, Edna must go to Mrs. Ratignolle's, and she promises: "'I shall come back as soon as I can; I shall find you here'" (109). However, regardless of the extent and the revelation of his feelings for Edna, Robert lacks the agency to join Edna against the dominant societal constructs, which con-fine women to subservient roles as mothers and wives. Although "[h]er seductive voice, together with his great love for her, had enthralled his senses, had deprived him of every impulse but the longing to hold her and keep her," Robert abandons Edna with a note: "I love you. Good-by—because I love you" (109, 112), and he symbolically joins the society that seeks to deny women the ability to think and act as individuals, by deciding what is best for her. Ultimately, Edna must take back her agency by subverting the decision Robert made for her, against her wishes. She returns to Grand Isle, having "done all the thinking which was necessary after Robert went away," despondent that "[t]here was no one thing in the world that she desired . . . no human being whom she wanted near her except Robert" (114-15). As Edna swims out into the Gulf, her thoughts reflect her conviction that "Léonce and the children . . . were a part of her life. But they need not have thought that they could possess her, body and soul" (116). Her "courageous soul" dared and defied the patriarchy that sought to control her; she fought for her independence until "her strength was gone" (116); she drowned.

Like Edna, Charlotte Rittenmeyer is a member of the wealthy, patriarchal social structure; however, Charlotte is able to consummate the love affair, albeit short-lived, that is denied Edna. In the almost forty years between these characters' lives, women gained the right to vote and a louder voice on social and political matters. Charlotte's husband, Francis "Rat" Rittenmeyer, allows her to leave him and her children for Harry Wilbourne. Unlike Léonce, who seeks to control Edna, Rat steps aside and enacts contingencies to insure Charlotte will be safe and allowed to return, if and when she desires. Despite his acquiescence to Charlotte's desire to leave, Charlotte and Harry still face many challenges to their love. Charlotte faces the continual struggle for independence and agency with mixed success at times, but ultimately, triumphs in having the final say over her own body.

Motivated, like Edna, by the desire for a love she had never known, Charlotte is more sophisticated and straightforward than Edna when meeting Harry. On the second meeting, during dinner at the Rittenmeyer house, Charlotte asks Harry what he wants to do about "it," and he responds: "'I don't know. I never was in love before'" (Faulkner 42). They continue to meet, and Charlotte confesses the affair to her husband; however, before Charlotte and Harry can consummate their affair, Charlotte stops and says: "'Not like this Harry. Not back alleys. I've always said that: that no matter what happened to me, whatever I did, anything, anything but not back alleys'" (46). Charlotte's concern about "back alleys" foreshadows the illegal abortion that will result in her death. Charlotte explains that since Rat is Catholic, there will not be a divorce, and "there's just one other thing." Harry assumes this "other thing" is her children, but Charlotte confesses she "wasn't thinking of them" because she "'know[s] the answer to that and . . . [she knows she] cant change that answer'" (48). The problem, Charlotte explains is:

> I dont think I can change me because the second time I ever saw you I learned what I had read in books but I never had actually believed: that love and suffering are the same thing and that the value of love is the sum of what you have to pay for it and any time you get it cheap you have cheated yourself. (48)

Charlotte knows they do not have enough money to move away and begin a life together; more specifically, Harry has no money. However,

Harry's discovery of a wallet with over twelve hundred dollars inside solves the financial issue, and they can begin their journey together the next morning.

Neither Charlotte nor Harry has experienced love. Harry has lived his life in single-minded pursuit of becoming a doctor, and Charlotte grew up in a home full of men. She tells Harry she loved her brother and, because she could not marry her brother, she married his roommate. Consequently, as Olga Vickery notes, "In their intense reaction to a world without love, they seek to create a world, quite independent of their environment, devoted solely to love" (163). Toward this end, they are forced, by the social and moral expectations of society, to fulfill the outward roles of husband and wife while remaining determined to avoid those roles within their personal relationship: "they are, in fact, attempting to create a world whose identity is dependent on its opposition to the world they have rejected" (163). However, because he lacks even the experience of a loveless marriage, Harry imagines "*the idea of illicit love is a challenge to them, because they have an irresistible desire to (and an unshakable belief that they can . . .) take the illicit love and make it respectable*" (Faulkner 82). However, Charlotte responds to this idea violently "grasp[ing] his hair . . . . hurting him . . . she knew she was hurting him. 'Listen: it's got to be all honeymoon, always. Forever and ever, until one of us dies'" (83). Philip Weinstein concludes: "Charlotte conducts her lover undeviatingly into the fatal conflagration ('grave-wound, womb-grave, it's all one') that is their erotic union" (195). Unlike Edna, Charlotte is able to take control and act in order to establish their love affair according to her rules, and "he needs to be directed . . . she knows from the beginning that it must be tragic" (195). Charlotte must control the relationship to avoid losing the love and finding herself back in a relationship like the one she had with Rat.

Like Edna, Charlotte's artistic abilities translate into income when she sells some of her sculptures and receives an order for more, but Harry acts according to expected patriarchal constructs when he tells Charlotte to keep the money because she earned it. Charlotte confronts him: "'You don't like the idea of your woman helping to support you is that it?'" (87). She emphasizes that the important thing is that they can continue what they have together as long as they are "worthy of keeping it" (88). Charlotte establishes her agency and her status as the feminist ideal's "New Woman," when she says: "'I like bitching, and making things with my hands. I don't think that's too much to be permitted to like, to want to have and keep'" (88). Her sculptures continue to sell for a time, but eventually the sales come to an end and Harry loses his job. This pending financial difficulty and a generous offer from McCord result in the first of several relocations. Vickery explains the repeated relocations as necessary for the protection of their love: "Whenever their environment begins to intrude, whenever they find themselves developing conflicting interests, they start looking for a new place or a new climate where their love will be safe" (163). Later, at the lake cottage, they are confronted by the social mores and expectations of others that intrude on them. Charlotte reminds Harry: "'Dont you know yet that we just don't look married, thank God'" (Faulkner 108). When supplies are running low, and things look bleak, McCord contacts them with news about an opportunity that brings them back to Chicago. Charlotte takes on the masculine role as the primary income producer while Harry stays home, eventually writing stories for confessional magazines. This domestication of Harry and his confessional story writing place him in the feminized position of subordination, an arrangement that allows them to live comfortably—too comfortably Harry decides. In an effort to regain his manhood, Harry takes charge and insists they are leaving because "'we have come to live like we had been married five years'" (127). He admits to having thoughts of her like those of a husband who wants the best for his wife, and he thinks he may begin to try to control her. Harry reminds her of what they "bought; what [they] are paying for: to be together and eat together and sleep together" (127), but that they are no longer doing those things. Weinstein argues that the lack of sustained "place" is the intentional avoidance of "a stabilizing history, populated by others one might come to know. . . . Fleetingly, other people and places flash by in 'Wild Palms,' like two-dimensional landscapes glimpsed on a speeding train. The train is the lovers' sexual bond(age): it has room for only two figures—Charlotte and Harry—and it is at home nowhere" (194-5). They "bought" a ticket to ride this "speeding train" toward their own destruction, and even the promise of death will not deter Charlotte's determination to remain with Harry when returning to Rat could save her life.

At the Utah mines, the Buckners greet them, and Charlotte soon learns that, like her and Harry, Billie and Buck were not always married. Billie advises Charlotte to make Harry marry her because "'It's better that way. Especially when you get jammed [pregnant]'" (180). Charlotte and Harry's relationship mirrors other aspects of Billie and Buck's. Most significantly, the abortion Charlotte convinces Harry to perform on Billie will open the door for Charlotte's later request. Harry does not want to perform an abortion on Charlotte, despite her rationale: "'I can starve and you can starve but not it'" (205). Joseph Urgo explains, "Charlotte . . . is compelled to abjure motherhood and construct an identity centered not on procreation but upon the cessation of maternity" (254). Agency is regained "[t]hrough the choice of abortion, [since] maternity becomes a matter of consciousness, no longer an exclusively natural function" (Urgo 255). Charlotte must reclaim her independence, which is a catalyst for her insistence on an abortion:

> The continuity of bodies, from mother to child, denies the autonomy of the female self, and the "hurt" that Charlotte seeks to abort is the pain of this intrusive, unwelcome qualification of her own independence. Charlotte has abandoned everything in her past to assure the complete autonomy of an unplugged self, to create herself and her destiny anew. When she becomes pregnant, she is threatened with the return of her former self, Mother Charlotte. (Urgo 258)

Harry delays performing the operation with promises of a pill that will cause the abortion. However, when he is unable to find a job, Charlotte reminds him of the "compact" he made to "'look for a job, a good job that will support the three of [them]'," but "'[t]hen if you haven't found a job by that time, you will do it, take it away from me'" (Faulkner 218). His attempts to gain control over the situation by postponing until it is too late fail. In response to his vehement refusals, Charlotte reminds him, "But you promised. . . . Don't you see there is nothing else" (218). Back in complete control, Charlotte talks Harry through the procedure as his hands shake, and she makes light of the situation: "'It's simple. It's funny. New, I mean. We've done this lots of ways but not with knives, have we? There. Now your hand has stopped'" (221). Charlotte dies of complications from the abortion, most likely as a result of Harry's delay in performing it. Aware of the risks, and illegality, of the abortion, Charlotte chooses to regain control of her body as a way to ensure her independence and agency.

In *The Awakening* and *The Wild Palms*, Chopin and Faulkner create women whose "behavior defies social convention and that moral code which considers the institutions of marriage and the family as sacred" (Vickery 164), reflecting the "New Woman" of the feminist ideal, despite their tragic ends. Furthermore, these women fulfill the definition of agency in that they act based on their own motivations for love and self-fulfillment. Ultimately, they take responsibility for the failure of these relationships, and they value the reward of experience and independence, which was made possible by their actions. While Edna's awakening results in suffering through the wisdom and self-awareness she gains, she accepts and rejoices in the year of understanding that accompanies this suffering. According to Edna, to live with self-awareness, possessed and controlled only by one's own soul, offers an existence far richer than a life lived according to the restricting "illusions" that are imposed by the expectations of others. Likewise, Charlotte and Harry value their relationship and the love they share; they suffer, and they pay for it. This acknowledged price is the reason Harry refuses to run and avoid capture or commit suicide to avoid punishment. These characters have all learned Faulkner's lesson: *"between grief and nothing I will take grief"* (Faulkner 324) because "perhaps it is better to wake up after all, even to suffer, rather than remain a dupe to illusion all one's life" (Chopin 112).

Notes

1. Davidson 1980 [1971], p. 46; Segal 1991, p. 113; Rovane 1998, p. 85; Mann 1994, p. 14.

2. In 1990, Noel Polk restored Faulkner's preferred title, *If I Forget Thee, Jerusalem*. Confusion regarding the title led to the reinstitution of the original title in 2003, with Faulkner's preference in brackets.

Works Cited

Ahearn, Lara M. "Language and Agency." *Annual Review of Anthropology* 30 (2001): 109-37.

Chopin, Kate. *The Awakening*. 1899. New York: Dover, 1993.

Faulkner, William. *The Wild Palms*. New York: Random House, 1939.

Kearns, Katherine. "The Nullification of Edna Pontellier." *American Literature* 63.1 (1991): 62-88.

Urgo, Joseph R. "Faulkner Unplugged: Abortopoesis and *The Wild Palms*." In *Faulkner and Gender: Faulkner and Yoknapatawpha, 1994*, ed. Donald M. Kartiganer and Ann J. Abadie. Jackson: UP of Mississippi, 1996. 252-72.

Vickery, Olga. *The Novels of William Faulkner: A Critical Interpretation*. Rev. ed. Baton Rouge: Louisiana State UP, 1992.

Weinstein, Philip. *Becoming Faulkner: The Art and Life of William Faulkner*. New York, Oxford UP, 2010.

Failing to Know Their Roles:
Examining Parallels Between Addie Bundren and Edna Pontellier

Both William Faulkner and Kate Chopin explore, through the characters of Addie Bundren and Edna Pontellier, the issue of what happens when women fail to meet their expected social roles. In *As I Lay Dying*, Addie fulfills her roles as mother and wife to some extent, but she also manages to subvert those roles in other ways. She serves not as an embodiment of the perfect mother but as a woman who is dissatisfied in her feminine role. Chopin showcases a similar character with *The Awakening*'s Edna Pontellier. Like Addie, Edna attempts to fulfill her traditional roles. However, she makes much larger strides away from those roles than Addie. Regardless of their differing situations, Addie and Edna both serve as examples of women who, essentially, fail to adhere to their roles as mothers and wives in favor of more independent and unconventional identities. Barbara Ladd notes that "marriage and motherhood were thought to be the means by which such unfeminine ambitions in women could be recorporealized, directed away from the urge toward individuation and back toward the idea of an enabling female self-sacrifice to the life of the race" (17). In the course of failing to meet these standards of marriage and motherhood, many of Addie's and Edna's actions create parallels, leading them both to the same ending—death.

Perhaps Addie's and Edna's failures to fulfill their roles as wives stem from the fact that they are both part of loveless marriages. Both women seem to take their husbands for no apparent reason other than they asked them to marry. When musing over her marriage in her one section of narration, Addie comments, "And so I took Anse. I saw him pass the school house three or four times before I learned that he was driving four miles out of his way to do it" (Faulkner 170). When Anse proposes marriage, Addie simply agrees. She shows no real emotion or attachment toward Anse, but she is not a fool. Realizing that she will not live well without a man who has a farm and property, Addie agrees to marry him. Edna, too, seems to have no real reason for marrying Léonce: "Her marriage to Léonce was purely an accident, in this respect resembling many other marriages which masquerade as the decrees of Fate" (Chopin 36). Like Addie, she enters into the marriage for reasons other than love.

Although Léonce falls in love with Edna, she does not return the affection. She finds him pleasant, but perhaps the real reason she marries him is because her family disapproves. Both Addie and Edna are dissatisfied with their marriages practically from the beginning, so we should not be surprised that they fail to uphold the roles of "good" wives. However, they are not without their sense of duty to their husbands.

Both Addie and Edna attempt, for a while at least, to fulfill their roles as wives as best they can. They do fit the traditional standards in the sense that they bear their husbands' children, take care of household matters, and perform their "wifely duties." Each woman also directly addresses this issue of duty to her husband. Addie notes: "I gave Anse the children. I did not ask for them. I did not even ask him for what he could have given me: not-Anse. That was my duty to him, to not ask that, and that duty I fulfilled" (Faulkner 174). Although Addie is not satisfied with her marriage to Anse, she still feels the need to fulfill some of her roles as wife. Hence, she gives him Cash, Darl, Dewey Dell, and Vardamann. She takes care of his children, and Anse as well, in an effort to fulfill this role. However, she remains unsatisfied because her "aloneness had been violated" (172). Rather than feeling more complete in her role as wife, she longs to become more isolated from her husband. She performs the actions expected of her not because she loves her husband and wants to, but only because she feels she should.

Like Addie, Edna also feels a sense of duty toward her husband, Léonce. Pondering the marriage, she feels that "as the devoted wife of a man who worshipped her, she felt she would take her place with a certain dignity in the world of reality, closing the portals forever behind her upon the realm of romance and dreams" (Chopin 37). Perhaps this idea, coupled with the fact that she did come to feel some amount of contentment with her husband, causes Edna to fulfill her role as wife for a time. After all, Léonce does see to her physical comforts and tries to keep her satisfied. She also bears his children and, before her island awakening, performs as he expects her. Based on the evidence, at one time Edna probably did accept guests on certain days and visit on other days, as she was expected. However, she, too, becomes dissatisfied with her marriage, which leads her to search for contentment elsewhere.

Addie and Edna share another common bond because both take part in adulterous affairs. Each becomes so dissatisfied with her life and her husband that she seeks out the arms of another man. For Addie, that man is Reverend Whitfield. Obviously unhappy with her marriage to Anse, Addie finds a secret thrill in her meetings with Whitfield. When thinking about their relationship, she comments, "I would think of sin as

I would think of clothes we both wore in the world's face, of the circumspection necessary because he was he and I was I; the sin the more utter and terrible since he was the instrument ordained by God who created the sin, to sanctify that sin He had created" (Faulkner 175). Not only is Addie excited by her encounters with Whitfield, but she also does not feel the need to hide those encounters from anyone else. In examining the situation, Ladd remarks that Addie "enters into an affair that is satisfying precisely because it is so transgressive, allowing her to violate social convention, law, *and* the fundamentalist religion that have betrayed her" (43). Addie even states that she did not try to hide her affair from Anse; she simply withheld the information from him. Although her relationship with Whitfield is only temporary, it does seem to offer her more satisfaction than her entire marriage to Anse. She also receives her greatest treasure—Jewel. Perhaps the main reason why she feels so strongly about Jewel is because he is the product of this temporarily satisfying relationship.

Edna, too, enters into adulterous relationships after she becomes dissatisfied with her own marriage. Although she initially feels some contentment with her husband, her growing dissatisfaction, which she discovers on the island, leads her into the arms of other men. Initially, Edna wishes to explore a relationship with Robert Lebrun. However, he is not willing to partake of an affair with her at the time and retreats to Mexico. Instead of Robert, Edna first enters into an affair with Alcée Arobin, a man with whom she becomes acquainted at the racetrack. She finds this relationship thrilling because she has never had a real sense of physical intimacy before, certainly not with Léonce. With Alcée, she can explore herself in ways never possible before. However, Edna's desire for Robert is not quenched through her relationship with Alcée, nor does she find satisfaction. When Robert finally returns, the two have a brief interlude, but even that fails to completely satisfy Edna's desire. Unlike Addie, Edna finds that these affairs do not really add anything to her life other than momentary excitement; she does not walk away with any type of "jewel." By entering into affairs with other men, these women certainly fail in their roles as "good wives." They deliberately commit adulterous acts against their husbands without real regard for the consequences. However, these events do seem to wear on them in the end, perhaps contributing in some way to their eventual deaths.

While Addie and Edna fail to be good wives, they also fail to be good mothers. Chopin presents the picture of a "mother-woman" early in *The Awakening*. These women "[flutter] about with extended, protecting wings when any harm, real or imaginary, threatened their precious brood.

They were women who idolized their children, worshiped their husbands, and esteemed it a holy privilege to efface themselves as individuals and grow wings as ministering angels" (Chopin 26). Neither Addie nor Edna fit into this category of women, as they do not fully dedicate themselves to their children or their husbands. Both women seem to have an almost bipolar feeling toward their children. At times, they feel some affection for them; at other times, they wish to be far away from them. For Addie and Edna, "motherhood breeds isolation rather than communion" (Clarke 48). Rather than drawing close to their children, they only wish to pull away.

Addie initially expresses some affection when she remarks: "And when I knew that I had Cash, I knew that living was terrible and that this was the answer to it" (Faulkner 171). In a sense, she feels some warm regards toward her unborn child. He seems to be compensation for her life with Anse. Of course, she also notes that, "motherhood was invented by someone who had to have a word for it because the ones that had the children didn't care whether there was a word for it or not" (171-2). While the first baby might have held some excitement, the following children do not. As Deborah Clarke notes, "Addie finds no comfort in maternity once it becomes repetitive" (37). Instead, it only adds to her dissatisfaction with life. Addie seems to express positive feelings only toward Jewel. When she finds that he has been working elsewhere, which results in his completing fewer chores around their own farm, she takes up for him. Rather than punishing him, she allows him to sleep and makes excuses for him. In this sense, she does seem to be more of a "mother-woman." On the whole, though, she fails to fulfill the role of mother completely.

Edna also fails to be a truly good "mother-woman" even though, as Marianne DeKoven notes, "the narrator describes Edna's relation to her children in unambiguously approving terms" (26). Although she only has two children, as opposed to Addie's five, she holds them in similar regards. She, too, has a wavering approach toward her children. Priscilla Leder notes that Edna realizes "the limitations of domesticity as exemplified by the confining roles of wife and 'mother-woman'" (237), which could be partially to blame for her uneven attitude toward her children. The narrator even notes that "If one of the little Pontellier boys took a tumble whilst at play, he was not apt to rush crying to his mother's arms for comfort; he would more likely pick himself up, wipe the water out of his eyes and the sand out of his mouth, and go on playing" (Chopin 26). This suggests that Edna lacks mothering tendencies. While at times she can be the picture of a perfect mother, smothering Etienne and Raoul with kisses and bonbons, she generally does not seem to have the maternal feelings which other women possess.

Perhaps Edna's disregard for her children is best expressed in the scene in which her husband tells her Raoul has a fever. Although Léonce is only testing her to ensure that she performs her duties as a mother, she responds negatively to the request. Thinking of the event, he "reproached his wife with her inattention, her habitual neglect of the children. If it was not a mother's place to look after the children, whose on earth was it?" (24). Edna fails to fulfill her role to such an extent that even her husband notices her inattention, which suggests that she often overlooks her boys. While she might lavish them with attention at some times, those rare moments do not make up for her lack of attention the rest of the time.

Perhaps Addie's and Edna's failures to fulfill their roles as mothers are only heightened by the fact that both are in contact with a woman who does fulfill her role. For Addie, that woman is Cora Tull who believes "a woman's place is with her husband and children, alive or dead" (Faulkner 23) and who exhibits this belief in practically everything she does. Ladd comments, "Cora's sensibility is simple and conventional, her talk an accurate representation of the dimensions of wifehood and motherhood in the late Victorian and early modern periods in the United States" (22). Cora even feels bad that she has neglected her own family by attending to Addie on her death bed. Furthermore, Cora serves as a type of moralistic voice in Addie's life, berating her for her failure to attend to her children fully. Addie remarks how "[Cora] would tell me what I owed my children and to Anse and to God" (Faulkner 174). Also, Cora would tell her she was not a "true mother" (173), which suggests that Cora is closer to that ideal than Addie. Since Cora tries to attend to her family as best she can, she does seem to be closer to the traditional mother role than Addie. When examining the two side by side, Addie's failures as a mother become even clearer than before. Ladd notes that "[Addie] differs from Cora Tull primarily in her sense of separateness, her rage, and her willfulness" (40). Unlike Cora, she cannot be content with her family life. Instead, she tries to find satisfaction in other ways.

Edna, too, falls short as a mother in comparison to her friend, Adèle Ratignolle. Adèle seems to be a perfect example of what a mother-woman should be, dedicating her life to her husband and the children she produces at the rate of one every two years or so. She is so devoted to her children that even though Edna manages to convince her to leave them for the afternoon, "she could not induce her to relinquish a diminutive roll of needlework, which Adèle begged to be allowed to slip into the depths of her pocket" (Chopin 32). Unlike Edna, Adèle cannot separate herself from her role as mother for even an afternoon. As Deborah Barker points out, she "has given herself to her children 'body and soul'—something Edna is not willing to do" (132). Whereas Adèle faithfully produces children and cares for them unconditionally, Edna rarely shows love for the two children she has. When placed next to Adèle, Edna's failure as a mother-woman becomes painfully obvious.

To fully understand why these women fail to be good mothers, we have to understand why they respond to their children as they do. Each woman seems to feel some anger towards her children because those children separate the mothers from their aloneness. Both women desire isolation and time for themselves. As a teacher, Addie escapes to a spring "where [she] could be quiet and hate them" (Faulkner 169), which suggests that she desires that separation from children even when they are not her own. While some women, like Cora, would feel more complete after bearing children, Addie finds that she only longs for her isolation more. Unfortunately, she could not because she "was three now" (173) rather than just one. After the birth of Cash, Addie is unable to reclaim any sense of aloneness, for which she shows some resentment. This resentment is perhaps the greatest contributing factor that leads her to feel negativity toward her children. As a result, she fails to meet their needs fully and perform well as a mother.

Edna also desires isolation from her children. Though she does love them, she relishes the solitary time she receives: "their absence was a sort of relief, though she did not admit this, even to herself. It seemed to free her of a responsibility which she had blindly assumed and for which Fate had not fitted her" (Chopin 37). Indeed, Edna seems to spend little time with her boys. Often they are left under the watchful eye of the quadroon rather than Edna. Perhaps this distance between Edna and her boys partially prevents her from fully assuming her role as mother. However, she seems to be suffocated when she has charge of them. During those times, she longs for freedom, which is why she is so relieved when they are away. Once the boys are gone, she finds "a radiant peace settled upon her when she at last found herself alone" (92). Edna only seems to be truly satisfied during these solitary moments when she is able to shirk her responsibilities toward her family. As Karen Simons suggests, "She cannot be a mother and have a self at the same time" (243). Like Addie, she seems to feel some resentment toward her children for encroaching on her sense of self.

Even though Addie and Edna fulfill their roles as mothers and wives at some points, their overall inabilities to perform as expected do produce some consequences. By the end of both novels, the women have become burdens to their families. Addie becomes a physical burden for her family as they attempt to transport her to Jefferson for her burial. Not only the distance to Jefferson but also her decaying corpse become burdens for the family as they make the journey. By the end of the trip, everyone is exhausted. Again, Addie has somewhat failed in her role as a "good" woman by requesting that she be taken to Jefferson. Rather than simply being buried close to home with Anse's family, as Cora suggests, Addie insists on being taken to Jefferson to be with her own family. In essence, this request serves as a type of retribution toward Anse and her family for the troubles they have caused her. Since they have invaded her personal space and demanded that she fulfill certain roles, she makes this final request as a way of getting back at them. Instead of making their lives easier, she becomes a burden and returns some of the hell that they have caused her throughout her life.

Edna, too, becomes a burden to her family, but in a much different way. She becomes not a physical burden, but a social and financial burden. Edna first becomes a social burden for Léonce when she stops performing certain social actions, such as accepting callers on a specific day and making calls during the week. By refusing to keep up with societal standards, Edna creates a problem for her husband. He then has to find a way to explain her unusual habits to others; thus she becomes bothersome for him. When she moves out of Léonce's house and into the pigeon house, she only furthers his frustration because explanations must be made for this move. In order to cover the fact that she has moved because she is dissatisfied with her life, Léonce tells everyone that the house is being worked on. In this sense, Edna becomes a financial burden to him as well. However, she "admired the skill of his maneuver, and avoided any occasion to balk his intentions" (Chopin 115). This suggests that, to some extent, she does not show total disregard for him. She still leaves him to manage the situation though. Like Addie, she becomes quite burdensome for her family, and they struggle to deal with the problems she creates.

In the end, Addie's and Edna's failures to fulfill their traditional roles only cause them distress. While they are, at times, satisfied with their actions, both eventually give up on life. For the most part, people believe that Anse essentially causes Addie to die. Peabody remarks, "He has wore her out at last" (Faulkner 41), which is the commonly accepted idea. Anse has depended on Addie to raise his family and, basically, take care of all the details of his life. However, I believe that she essentially gave up on life. Anse seems to be somewhat aware of the fact that Addie has chosen to die as well. He states: "Her mind is set on it . . . I reckon she's bound to go'" (33). This statement suggests that she is giving up on life rather than dying from any specific illness. As Diane Roberts notes, "there is no sense that she is 'fulfilled,' she is simply ready to die" (198). There really seems to be nothing left in life for Addie. Perhaps, as Peabody suggests, she has been worked, literally, to death. However, I believe that as a result of her dissatisfaction with life, which led to her failure to complete her roles as mother and wife, she chooses to die. Rather than live in a loveless marriage and take care of her children, Addie chooses death. She could not bear her dissatisfaction any longer.

Edna, too, seems to choose death over life. Like Addie, she basically gives up in the end of the novel. In some ways, she seems to have found the freedom that she so desired. However, she is still unsatisfied with her life. She had hoped that her relationship with Robert, which she had long dreamed of, would bring her some satisfaction. When it fails to do so, she seems to lose some of her sparkle. Even though she thinks of her family right before she walks into the ocean, those thoughts are not enough to keep her alive. While they may give her some comfort, they do not give her enough joy to prevent her death. Thinking of her family, she notes, "They were a part of her life. But they need not have thought that they could possess her, body and soul" (Chopin 137). However, her suicide is somewhat troublesome to readers. As Ruth Sullivan points out, "The implication is that Edna's suicide is far from being the courageous act of a strong and free woman" (152). Perhaps Edna's suicide occurs not only because she longs to be completely free from her current life but also because she has given up on life. Like Addie, Edna's dissatisfaction with her current situation in life is a contributing factor in her decision to walk into the ocean and never return.

Though Addie Bundren and Edna Pontellier might seem to be in vastly different situations, the two women partake in similar circumstances. Both enter into loveless marriages that eventually lead to dissatisfaction in their lives. As a result of that dissatisfaction, they fail in their roles as wives and mothers. While both women might achieve some degrees of happiness throughout their lives, they never find real contentment with either their husbands or their children. As a result, they find themselves giving up on life in the end. While they might fail to fulfill their roles by society's standards, in their own minds they only do what they feel is necessary to survive in situations that are less than satisfactory. Perhaps they realize that it is easier to end their lives than to continue on the same path of dissatisfaction each day.

Works Cited

Barker, Deborah. *Aesthetics and Gender in American Literature: Portraits of the Woman Artist*. Lewisburg: Bucknell UP, 2000.

Chopin, Kate. *The Awakening*. Case Studies in Contemporary Criticism. Ed. Nancy A. Walker. New York: Bedford St. Martin's, 1993.

Clarke, Deborah. *Robbing the Mother: Women in Faulkner*. Jackson: UP of Mississippi, 1994.

DeKoven, Marianne. "Gendered Doubleness and the 'Origins' of Modernist Form." *Tulsa Studies in Women's Literature*. 8.1 (1989): 19-42. JSTOR. Kent Lib, Cape Girardeau. 19 Apr. 2008 <http://www.jstor.com>.

Faulkner, William. *As I Lay Dying: The Corrected Text*. New York: Vintage, 1957.

Ladd, Barbara. *Resisting History: Gender, Modernity, and Authorship in William Faulkner, Zora Neale Hurston, and Eudora Welty.* Baton Rouge: Louisiana State UP, 2007.

Leder, Priscilla. "Land's End: *The Awakening* and Other 19th Century Literary Traditions." In *Critical Essays on Kate Chopin,* ed. Alice Hall Pertry. New York: G.K. Hall. 1996. 237-50.

Roberts, Diane. *Faulkner and Southern Womanhood*. Athens: U of Georgia P, 1994.

Simons, Karen. "Kate Chopin on the Nature of Things." *Mississippi Quarterly* 51.2 (1998): 243-52.

Sullivan, Ruth, and Stewart Smith. "Narrative Stance in Kate Chopin's *The Awakening*." In *Critical Essays on Kate Chopin*, ed. Alice Hall Petry. 147-58.

A Fable of Labor: Class Struggle, the Specter of Class Consciousness, and Faulkner's Unread Hostility to Capitalism

During the decade in which Faulkner published *A Fable*, he expressed on a number of occasions his frustration with the artist's distance from political and social activism. As Joseph Blotner records, a number of events "would reinforce [Faulkner's] feeling that he would have to speak out . . . on political issues rather than confining his utterances only to art" (447), and in 1954, Faulkner spoke at length about the powerlessness of the "harmless artists" who "stay out of trouble" (596). In 1953, Faulkner remarked that "we are all capable of revolt and change" (Blotner 571), and in 1955, he published *A Fable*, a novel about a mutiny during World War I; the novel constitutes Faulkner's most overt exploration of active rebellion and arguably his most radical indictment of capitalism and class struggle. On one level, *A Fable* provides insights into military life and evokes real events during and around World War I, most centrally the 1914 Christmas truce when the whole front line ceased fighting in order to sing Christmas carols,[1] but as the title suggests, at the same time *A Fable* operates on the level of allegory. While scholars have written relatively little on *A Fable* compared with other works by Faulkner, those who have carefully read the novel and do not dismiss it as a catastrophe have not recognized or considered Faulkner's use of World War I and the Christ story to both displace and symbolize the conditions of labor under capitalism.

Faulkner insisted that *A Fable* was "not a pacifist book." In fact, he said, "if this book had any aim or moral . . . It was to show by poetic analogy, allegory, that pacifism does not work; that to put an end to war, man must either find or invent something more powerful than war and man's aptitude for belligerence and his thirst for power at any cost, or use the fire itself to fight and destroy the fire with" (Blotner 585). While scholars have most often presented Faulkner's politics in terms of his adhering to a conservative, non-violent, gradualist approach to race relations in the South, discussion of Faulkner's relationship to labor politics and labor unrest remains scant indeed. As I and David Anshen have argued elsewhere, Faulkner's whole oeuvre can be seen to constitute a sustained critique of the dehumanizing nature of the capitalist and imperialist

133

logic, but this aspect of Faulkner's writing has remained almost entirely unexamined.[2] While *A Fable* might, debatably, not demonstrate the linguistic and character complexity that has made other Faulkner novels such treasures for formalist and psychoanalytical readings, read politically, Faulkner's *A Fable* emerges not as an odd divergence from his other work, or, worse, as a failure, but instead as perhaps his most radical account of the nature of labor under capitalism as well as the use of the military to support industrial production on the backs of the working class.

Surprisingly, studies that have recently catalogued representations of labor in American fiction, while including Norman Mailer's 1948 World War II novel, *The Naked and the Dead*, have excluded Faulkner's *A Fable* despite its many obvious military/labor correlations, such as front line/ assembly line, military regimentation/labor regimentation, and mutiny/ strike. This scholarship has overwhelmingly rejected Faulkner as a writer who can contribute to an understanding of labor. In *Labor's Text: The Worker in American Fiction,* a supposedly comprehensive study of rep-resentations of work and labor in American literature, Laura Hapke praises the "worker subtext" in what she calls Mailer's "detailed analysis of a military hierarchy" (270), identifying a significant encoded explora-tion of "class hierarchy," "class rage," and "the burden of class prejudice" (272-3) in his novel, but ignores *A Fable* and mentions Faulkner only to dismiss him as a writer who erases "the humanity of the poor white farming classes" (311-12).[3] Faulknerians, meanwhile, although recogniz-ing *A Fable* as an allegory that engages the themes of authority, empire, and militarization, have not read *A Fable* as an allegory of labor.[4] And yet Faulkner's *A Fable* contains a striking rumination on the nature of alien-ated labor and a brutalized proletariat and persuasively challenges the omission of Faulkner in histories of literary representations of labor.

Biographers of Faulkner, as well as his own public statements, have illustrated Faulkner's strong disgust with Hollywood and the broader cul-tural move toward passivity and homogenization during the years 1943 to 1954, when he wrote *A Fable*.[5] His alignment, if not explicitly anti-capitalist, was ideologically and artistically with the radical independent spirit of earlier left-labor fiction, and his 1954 novel shares much with this radical literary genre;[6] if mainstream culture distrusted labor activ-ism and working-class people, Faulkner's attraction to a lawless and vital world of manual labor, union protest, and the struggle of the common man manifests itself both in his life and writing. When Faulkner received a phone call in 1950 from Sven Ahman telling him that he had won the 1949 Nobel Prize and asking him if he was looking forward to receiv-ing it in Stockholm, Faulkner replied quite seriously, "I won't be able to come to receive the prize myself. . . . It's too far away. I am a farmer down here and I can't get away" (Blotner 523-4). Echoing other examples of Faulkner's resourceful ability to imaginatively reinvent himself, his comment on this occasion implies the pleasure he took in personally resisting the pomp and circumstance that forgets the material reality of human labor. Faulkner, on many other occasions, cast himself as a "badly wounded" (67) R.A.F officer by limping around Oxford, Mississippi, in a "uniform of a rank he had not attained" (Blotner 66), a reminder of Faulkner's disappointment over not having the opportunity to make the front lines in either of the world wars that fell during his lifetime. If these charades humorously suggest Faulkner's interest in both common labor and military combat, Faulkner's portrayal of military rank and hierarchy in *A Fable* provides a remarkable metonymic portrayal of class division, alienated labor, and the repression of class consciousness, both existing in the military in perhaps especially sharp form but also as the most basic aspects of capitalism worldwide.

Faulkner identifies the location of *A Fable* as World War I France, but it serves as a place undeniably analogous to the capitalist landscape of America and elsewhere, to a stage of technological modernity, alienation, mechanization, and class division that need not necessarily be identified with any particular place. Much Cold War labor fiction constituted a response to the McCarthy period and government agencies of ideological repression such as the HUAC that fostered a cultural climate in which sympathy for labor became equated with support for Soviet-style Communism and which in turn forced left-labor fiction into virtual silence and drove concern for the worker's story into subplot. As Hapke has recorded, with "a new caution about labor writing, even among its ardent practitioners, [books] published in the postwar or first cold-war decade, even the more daring novels containing workingmen and women, sent allegorical or coded messages about them, de-emphasized social class, or placed class struggle in an earlier decade" (253); even the most left-wing leaders and spokesman, fearful of blacklists, became "ideologically aligned with those who praised worker concessions to employers in the name of American individualism and classlessness" (251). Any knowledge of this literary history instantly invites readers to consider the possibility of displacement of labor in the emphasis on allegory and World War I France in Faulkner's *A Fable*. Directly linking the military mutiny at the center of the novel to more general class defiance, the division commander of the mutinous regiment immediately compares the thirteen men who instigate it to "a group of peasants in a half-mown field suddenly shouldering their scythes and lunch-pails and walking off" (715).

Faulkner begins *A Fable* with a vivid description, not of military life but of a civilian crowd; he describes them as a "dense seething voiceless lake" (671), "passive" and "unintelligible" (671), a "human river" that "made no sound" (670) and that "made no effort to avoid" the cavalry on horseback and "which accepted" them "as water accepts a thrusting prow" (671), a "vast seething moiling spiritless mass" (693), "inattentive" and "passively contemptuous" (671). These images, on the one hand, evoke an America characterized in the 1940s and '50s by the conflation of labor militancy with communism, the dissolution of unions, what Hapke calls a "defanged proletarian identity" (260), and the increasing success-ful efforts to silence wildcat strikes, protests, and any dissenting voices. However, Faulkner's descriptions of the masses here imply something else too; the two references to "seething," for example, powerfully suggest that the masses, quiet, repressed, and spiritless for now, exist on the verge of erupting, capable of exploding, enraged and furious; like a seemingly calm "river" concealing a forceful and dangerous current beneath its surface, Faulkner evokes the crowd as voiceless and spiritless, but not permanently and inherently passive. In fact in the opening scene of the novel, while not breaking the cavalry line charged with policing the *Hôtel de Ville*, the crowd does manage to push them back and fling them aside, indicating the tenuous nature of policing a potentially collective majority like the working class, a force already strong simply in terms of numbers, "irresistible" in some sense, at least "in the concord of its frail components" (670).

While the cavalry cannot contain the crowd, the sergeant supposedly in charge of the cavalry also proves ineffective, even impotent; he shouted but it "was not a command, because the troop did not stir. It sounded like nothing whatever in fact; unintelligible: a thin forlorn cry hanging for a fading instant in the air like one of the faint, sourceless, musical cries of the high invisible larks now filling the sky above the city. His next shout though was a command. But it was already too late" (671). The sergeant's inability to direct the cavalry insinuates the precarious nature of the con-trol an alienated boss has over workers. The sergeant has escaped from a class that he can only associate with poverty and degradation, an escape signaled by the "symbolical candy–stripes" (675) of status and recog-nition plastered across his breast, but the escape remains a dubious one that replaces poverty with regimentation, physical danger, and estrange-ment: he "had accepted, relinquishing volition and the fear of hunger and decision to the extent of being paid a few sure sous a day for the privilege and right, at no other cost than obedience and the exposure and risk of his tender and brittle bones and flesh" (675). Such obedi-

136

ence brings to mind Truman's 1947 Employee Loyalty program conveniently capitalizing on the red scare to gain the submission of workers. The sergeant's separateness from the crowd by his new position feels like "isolation" and "insulation," while "the stripe and bars and stars and ribbons" resemble the claustrophobia of "an armored ship" (675). Faced with a "kinless and nameless girl" who has fainted in the crowd,

> it seemed to the sergeant with a kind of terror that it was himself who was the alien, and not just alien but obsolete; that on that day twenty years ago, in return for the right and the chance to wear on the battle-soiled breast of his coat the battle-grimed symbolical candy-stripes of valor and endurance and fidelity and physical anguish and sacrifice, he had sold his birthright in the race of men. (675)

The sergeant has become isolated, lost, divided from other workers by upward social mobility and obedience to those who pay his wage, and he is unable to take the time to empathize with the girl he has to pick up off the street "not roughly, just impatient at the stupidity complicating ineptitude of civilians at all times, particularly at this one now which kept him from his abandoned post" (672).

The sergeant embodies both what Marx identifies as the passivity, alienation, and repression of human spirit inherent in class division, and also what Hapke and others document as a '40s and '50s defined by "bland individualism," the "happy worker" (249-51), the "nonideological" workingman, "consumers and their desire to acquire badges of passing for middle-class," badges that "replaced the old fire" (255-6) with "high wages at the cost of spiritual sterility" (256), and "those who sell their souls to the company store" and are "well paid to do so" but who also "undergo a sort of voluntary imprisonment in which discontent, aimlessness, and self-minimization are givens" (255). Faulkner's "perfect soldiers" appear as patriotic, loyal, and honorable "self-made men" (685), but also as workers who vividly convey the delusion and ideological passivity that Marx and others have characterized as the inevitable condition of labor under capitalism prior to the development of class consciousness, "tall shadows" (670) of men, anonymous silhouettes of the craftsmen they once were.

Faulkner offers an especially detailed characterization of the division commander (Gragnon) who leads the attack "already doomed in its embryo" (686) and that results in the mutiny by the Christlike corporal and his twelve followers. Gragnon constitutes simultaneously a sympathetic victim of worker ascension and a disturbing embodiment of class brutality, a "self-made man who had risen from the ranks" with nothing other than what he "earned himself by his own efforts and record" (684). There "seemed no limit to his destiny save the premature end of the war itself" (684), and yet despite his loyal service, suddenly "something happened" and "the opportunities ceased" even though "he had not changed" and "was still competent, still unhampered and complete" (685), and he had been given "the next star for his hat and not only the division which went with it but the opportunities too, indicating that his superiors still believed that at any moment now he might recover, or rediscover, the secret of the old successfulness" (685). Not only has the military passed him over for promotion but the work it has committed him to has reduced him to a state resembling a working-class stiff who "simply followed the jerking watch-hand" (689). Powerless to challenge the senseless assignment authority has ordered him to carry out, one which will result in the collapse of the "[w]hole line" (690) and probably his own demise back into the lower ranks where people aren't "even paid" (688) for risking their lives on the job, Gragnon embodies the American fable of classlessness and exceptionalism inverted, the Ben Franklin/Horatio Alger success story gone awry.

Tricked into leading "the cheapest attack" there is for "a ribbon," Gragnon is a grossly alienated managerial figure with "synchronized watch in hand" looking down "as from a balcony seat at the opera. Or box seat, and not just any box, but the royal one: the victim by regal dispensation watching in solitary splendor the preparations for his execution" (687). Gragnon's literal execution by the Marshal results from his blind, machine-like obedience to the discipline and standardization implemented both in military life and the industrial workplace. He goes through with the futile attack he is ordered to carry out, not because of greed or desire for a promotion but out of a sense of inflexible responsibility and duty to the rules of the military, out of mindless compliance to the rules that have defined his life; as the German General, Bidet, observes, "it wasn't we who invented war. . . . It was war which created us. From the loins of man's furious ineradicable greed sprang the captains and colonels to his necessity" (715). Myra, the woman who raises the corporal, echoes his words later in the novel when she says, "people . . . don't choose evil and accept it and enter it, but evil chooses the men and women" (931). Confirming this wisdom, Gragnon has become totally co-opted by the system, by the military logic that ensures the necessary policing of those below him, and in calling for the execution of the whole mutinous regiment (three thousand men) resembles an out-of-control machine, "carrying inside him like a liquid sealed in a vacuum bottle that cold, inflexible undeviable determination for justice" (699) and "incapable of hoping: only of daring, without fear or qualm or regret within the iron and simple framework of the destiny which he believed would never betray him so long as he continued to dare without question or qualm or regret" (686). He believes he "could have done nothing else: Not for my reputation, not even for my own record or the record of the division I command, but for the future safety of the men, the rank and file of all the other regiments and divisions whose lives might be thrown away tomorrow or next year by another regiment shirking, revolting, refusing" (703). Unable to identify himself or anybody else as victimized by the very system his regiment rebels against, Gragnon actually believes that his wish for such an extreme act of discipline is in the best interest of his men.

Gragnon also believes in false solidarity based on nationalism, one which blinds men of all rank and class to the possibility of class solidarity across races and nations; "the troops"—he says "all of them"—were "defying, revolting, not against the enemy, but against us, the officers, who not only went where they went, but led them, went first, in front, who desired for them nothing but glory" (703); the mutiny reveals the lurking possibility of class war beneath and obscured by national fraternity and wars between nations. While Gragnon recognizes the mutiny as simply an unacceptable violation of authority and hierarchy, and one that by momentarily stopping the war threatens the whole "edifice of politics and economy on which the civilized concord of nations is based" (739), Bidet understands that even more importantly, the proletariat of the lower ranks must not recognize their own power; "they may even stop wars," he says, "let the whole vast moil and seethe of man confederate in stopping wars if they wish, so long as we can prevent them learning that they have done so" (715). Later, the runner, a rather misguided activist who also succeeds in starting a rebellion makes a similar observation: "they cant afford to let it stop like this. I mean let us stop it. They don't dare. If they ever let us find out that we can stop a war as simply as men tired of digging a ditch decide calmly and quietly to stop digging the ditch—" (954). It is precisely the prevention of such class consciousness that governs the Old Marshal's decision to refuse Gragnon's demand to kill three thousand men (an act likely to initiate further revolt) and to execute him instead.

The three most powerful generals, including the Old Marshal (the corporal's father and who stands symbolically in opposition to him), emerge from behind an array of hollow signifiers of power and importance, the "clash of rifles," the presentation of arms as their car approaches, and the "glitter of aides" (678); they come into sight as "three old men," one of which is the Generalissimo who held supreme command over all three armies, British, French, and American, and who Faulkner exposes as a "slight gray man with a face wise, intelligent, and unbelieving, who no longer believed in anything but his disillusion and his intelligence, and his limitless power" (678). Faulkner depicts the same three men as "three gaudy panoplied old men" identified by the mutinous regiment "not merely by their juxtaposition to the three flags but by their isolation, like that of three plague carriers in the empty center of an aghast and fleeing city, or perhaps the three survivors of a city swept by plague, immune and impervious" (680). Power has alienated these men from the rest of humanity to an even greater extent than the positions of superiority held by the sergeant and division commander. Faulkner portrays the Old Marshal, the most powerful figure in the novel, a representation of "limitless power" (678), as "a gaudy toy in his blanched and glittering solitude" (968) and "like a masquerading child beneath the illusion of crushing and glittering weight of his blue-and-scarlet and gold and brass and leather" (925), a uniform "which looked like a wife had got it out of a moth-balled attic trunk and cut some of it off and stitched some braid and ribbons and buttons on what remained" (947). The German general admits plainly that the top generals exist as nothing more than pawns for the alliances of capitalists and imperialists based on favorable trading agreements, for "the politicians, the civilian imbeciles who compel us every generation to have to rectify the blunders of their damned international horse-trading . . . the same blunder because it is always the same alliance: only the pieces moved and swapped about . . . the alliance which will conquer the whole earth" (947-8).

Faulkner wrote and published *A Fable* during a Cold War that ensured the ongoing existence of a huge military-industrial complex in the US, one that manifested itself in about 1,700 US military installations around the world, and as Richard Godden explores in depth, Faulkner's *A Fable* provides numerous images of the ways in which capital has driven military policy since World War I.[7] The mutually dependent relationship between military combat involving the deaths of thousands of workers, and the interests of capital and a bourgeois elite, becomes apparent in Gragnon's optimism over his resignation: "'Oh. The war,' he says, 'No, it's not over. They'll have something I can do as a civilian . . . maybe I could even run a production line . . . in a munitions plant'" (714). In addition, the Marshal, ultimately responsible for resuming the war after the mutiny even if it means forming an alliance with the enemy, has inherited a vast fortune from his godfather, "the board chairman of a gigantic international federation producing munitions" (893). The image of the corporal and his followers imprisoned in an abandoned factory also points to the necessity of war to fuel industrial production. As Chalmers Johnson puts it in *The Sorrows of Empire*, elite people "hold military and civilian posts in the imperial power, trade with the dominated peoples on structurally favorable terms, manufacture weapons and munitions for wars and police actions, and provide and manage capital for investment" (28), and "once the military has acquired a base, it is extremely reluctant to give it up. Instead, new uses are found for it" (35), especially since these bases became "a rich source of places to 'retire' for high-ranking military officers" (57). The lieutenant colonel explains war and the military in terms of

> the men who have hopes of being recorded as victorious prime or cabinet ministers furnish men for this. The men who in order to become millionaires, supply the guns and shells. The men who, hoping to be addressed someday as Field Marshal or Viscount Plugstreet or Earl of Loos, invent the gambles they call plans. The men, who, to win a war, will go out and dig up if possible, invent if necessary, an enemy to fight against. (Faulkner 726)

Readers of *A Fable* surely cannot miss the parallel between the necessity to deal effectively with the corporal's rebellious regime in the name of saving civilization and the US determination to repress proletariat rebellions at home, in Latin America, and elsewhere during the Cold War years, in the name of staving off a Soviet conquest.

Significantly, Faulkner does not present The Old Marshal as evil despite his limitless power, defense of war, and decision to execute the novel's Christ/hero figure; the Marshal is not a greedy or even power hungry man, but commits himself to defending and saving a civilization built on greed, destruction, and unequal power relations; he embodies the "oppression and anguish of responsibility" (1002). Whether he likes it or not, he stands as heir to a whole history of capitalist power and ambition, "a splendid fate which . . . he could not escape" (893),

> that of being not only the nephew of a Cabinet Minister, but the godson of the board chairman of that gigantic international federation of producing munitions which, with a few alterations in the lettering stamped into the head of each cartridge-and-shell case, fitted almost every military rifle and pistol and light field piece in all the western hemisphere and half the eastern too" (893).

In addition, he has become heir to his mother's sister's husband's fortune, that of a "Cabinet Minister who was himself a nobody but a man of ruthless and boundless ambition, who had needed only opportunity and got it through his wife's money and connections" (893) and so the Marshal is destined "given any sort of opportunity for any kind of military debacle worthy of the name" to be "a marshal of France when the nation buried him" (896). In saving civilization created out of man's own free will, the god-like Marshal remains unable to stop or sever himself from the dystopia that Faulkner describes as a future characterized by man's "enslavement to the demonic progeny of his own mechanical curiosity" (992) to building "aircraft bigger and faster and capable of more load and more destruction," until he realizes that it is not "notions of national boundaries he is contending with, but the very monster itself which he inhabits" (993).

The corporal, in contrast to the Marshal, refuses all that civilization stands for (quite literally during the three-temptations scene when the Marshal offers him wealth, power, and finally his life in exchange for a negation of his rebellion against civilization). He engages in a politically lawless act out of the conviction that, as the lawyer understands as he watches the crowd pour into the courtroom for the trial of the sentry and the others accused of stealing the oil baron's racehorse, "the mark of a free man was his right to say *no*" (825). Later the old porter (the A.S.C Private), who recognizes the corporal as Christ reiterates these words when he tells the runner, "all we ever needed to do was just to say, Enough of this;—us, not even the sergeants and corporals, but just us, all of us, Germans and Colonials and Frenchmen and all the other foreigners in the mud here, saying together: Enough. Let them that's already dead and maimed and missing be enough of this" (727). In France only to look for his missing son, the old porter recognizes the power of the proletariat, "of thirteen men in horizon blue" (728), to bring the whole war to an end. The fact that it is the old porter who tells the runner of the thirteen mutinous men suggests that he possesses the knowledge of salvation in rebellion against the laws and hierarchy of a status quo that strips men of individuality and humanity, and that kills them too. While the runner remains cynical that authority will take notice of just thirteen men, and Bidet concerns himself with the need to contain the proletariat by keeping the knowledge of their power from them, the porter, like the corporal, believes in the ability of the individual to make a difference: "'Wasn't it just one before?' the old porter said. 'Wasn't one enough to tell us the same thing all of them two thousand years ago'" (727).

A revolutionary figure, the Christ corporal in *A Fable* operates as a mythical slate for imagining and inventing the possibility of redemption of the human spirit through resistance, for imagining salvation in resisting an economic and technological logic that strips men of their essential spirit and life.[8] In addition, in a time when communists were labeled godless, what better way to displace an unacceptable challenge to capitalism than in the figure of Christ? Salvation, in *A Fable*, does not lie with those with limitless power, with the Old Marshal, but with the infantry, the proletariat saying *no* and *enough*.[9] This will inevitably involve a confrontation between power and the oppressed, as Myra understands when she says, "'victory . . . would be that day when at last you would see one another face to face,'" the corporal "in his humble place," and the Marshal in his "high and matchless one" (944), and this time it ends with the death of the corporal. Faulkner's corporal represents the action and spirit that had largely disappeared from the landscape of labor by the 1950s. The corporal's disciples are drawn to him because of his revolutionary "spirit," and if the opposition between American freedom/democracy and communism consumed the resistance of labor during the time Faulkner wrote *A Fable*, the corporal's resistance to co-option by the system or a national enemy earns him his role as hero. This does, however, require his martyrdom as it did Christ's all those thousands of years ago; Faulkner's corporal embodies a high ideal, one that most men, Faulkner recognizes, will fall short of because they are men and because the system does a good job of repressing resistance to it.

The mutinous regiment, the infantry and proletariat, "the small clump of battle-stained horizon blue" (855) persuaded by the corporal to resist carrying through an attack intended to fail and which would result in their deaths, emerge as oppressed, dehumanized, divided, and alienated from each other, as well as from other ranks, most of them "packed like cattle . . . stained from the front lines, with something desperate and defiant in the unshaven and sleepless faces which glared down at the crowd as if they had never seen human beings before" (679). The corporal and his twelve followers also appear as something less than human: "manacled, chained to one another and to the lorry itself like wild beasts, so that at first they looked not merely like foreigners but like creatures of another race, another species; alien, bizarre, and strange, even though they wore on their collar tabs the same regimental numerals, to the rest of the regiment" (681), and then even among these thirteen, four "were really foreigners, alien not only by their gyves and isolation to the rest of the regiment but against the whole panorama of city and soil across which the lorry was rushing them" (681). Brutalized by authority for striking against dehumanizing labor and condemned by their own rank and file who prefer to avoid conflict and their own brutal impression, imprisonment, and execution, the corporal and his followers symbolize the challenges to collective resistance as well as its potential.

Read as an allegory of labor, *A Fable's* "horsethief" episode becomes less of a digression than scholars have previously supposed. In many ways, Harry the horse groom (later the sentry) functions as a kind of inverted corporal; in flouting the rules, in this case of ownership, rules of capital that do not value his genuine love for a racehorse, Harry and his followers find themselves in a whole lot of trouble for taking the three-legged racehorse bought by a millionaire oil baron. The horse groom in an important sense, like the corporal, remains alien and misunderstood because he stands outside of the logic of capitalism; the community assumes he has made immense amounts of money from stealing the racehorse when in actuality his main interest in the racehorse stems from love, and as the lawyer announces, "he hasn't got any money. He doesn't even know where any is . . . because there never was any and what little there might have been, that cockney swipe threw away long ago on whores and whiskey" (831). Like the corporal, Harry and his cohorts (a negro boy and Sutterfield, a Baptist preacher) find themselves castigated both by authority and a mob-like majority for refusing to accept a dehumanized system. While the corporal dies rather than succumb to co-option by the system, Harry gets contained by it, participating in the capitalist logic that he once existed outside of. In order to induce him and his fellow criminals into conformity, the status quo even frees them from prison, based on the understanding that they, like any other American, had the right to make as much money as they could by any means they could; as Keen Butterworth puts it, "to defend the American tradition of Rapine— of Harry's and Sutterfield's right to make as much money as everybody thinks they have no matter how they did it" (53). This is exactly what Harry does when he gets into the army and discovers the opportunity to make money from soldiers willing to bet their life insurance policies.

If Harry embodies a parallel to the corporal but becomes co-opted by the logic of capitalism, the runner also parallels the corporal by rebelling and inciting others to rebel, but he represents a flawed idealism compared to that of the corporal; he stands as the activist who so often exists alienated from the humanity he wants to transform and who misunderstands man's unwillingness to fight against injustice. The runner mourns "the lost free spirit of man" (802) and hates what he perceives as the passivity of men, their acceptance of their condition; he hates the "unresisting, undemanding passivity" (728) of the masses; "I hate man so" he tells the company commander, "the smell . . . not the dead bones and flesh rotting in the mud, but because the live bones and flesh had used the same mud so long to sleep and eat in'" (721). He doesn't understand man and tries to turn the corporal's strike into a revolution which ends in the disastrous destruction of a whole battalion because it is an act that represents "not the wrong truth but the wrong moment for it" (742). He fails to understand that the development of a collective class consciousness is a historical process, not something that he can initiate overnight. He himself cannot escape the capitalist logic that prevents widespread class consciousness in the humanity he hates. This is exemplified most explicitly by his objectification of the prostitute whom he uses as a commodity to get decommissioned, a girl "willing to help him for a price—a price twice what she suggested" (723), an act that stands in vivid contrast to the corporal's act of proposing to a whore from the slums of Marseilles.

Levine, a young Jewish pilot, also adopts a form of flawed idealism, one signaled by the heroic war stories he read as a child, and one that leads to suicide as an escape from what he perceives as an imperfect world. Neither Levine nor the runner understands what Sutterfield, the preacher in the horsethief episode, explains and what the corporal and Faulkner both know, which is that "evil is a part of man, evil and sin and cowardice, the same as repentance and being brave. You got to believe in all of them, or believe in none of them. Believe that man is capable of all of them, or he aint capable of none" (854). But *A Fable* ends with the runner (not the corporal), deformed and brutally beaten down by both the masses and by the police, and yet still remaining defiant. If the corporal represents an ideal revolutionary spirit set before man, the specter of the potential for collective class consciousness, and the Marshal represents a defense of civilization that seeks to crush resistance of any kind, the runner perhaps provides an image of the imperfect but subversive spirit of man struggling, failing, resisting, and enduring, of man perhaps "not triumphant; just indomitable, with that side of his ruined face capable of laughing" (1071) and saying, "Tremble, I'm not going to die. Never" (1072).[10]

A Fable contains a subtext that shares much with working-class narratives. As Renny Christopher, a member of the National Advisory Board of the Center for Working-Class Studies at Youngstown State University, argues, working-class narratives involve protagonists' "alienation, despair, and impulses to suicide," and "the writers' refusal to endorse the protagonist's arrival in the middle class as an unquestionably positive outcome" (80). Christopher asserts that "the writing of these narratives which refuse the happy ending dictated by the American myth is . . . a political act" (80), a "revolutionary and unpalatable" (82) assertion in America that hard work, success, and loyalty to the company will destroy the individual. As Christopher exemplifies, upwardly mobile characters in these texts "thoroughly lose [themselves] in the course of [their] journey upward through the class structure" (82) unless they revolt against it. The ways in which a capitalist world, in Christopher's words, a world that remains "hollow, empty, and devoid of meaning" (82) and that leaves "wounds of consciousness" (80) in all those who encounter it, can be traced throughout *A Fable* as the novel combines many of the elements of the 1930s proletarian novel with the concerns of the labor fiction of the '40s and '50s, such as the search for salvation and the martyred alienated radical.[11]

Perhaps in imagining salvation in class struggle against the economic logic that governs labor and military combat under capitalism, Faulkner, in writing *A Fable,* engaged the nature and significance of silencing worker protests, as well as of expanding military bases during the Cold War years. Faulkner may not have been a conscious Marxist, but he does represent the insufficiency of a capitalist logic in meeting human needs, and his 1954 novel, like many of his public speeches,[12] calls for the individual to revolt against the exploitation and dehumanization inherent in capitalism and any other system that violates the basic rights of humanity. If, despite his attempts to enlist in the military, Faulkner failed to make the military front line during the two world wars of the twentieth century, it might be argued that in writing *A Fable* Faulkner found his literary front line in a battle against the silencing and obfuscation of labor and any dissenting voices.

Notes

1. Faulkner would have been aware of other revolts taking place around this time, such as the series of rebellions and uprisings between 1918 and 1922 against the Bolsheviks by left-wing groups like the Socialist Revolutionaries and Mensheviks.

2. See the 2008 summer issue of the *Mississippi Quarterly,* "Faulkner, Labor, and a Critique of Capitalism," co-edited by Caroline Miles and David Anshen.

3. Sylvia Jenkins Cook's *From Tobacco Road to Route 66: The Southern Poor White in Fiction* also sets aside Faulkner as an author who stereotypes poor and laboring folk, and in *Natural Aristocracy: History, Ideology, and the Production of William Faulkner,* Kevin Railey concludes that Faulkner's "identification with the ruling class explains, in a preliminary way, why Populist, working-class, and integrationist voices are absent from Faulkner's canon" (45). It should also be noted that John T. Matthews has looked at Faulkner in the context of proletarian literature, most notably in his essay, "Faulkner and Proletarian Literature," but he has not paid attention to *A Fable.*

4. Keen Butterworth's useful *A Critical and Textual Study of Faulkner's A Fable* views the novel primarily as a representation of the "timeless conflict between the individual and authority" (82), Barbara Ladd reads it as a book about empire and memory as resistance, while Richard Godden's excellent chapter on *A Fable* in his recent book *Faulkner: An Economy of Complex Words* focuses on the novel as an "allegory that engages with the military even as militarization in a plethora of guises—as 'military keynesianism,' the 'military-industrial complex,' 'internal preparedness'—moves to the center of America's political and cultural economy" (156). While Godden's study of *A Fable* remains most interested in the figure of the Jew and the way this figure operates as other in the context of militarization, he does highlight Faulkner's recognition in the novel that a modern capitalist state relies on war, death, and destruction to maintain economic production and industrial growth.

5. See Joseph Blotner, *Faulkner: A Biography*, 456-57,465-9.

6. While I am using the term "labor fiction" throughout this paper to refer broadly to any literature about work and the worker, here I am referring to a particular sub-genre of radical labor fiction published between 1900 and 1954. For more on how to define and distinguish between these terms, see Laura Hapke's summary of these distinctions in *Labor's Text: The Worker in American Fiction*, 5-6. Also see Paul Lauter, "American Proletarianism," in *The Columbia History of the American Novel*, and Barbara Foley, *Radical Representations: Politics and Form in U.S. Proletarian Fiction, 1929-1941*. Also see Walter Rideout's *The Radical Novel in the United States, 1900-1954*.

7. See Richard Godden's two chapters on *A Fable* in *Faulkner: An Economy of Complex Words* for a more detailed explanation of militarism, the military-industrial complex, and the way in which they figure into *A Fable*. Godden describes the processes of devaluation and creative destruction "inherent in the 'competitive' and 'progressive' rhythms of capital accumulation, "a technological fix represented by the Marshal meeting with the German general and recognizing that "like military products, his military workers (the Allied Forces) should where necessary be devalued so that the permanent arms economy may be ensured permanently"(173).

8. The corporal might also be read as reminiscent of the revolutionary Christ figure in Latin American Theology. Faulkner went to Latin America on a number of occasions during the Cold War years and expressed his admiration for the spirit and history of Latin Americans in Latin America. See his "Address at the Teatro Munciple" (Faulkner, *Essays* 285-6) and Blotner, 590. Central to Liberation Theology was the recognition that "the process of liberation requires the active participation of the oppressed"; this, says Gustavo Gutierrez, "is one of the most important themes running through the writings of the Latin American Church. . . . It is the poor who must be the protagonists of their own liberation" (113). For more on the relationship between Faulkner and Latin America, Deborah Cohn's work on Faulkner and Latin America is particularly notable.

9. It might be noted that Marxists speak of salvation, the proletariats messianic vocation, and what Marx referred to in *The Communist Manifesto* as the "new social Gospel" (84); as Karl Lowith puts it, Marx's "historical materialism is

essentially, though secretly, a history of fulfillment and salvation in terms of social economy" (Bender 178).

10. The runner's words here have an uncanny likeness to Marx's comment at the end of *The Communist Manifesto*, "let the ruling classes tremble. . . . The proletarians have nothing to lose but their chains" (86).

11. See Hapke, 192-227.

12. See, for example, the speech Faulkner gave to the 1951 graduating class at University Class High School in Oxford, Mississippi. Faulkner promoted the courage to "resist any who would reduce man to one obedient mass for their own aggrandizement and power" and to "refuse always to be tricked or frightened or bribed into surrendering," to accept "not just the right, but the duty too, to choose between justice and injustice, courage and cowardice, sacrifice and greed, pity and self" (Faulkner, *Essays* 123).

Works Cited

Bender, Frederick L., ed. *Karl Marx: The Communist Manifesto*. New York: Norton, 1988.

Blotner, Joseph. *Faulkner: A Biography*. New York: Vintage Books, 1991.

Butterworth, Keen. *A Critical and Textual Study of Faulkner's A Fable*. Michigan: UMI Research Press, 1983.

Christopher, Renny. "Rags to Riches to Suicide: Unhappy Narratives of Upward Mobility: *Martin Eden, Bread Givers, Delia's Song, and Hunger of Memory*." *College Literature* 29.4 (2002): 79-108.

Cohn, Deborah. "William Faulkner's Ibero-American Novel Project: The Politics of Translation and the Cold War." *Southern Quarterly* 42.2 (2004): 5-18.

Cook, Sylvia Jenkins. *Tobacco Road to Route 66: The Southern Poor White Fiction*. Chapel Hill: U of North Carolina P, 1976.

Faulkner, William. *A Fable. William Faulkner: Novels 1942-1954*. New York: Library of America, 1994. 665-1072.

———. *Essays, Speeches & Public Letters*. Ed. James B. Meriwether. 1966. Expanded issue, New York: Random House, 2004.

Foley, Barbara. *Radical Representations: Politics and Form in U.S. Proletarian Fiction, 1929-1941*. Durham: Duke UP, 1993.

Godden, Richard. *Faulkner: An Economy of Complex Words*. Princeton: Princeton UP, 2007.

Hapke, Laura. *Labor's Text: The Worker in American Fiction*. New Jersey: Rutgers UP, 2001.

Johnson, Chalmers. *The Sorrows of Empire*. New York: Metropolitan Books, 2004.

Kartiganer, Donald M., and Ann J. Abadie, eds. *Faulkner in Cultural Context: Faulkner and Yoknapatawpha, 1995*. Jackson: UP of Mississippi, 1997.

Ladd, Barbara. "'The Anonymity of a Murmur': History, Memory, and Resistance in Faulkner's *A Fable*." In *Resisting History: Gender, Modernity, and Authorship in William Faulkner, Zora Neale Hurston, and Eudora Welty*. Baton Rouge: Louisiana State UP, 2007. 79-107.

———. *Resisting History: Gender, Modernity, and Authorship in William Faulkner, Zora Neale Hurston, and Eudora Welty*. Baton Rouge: Louisiana State UP, 2007.

Lauter, Paul. "American Proletarianism." *The Columbia History of the American Novel*. Ed. Emory Elliot. New York: Columbia UP, 1988.

Matthews, John T. "Faulkner and Proletarian Literature." In *Faulkner in Cultural Context*: *Faulkner and Yoknapatawpha*, *1995*, ed. Donald M. Kartiganer and Ann J. Abadie. Jackson: UP of Mississippi, 1997. 166-90.

Railey, Kevin. *Natural Aristocracy: History, Ideology, and the Production of William Faulkner*. Tuscaloosa: U of Alabama P, 1999.

Rideout, Walter. *The Radical Novel in the United States, 1900-1954*. New York: Columbia UP, 1992.

Deconstructing Immortality and Decay in Faulkner's *A Fable*

When William Faulkner delivered his Nobel Prize acceptance speech on December 10, 1950, some of the immortal words he chose to utter from his "pinnacle" were on the topic of immortality. They were variations on words spoken by one of Faulkner's own characters, the Old General, near the end of *A Fable*, which was still in progress at that time. The fatalistic Old General plays the Devil's role in the crucial Temptation scene, and he is usually interpreted as "an evil force against which good human forces ought to fight" (Urgo 110) or at best a combination of the dark and light forces in human nature (King 206). He believes "in nothing whatever save man's . . . folly" (196), but must nevertheless express man's folly and vice as "enduring" and "deathless" and even insist that "the quality mark and warrant of man's immortality" is "his deathless folly" (298). According to Urgo, the Old General cynically uses "the language of the rebel and the life of the martyr . . . to justify the authority of the ruling powers" (112), including himself. Faulkner's own authority was increasing when he delivered his famous speech; his own "puny and inexhaustible voice" was becoming monumental, though, some argue, less rebellious (Végsö 102). At any rate, Faulkner is less cynical than his character, professing faith in "the verities of the human heart" that will endure beyond even the impulse to speech, and, presumably, our immortal folly. He closes *A Fable* with the insistence of the English Runner, representing the "active" part of man's conscience (Faulkner "Note" 163), that he was "not going to die. Never" (370).

Immortality and endurance are major themes in Faulkner's works, and it is not surprising to find immortality foregrounded in a novel that is considered a loose allegorical representation of Christ's sacrifice, with the martyred Corporal Stefan as Jesus embodied in a World War I soldier. As Faulkner told an acquaintance, "it's about Jesus Christ coming to earth during the World War" (Server 119). Throughout *A Fable*, Faulkner displays parallels with the story of Christ that seem obvious until they are examined more closely. Most critics agree that the parallels to the biblical story are not consistent (King 202; Kartiganer 640-41), and Faulkner himself asserted that the Christian allegory in *A Fable* was more structural than moral or symbolic, that "the Christian legend is part of any Christian's background . . . I assimilated that, took that in without even knowing it. It's just there. It has nothing to do with how much of it I might believe or disbelieve—it's just there" (Butterworth, *Critical* 14-15). He compared using the Christian story to structure his novel to the purpose that a carpenter finds "in building square corners in order to build a square house" (Butterworth *Critical* 14), but a novel is more flexible than a house. He also said, "Whenever my imagination and the bounds of that pattern conflicted, it was the pattern that bulged . . . the pattern shifted and gave" (*Faulkner in the University* 51-2). But the action of Faulkner's imagination goes further, beyond bending and bulging familiar patterns to dissolve and deconstruct obvious oppositions, most notably that between war and pacifism, creating a novel that is often misunderstood by readers who oversimplify its message (Butterworth, *Critical* 4, 13; King 205).

Joseph Urgo believes that *A Fable* is an apocrypha, an alternative to the canonical Christian story which stresses "Christ's vitality as a model for rebellion and insurrection against authority . . . replacing the martyr with the rebel" (104-5). This makes it possible for Faulkner to include multiple, conflicting viewpoints concerning immortality which enrich, rather than limit or directly express his own. Urgo's interpretation stresses the radical nature of Faulkner's project. Another interpretation is that this work, like others by Faulkner, plays its part in a movement of deconstruction working to erase the dichotomy of mortality/immortality and to make interchangeable or reversible the values of good and evil which they previously carried. Both the martyr and the rebel are represented in this novel by different characters who present different aspects of corporeality, immortality, and endurance. The martyr exchanges corporeality for spirituality, which one would traditionally expect to broaden and augment human power. The rebel has traditionally used power to inspire a more focused, insistent force for reform. The martyred corporal and the rebellious Runner represent these two aspects of power in opposition to the Old General's vision of immortal mankind emerging from the ruins of apocalyptic destruction to continue planning, even after "the last ding dong of doom" to build "something higher and faster and louder" that will still "fail to eradicate him from the earth" (299).

These differently nuanced aspects of endurance display ambivalence about immortality, and this novel shares that ambivalence with other modernist works. The image of the uprooted or unburied, obviously decaying corpse, prime symbol and evidence of mortality, is a common one in modernist writing, prevalent not only in other works by Faulkner such as "A Rose for Emily," *As I Lay Dying*, and *Intruder in the Dust*, but also in classic high modernist works such as Eliot's *The Waste Land* ("that corpse . . . in your garden") and Joyce's *Ulysses* ("poor dogsbody's body"). Eugène Ionesco's play *Amédée, or How to Get Rid of It*, published the same year as Faulkner's *A Fable*, features an unexplained but inconveniently expanding corpse in a couple's apartment. These bodies are radically different from the intact and incorporeal images of the risen Christ or even the ghosts and spirits of Romantic and Gothic writing. Though they also carry the value or threat of revelation, it is usually of a more humble, unpleasant, unwelcome, or even comic set of truths.

In the context of these literary signals of change in the value of mortality itself, Faulkner alters the story of the risen Christ to give a positive value to the decaying body of the Corporal. In the Christ story, the offensive corpse disappears altogether, completely transformed into a perfect but insubstantial type of the man; it is only after this transformation that the doubting, denying disciples can gather together to celebrate the significance of his life in a new religion. In Faulkner's loosely anchored allegory, the Corporal's corpse has a floating market value of its own, but his identity and the significance of his life are lost in a series of transactions that transform the very meaning of his death.

The implication that the Corporal is more valuable dead than alive is carried forward from the time of his interview with the Old General (the Temptation scene) through to the end of the novel. The Corporal, who is the unacknowledged son of the Old General, conspired with a group of French soldiers to stop the fighting, and the Germans on the other side of the line joined them in this gesture, creating an unofficial cease fire, a temporary end to the war. When the Old General is trying to tempt him to betray his fellow conspirators, accept his own protection, and live, he acknowledges the potential power of martyrdom, saying: "to me, your death is but an ace to be finessed, while to you it is the actual ace of trumps" (295). The Corporal resists his father's offers and is executed, and the darkly comic progress of his dead body is accompanied by an escalation of his value. His dead body brings to his impoverished sister and her family a free passage back home, accompanied by a medal and a signed paper. The signature is presumably that of the General himself, and the document is pronounced potent enough to pass them through any "pearled and golden gate" (328). Later, his corpse, blasted out of its grave and into a neighbor's field by more shelling, is "resurrected" and sold by that neighbor as the culminating exchange in a series which provides brandy for a group of soldiers. Ironically, they are in need of the comfort of spirits because they have just descended into the catacombs at Verdun in search of a corpse for an Unknown Soldier's monument, which they sold for the brandy. There is further irony: the body of the Corporal, who has been executed because he has opposed himself to war, is used as the replacement to represent the Unknown Soldier.

Thus, mortality acquires not only an exchange value, but also a symbolic one, in the form of the monument above him:

> The vast and serene and triumphal and enduring Arch . . . lifted toward the gray and grieving sky, invincible and impervious . . . crowning the city: on the marble floor, exactly beneath the Arch's soaring center, the small perpetual flame burned above the eternal sleep of the nameless bones. . . . (367)

The use of the pacifist Corporal to occupy the tomb of the Unknown Soldier is possible only because of the Corporal's corporeality. Decayed beyond recognition, his body can be transformed for any symbolic purpose, making his mortal remains more adaptable for the human version of immortality enshrined than a fully incorporeal but resurrected and recognizable spirit would be. The Corporal's mortal body has been given to maintain his bond with those he led in the war against war, has been sold to provide liquor to comfort and fortify the surviving soldiers who must endure the reek of the carnage he tried to end, and has finally come to occupy the place one would expect to be occupied by Christian images of immortality—that of a general palliative which helps diminish the pain of war, sentimentalizes and beautifies it, and makes its continuance possible.

In contrast to the portrayal of corporeality, immortality in *A Fable* is presented as downright tough and ugly. It is represented in its positive manifestation by the Runner, who makes a dramatic gesture in remembrance of those who tried to stop the war and closes the novel with a declaration that he will never die. Faulkner calls him a "living scar," the "active" conscience, one who takes the attitude that "there is evil in the world and I'm going to do something about it" ("Note" 163). Unlike the Corporal, the Runner survives as a witness to the effort to end the war as well as to its betrayal; the runner is too ugly and offensive to assimilate or break down, and he is too tough to kill. He is a human monument to the attempt to wage peace, equivalent to the ugly and enduring marble monuments that glorify war (Polk 113).

A more negative and very interesting representation of immortality comes from the Old General, as he describes the "deathless" and "enduring" vice and folly of mankind. He describes a future in which man's inventiveness, his "puny and inexhaustible voice still talking, still planning . . . after the last ding dong of doom . . . to build something higher and faster and louder" (299) will enable him to outlast even "his enslavement to the demonic progeny of his own mechanical curiosity," who will seem, at least for a time, to be immortal

> because by that time his wars will have dispossessed him by simple out-distance; his simple frail physique will be no longer able to keep up. . . . It will be his own Frankenstein which roasts him alive with heat, asphyxiates him with speed, wrenches loose his still-living entrails in the ferocity of its prey-seeking stoop. (298-9)

The scenario of humans plagued and outlasted by the products and waste of their technology, already appearing in literature by the time *A Fable* was written, will become an increasingly common literary trope as the century progresses. A new dichotomy between that which is natural, subject to decay and therefore good, opposed to the artificial, everlasting, and poisonous, was becoming established in literature and would break out into popular culture in the 1960s with symptoms as wide-ranging as fear of nuclear contamination and Jessica Mitford's scathing condemnation of the burial and embalming industry in *The American Way of Death* (1963). In this novel, though, it is only the evil genius of the Old General which is able to grasp the relationship between increasingly technological and increasingly unstoppable warfare and the durability of his own career and reputation. He says he is "ten times prouder of that immortality which [man] does possess than ever he of that heavenly one of his delusion" (299).

The Corporal's family does not have to share this vision of a future dominated by the unstoppable machinery of technology and war in order to feel its growing presence in their own lives. His sister's husband is concerned with the effect of war on his land, the effect of the durable technology of war on the natural cycles of growth and decay. The sister herself is convinced that "it was the farm, the land which was immune even to the blast and sear of war," and that "restoring" the land would "palliate the grief" and "would affirm that he had not died for nothing" (337). But a new round of shelling blasts his decaying corpse out of the ground, enabling a neighbor to find and sell it to symbolize commitment to a war effort the Corporal condemned and betrayed, leaving the land planted only with unexploded shells.

Another aspect of this valuation of a naturally decaying body appears in the train of thought followed by the Corporal's fellow conspirators as they speculate about the use and value of their bodies after they are executed. During their "last supper," they imagine the future riches of those decaying bodies: "that gardenplot manured with the concentrate of this meal . . . the manure of traitors . . . the carrion we'll bequeath France tomorrow" (284). Ironically, this recalls the conception of Major "Mama" Bidet's (who planned their battle to earn a promotion) of the soldier

> as a functioning machine in the same sense that the earthworm is: alive purely and simply for the purpose of transporting, without itself actually moving, for the distance of its corporeal length, the medium in which it lives, which, given time, would shift the whole earth that infinitesimal inch, leaving at last its own blind insatiate jaws chewing nothing above the spinning abyss. (43)

Besides unintentionally providing us with an amusing representation of deconstruction, this image also reminds us of the transforming power of the earthworm, which digests the indigestible and does, in fact, help to increase the fertility of the soil, unlike the equally robotic and blind war machinery imagined by the general.

By its end, *A Fable* has shown the Corporal's mortal remains plucked from the home soil it is enriching to become a symbol for eternal war. The Christian dichotomy of the valueless mortal body set against the perfection of immortality has been effaced, and Faulkner's novel has demonstrated a shift in the traditional significance of opposing evil with martyrdom.

Works Cited

Butterworth, Keen. *A Critical and Textual Study of Faulkner's* A Fable. Ann Arbor, Michigan: UMI Research, 1983.

Butterworth, Nancy, and Keen Butterworth. *Annotations to Faulkner's* A Fable. New York: Garland, 1989.

Faulkner, William. *A Fable.* 1954. New York: Vintage Books, Random House, 1978.

———. *Faulkner in the University.* Ed. Frederick L. Gwynn and Joseph L. Blotner. New York: Vintage Books, 1965.

———. "A Note on *A Fable.*" In *Faulkner Miscellany*, ed. James B. Meriwether. Jackson: UP of Mississippi, 1974. 162-3.

Kartiganer, Donald M. "'So I, Who Had Never Had a War . . .': William Faulkner, War, and the Modern Imagination." *Modern Fiction Studies* 44.3 (1998): 619-45.

King, Roma A., Jr. "*A Fable*: Everyman's Warfare." In *Religious Perspectives in Faulkner's Fiction*, ed. J. Robert Barth. Notre Dame: U of Notre Dame P, 1972.

Polk, Noel. "Scar." *Faulkner and Welty and the Southern Literary Tradition*. Jackson: UP of Mississippi, 2008. 106-32.

Server, Lee. "'The Thieves' Market: A. I. Bezzerides in Hollywood." *The Big Book of Noir*. Ed. Ed Gorman, Lee Server, and Martin H. Greenberg. New York: Avalon, 1998.

Urgo, Joseph R. *Faulkner's Apocrypha: A Fable, Snopes, and the Spirit of Human Rebellion*. Jackson: UP of Mississippi, 1989.

Végsö, Roland. "Faulkner in the Fifties: The Making of the Faulkner Canon." *Arizona Quarterly: A Journal of American Literature, Culture, and Theory* 63.2 (2007): 81-107.

"You'll Never Find a Woman Who is Worthy of You": Freud's *The Interpretation of Dreams* and the Effects of Oedipal Impulses in William Faulkner's *The Sound and the Fury*

In his 1992 article "Horace Benbow and the Myth of Narcissa," John T. Irwin briefly comments on Quentin's incestuous relationship with his sister Caddy in *The Sound and the Fury* and relates it to the classical figure of Narcissus. The Freudian implications here are great—as often seems to be the case with Faulknerian relationships—though the focus of pschological criticism seems to fall on this incestuous brother/sister bond. By extending the discussion of incestuous relationships as they relate to classical Greek figures to include Jason Compson and his mother, further connections can be drawn between William Faulkner's *The Sound and the Fury* (1929) and Sigmund Freud's *The Interpretation of Dreams* (1899). Such connections position Jason as a figure comparable to King Oedipus and—more appropriately—to Prince Hamlet, as these are the two literary figures Freud examines in his landmark publication in question.

To examine the impact of *The Interpretation of Dreams* on *The Sound and the Fury*, equal consideration must be given to the writing of both men. Gary Storhoff notes that criticism of Faulkner has become "overwhelmingly Freudian in approach" (524) and quotes Donald Kartiganer as having said that "the theory of psychoanalysis-according-to-Sigmund-Freud, much of which has long since been dis-carded by practitioners and scholars in the field of psychology . . . [is] the indispensable body of thought" in Faulknerian studies (Kartiganer vii). Freud's theories—when used in reference to the treatment of psychological patients—have fallen by the wayside in recent decades. With our improved knowledge of cognitive functions and biological factors that influence psychological behavior, and the advances that have been made in medicine, analyzing a person's unconscious desires has not proven to be the most efficient or effective way to treat a psychological ailment. The clinical usefulness of these theories aside, their influence on literary studies must be acknowledged, particularly, as Kartiganer suggests, in relation to a study of Faulkner's work.

A large area of the critical conversation taking place in relation to Faulkner's writing and the psychological lives of his characters, however, is dedicated to speculation as to whether Freud's work provides a source of motivation for Faulkner's characters; however, Freudian writing argues that this is not necessary for an author to create such psychologically astute characters as Faulkner's. In the introduction to *The Interpretation of Dreams*, Ritchie Robertson notes that Freud's impact on the creation of literature is actually less than is often supposed and that Freud himself would admit that "creative writers anticipated his findings by their own psychological intuition. Writers do not create by anxiously following the instructions of a psychological theorist" (xxxiii). Robertson's argument here indicates that the appearance of Freudian theory in a piece of literature is the result of neither coincidence nor an author's attempts to follow a prescribed structure for formulating a text. Instead, an inherent intuition of Freud's theories manifests on the page. After all, Freud did not invent his theories—he merely *presented* them. To illustrate this, we can turn to Ineke Bockting's work which explores Quentin's fixations and other aspects of his personality in order to prove that he displays signs of schizophrenia. Studies such as Bockting's help to strengthen the argument that Faulkner did not have to have read Freud in order to create characters that demonstrated certain neuroses. Given the timeline—*The Sound and the Fury* being published in 1929 and schizophrenia not becoming widely studied until much later and not explored directly by Freud himself—Faulkner could not very well have spent time reading journals or other psychological writing on schizophrenia. Yet he was, as Bockting's work displays, able to create a character whose personality resembled this psychosis closely enough to create a compelling argument.

In psychoanalytic criticism of any piece of literature, it is common for a critic to be tempted to treat characters as patients instead of employing Freud's writing as a framework of literary theory. Frederick Crews argues that, because of this, Freudian criticism can easily morph into "a grotesque Easter-egg hunt" in which a critic works diligently to "find the devouring mother, detect the inevitable castration anxiety, listen, between the syllables of verse, for the squeaking bedsprings of the primal scene" (166) in order to detect just where the development of a given character's psyche was irreparably damaged, thus causing any number of irreversible psychoses. For our purposes, this "grotesque Easter-egg hunt" can be avoided by directly relating the novel to Freudian writing. As Kartiganer notes, the influence of Freud's theories on literary studies has proven to be long-lasting—an argument particularly compelling in an analysis of the intricate Oedipal relationship between Jason Compson and his mother.

That Freud's theories are "indispensable" cannot be denied. Closely related to this type of study is a discussion of Jason's Oedipal complex as it relates to *Hamlet* and *King Oedipus*—the two pieces of literature that Freud utilized in *The Interpretation of Dreams*. These works far preceded his own and so, as Freud argues, the psychological complex they demonstrate must have existed in the human psyche long before his theories were published in order to have manifested in works of literature from such different historical eras and geographic settings. That criticism of Faulkner's work sometimes speculates as to his tangible knowledge of Freud's work and thus overlooks the connections between the writing of these two contemporaries is unfortunate. Throughout his career, Faulkner denied these assumptions and was quoted as having said, "I have never read [Freud]. Neither did Shakespeare. I doubt if Melville did either, and I'm sure Moby Dick didn't" (Faulkner, "Interview" 251). In another interview, he is reported to have said, "What little of psychology I know the characters I have invented and playing poker have taught me" (Gwynn 268). Though he did not "invent" the complex to be discussed here, these two quotes indicate that during the Modernist movement when Freud's writing was being translated into English—and for a great span of time preceding—novelists were turning their focus inward to the psychological lives of the characters they created. Psychological language and concepts were simply a part of the world out of which Faulkner's writing was born. In studying Jason Compson's Oedipal complex, the critic should acknowledge that his obsession materializes from factors present in every human psyche—that to create the characters, the author must have possessed the same innate qualities that lead to the character's neurosis. The same is true of the reader who identifies with and understands the characters' plights. As mentioned above, Freud did not *invent* these urges— he merely *presented* them as part of a theory. This connection between author, audience and character allows for a detailed psychological analysis of the text and sheds light on similarities between Jason Compson and these figures of classical literature.

Freud used *King Oedipus* and *Hamlet* to demonstrate the basis for the origin, formation, and effects of the Oedipal complex in children but also to reveal that such phenomena were present in the human psyche centuries before he had formed his theories. He argues that "the ancient world has provided us with a legend whose far-reaching and universal power can only be understood if we grant a similar universality to the assumption from child-psychology" that psychoneurotic children exhibit the failings of repression that function well in most children and therefore exhibit active desires that would generally lie dormant were the repressive tendencies to be in functioning order (201). Because the characteristics of the Oedipal complex are not always readily apparent, many critics of Freud's psychoanalytic theories take issue with this complex. Having never felt a tangible desire to kill his father and sleep with his mother, no man could see the validity of such a concept without understanding the process of repression. Furthermore, Freud expressly states that "psycho-neurotics are only revealing to us . . . what goes on less clearly and less intensely in the inner life of most children" (201), thus suggesting that though we may not clearly exhibit such desires, we should not deny their existence within us, as they have been observed in children whose repression processes have failed and are therefore demonstrating "psychoneurotic" tendencies.

Jason Compson's relationship with his mother demonstrates not only his Oedipal complex but also his need for a father-surrogate, and has spurred a great distrust of women that dominates his adult life. Jason displays the two key ingredients of this complex in his section of the novel: one aspect being that his relationship with his mother in his adult life is one in which she consistently suggests through conversation as well as unspoken gestures that he is sexually fixated on her and illustrates that this is a fixation she encourages; the other being a hatred for his father, as evidenced by the lacing of each memory or mention of him with distaste and rivalry—a trend often noticed and commented on by Mrs. Compson. As a child his repression processes did not *quite* fail him, and as an adult they are not as effective as Freudian theory would suggest they should be in order for him to lead a normal and healthy life. The objective of the Oedipal complex is not, after all, to be able to act on forbidden desires, but rather to repress them successfully. Because the goal is not to *realize* these desires, we can group Jason's relationship with his mother together with what Irwin refers to as Faulkner's trend of "unattainable beloved[s]" in his article appropriately entitled "Not the Having But the Wanting" (54).

Kathleen Moore discusses several aspects of Jason's Oedipal complex by using Freud's theories to explore Jason's adult mindset and the psychological past that lead to his current neurosis. Moore uses these points to speculate as to why his narrative section shows him to be wife-less and distrusting of women, though still a servant to his mother's wishes. He exhibits an unusual closeness to her, which is exemplified by the scene in the final chapter of the novel in which Miss Quentin, who has been locked in her bedroom, has escaped through the window, causing Jason to fight with his mother for the key that will open the door. This scene, as noted by Philip Weinstein, is characterized by sexual connotations as the high levels of emotion that are displayed are exemplified by rage and passion. Jason falls to "pawing at the pockets of the rusty black dressing sacque" his mother is wearing, while his mother resists, protecting the keys in her pocket (Faulkner 281). The touching of his mother in a moment of passion, Mrs. Compson's choice of garment, and the provocative wording Faulkner utilizes strongly indicate that Jason's repressive capabilities are faltering here. In this flicker of wavering repression and enraged struggle, the reader is given the sense that Jason's hand entering her pocket to take the key was as personal and powerful as if a sexual relationship were being enacted, though in the end no such relationship is realized. This suggestion of Oedipal urges characterizes Jason's relationship with his mother throughout the narrative.

We cannot assume that Jason's repressive capabilities have just *happened* to have become impaired; nor can we assume that this Oeidpal relationship was not cultivated, at least in part, by Mrs. Compson herself. Her choice of garment and her insistence on fighting Jason in the aforementioned scene indicate that the Oedipal relationship the two share has not gone unnoticed by her. Furthermore, she displays an attachment to Jason that she does not harbor for her other children, repeatedly saying, "I thanked God it was you left me if they had to be taken" (226). The "they" here refers to Quentin (who was taken by suicide), Caddy (who was disowned for her promiscuity), and Benjy who is discarded completely because of his handicap. Jason is the only child to whom she lays any claim, and she separates him from the rest of the family, declaring that he is "a Bascomb, despite [his] name" (182), not a Compson like her husband and the rest of her offspring by whom she feels victimized. Her efforts here indicate that she sees herself sharing a relationship with Jason that is beyond that which she shares with the rest of her children—indeed, that is beyond that which she shared with even her husband—and suggests that she wishes Jason to harbor this view of the rest of the family as well. This separation of mother and son from the rest of their family allows for a sense of intimate privacy and understanding that is not characteristic of a mother-son relationship.

Jason's distaste and resentment that defines his relationship with his father is not surprising in light of the manipulative nature displayed by Mrs. Compson. His narrative is laced with indications of his resentment for his father's alcoholism, and references to how he had nothing to gain from being born a Compson because his father "drank it all up" (197).

Mr. Compson is portrayed as a nihilistic and disparaging man who drank constantly and felt very little need to maintain his family's good name. His one attempt at salvaging the family's reputation is when he sells the pasture that was to be Benjy's inheritance, in order to send Quentin to Harvard. Jason's obvious resentment that he "never heard of him offering to sell anything to send me to Harvard" (197) seems to be encouraged by Mrs. Compson. She alludes to her early knowledge that Mr. Comspon "would never realize that [Jason was] the only one who had any business sense" (221), thus furthering her attempts to separate Jason from his father, not only in name, but by also demolishing any inkling Jason could have retained of the idea that his father may have loved him and held any confidence in him at all.

Upon Jason's father's death, his place within the family structure had to be filled in order to maintain the function of his Oedipal complex. The objective of the Oedipal complex is not, as mentioned above, to realize forbidden desires but rather to repress them successfully. Jason's repressive acts may not be wholly successful, but his complex allows him to operate within his environment in a way to which he has grown accustomed. In order for the complex to function as he is used to it functioning, and because he knows on an unconscious level that he must never be able to possess his mother in the way in which he desires, Jason must replace his father so that he can have some dominant male figure to compete against for his mother's affection. Jason attributes this role to Uncle Maury and subsequently transfers his hatred for his father to this surrogate with the help of his mother's manipulation. This displaced relationship becomes apparent as Jason remembers the day of Quentin's funeral when his mother was repetitively expressing her relief that Jason is "not a Compson except in name" because he and Uncle Maury are all she has left. Jason responds, "I could spare Uncle Maury myself" (197), and then goes on to describe with obvious disgust the way his uncle strokes his mother's hand in an attempt to comfort her. His descriptions are laced with connotations of jealousy and loathing as he obviously believes that he can comfort his mother just as well, if not better, than this man who has intruded on their relationship. Again, however, Jason's impulses are not without provocation as here, too, we see Mrs. Compson's attempts to reorganize the family structure in order to create one more amenable to her desires. She first reinforces that Jason is only a Compson in name and later insists that Uncle Maury is "the nearest thing to a father [Jason has] ever had" (259). These three—Jason, Uncle Maury and Mrs. Compson— are all associated with the "good" family name of Bascomb. Jason does not possess this name but is entitled to it and its prestige only through his closeness and loyalty to her.

Noel Polk writes often of Faulkner's men and their need to control the sexuality of the women with whom they are involved, generally relating this desire to Quentin and Caddy when discussing *The Sound and the Fury*. Jason also possesses this desire, though it is directed toward Mrs. Compson and what he perceives to be a potential sexual relationship between her and Uncle Maury. In his 2003 article "Faulkner and Crime Fiction," Polk writes that the brothers in Faulkner's fiction want to kill their sisters' suitors "simply to control their sister's sexuality" (16) but he had previously noted in his 2001 article "Testing Masculinity in the Snopes Trilogy" that "Quentin cannot be a 'man' in *The Sound and the Fury* because he cannot control his sister's sexual life, because he cannot shoot a gun or hold a knife, because he cannot live up to a 'tradition' that insists that males behave in certain ways" (5). Jason faces a similar dilemma in his relationship with his mother. The scene in which he reflects on Uncle Maury's attempts at comforting his mother at his father's funeral indicates Jason's desire to control his mother's sexual life by preventing what he fears may develop into a sexual relationship. The Compson family is a rather isolated one, so Jason may not see his mother interact with many men outside of the family, allowing this type of jealousy to flare up during Quentin's funeral. His attempts to control not only his mother's relationships with other men, but also his Oedipal attraction to her illustrates, as Polk points out, "the problematics of masculine enactment and empowerment [in] Faulkner's work" (5).

Jason is not in sole control of the incestuous relationships that have formed within this family. Mrs. Compson's attempts at reconfiguring her family structure do not stop at reassigning roles; she must also reinforce them. Her obvious distaste for her late husband and his way of conducting personal and public affairs leads her to avoid allowing Jason to see any similarities between himself and his father, and, because of her pride for her own family line, she would prefer that Jason attribute bits of himself to his uncle, even if that which is being attributed is a negative quality. When Jason takes on the responsibility of disciplining the now hard-headed Miss Quentin in her teenage years, his mother expresses great concern that he will be too rough in his efforts, reminding him that he has "Uncle Maury's temper" (222). She attributes personality traits of Jason's to an inheritance from Uncle Maury, but fails to allude to similarities Jason may have with his own father. When Mrs. Compson can be sure that Jason has developed the same distaste for her brother as she had perhaps ensured that he had for his father, she begins to acknowledge this dynamic, repeating "I know you begrudge him" (225), making Jason's distaste for him all the more tangible. Even within the constructs of the family structure she has tailored herself, she cannot help but demolish any relationship he may have with someone else that has the potential to be stronger than the bond he has with her.

This destruction of relationships is not limited to Jason's connection to his father and his subsequent father-surrogate, but extends to his siblings, as well. Though she has discarded Benjy long ago, Mrs. Compson laments the past she has with Caddy and Quentin, saying, "They were always conspiring against me. Against you too, though you were too young to realize it. They always looked on you and me as outsiders, like they did your Uncle Maury" (261). Jason does not seem to have been too young to realize that they were isolating themselves—or, at least, that his mother felt this way. The two sections of the novel that precede Jason's narrative section depict him as a mean-spirited boy who was full of hatred and quick to hold grudges. He would run to his mother as soon as he had gathered information on the mischief about which his siblings were conspiring, as if his concern with fitting in with them was less substantial than his concern for pleasing his mother. One is left to question whether he formed these propensities on his own accord at such a young age or if promptings from his mother have had a consistent and vastly influential presence in his life. According to Mrs. Compson, Jason is as much an outsider to Quentin and Caddy as she and Uncle Maury are, and by bemoaning her and Jason's lacking relationship with the other two children, she reinforces this new, pseudo-incestuous construct in which mother, father, and son are united by their isolation.

This unnatural, manipulative closeness between Jason and his mother offers an explanation as to why we find Jason wife-less in his adult life, untrusting of women, and unable to leave his mother. Polk argues that Faulkner's men "construct an ideal woman or, rather, they bemoan the failure of a particular woman to live up to some ideal of womanhood that they first impose on her and then judge her by how far short of it she falls" (8). This serves as an accurate description of Jason Compson at the point at which we meet him in the novel. Upon receiving a letter from Caddy, he declares that he "make[s] it a rule never to keep a scrap of paper bearing a woman's hand" (Faulkner 193). He then goes on to claim that he often sees a woman in Memphis named Lorraine when he is able to get to town. Jason mentions that she asks repeatedly that he write to her, but that he has made it a rule not to write to women at all. Such a request seems indicative of the fact that Lorraine may be after something more than a sexual relationship. Jason creates distance between himself and this relationship by responding to these requests by saying "anything I forgot to tell you will save till I get to Memphis again" (193-4) in order to maintain his isolation within his established, tailor-made family structure. He adds, however, that he does not mind if she writes to him as long as no one (i.e., his mother) can distinguish the source from which the letter is coming, and is clear in his orders that she never try to call him on the telephone. We know, then, that Jason does not mind being contacted by a woman, but can assume that he must put limitations on this contact because he anticipates the jealousy that could ensue if his mother were to find out that he may be cultivating romance. He expresses these concerns to his mother, saying, "if I was to get married you'd go up like a balloon and you know it" (246). She responds by stating that she wants happiness for her son and that she does, in fact, want him to have a family of his own, but adds, "I'll be gone soon and *then* you can take a wife but you'll never find a woman who is worthy of you" (246-7, emphasis mine). He is, after all, a Bascomb underneath his Compson name, and no woman can complement such status unless she were herself a Bascomb. (One cannot ignore here the established fact that Mrs. Compson is one of the only Bascombs left.) That this conversation is just one in a string of similar discussions that have been present throughout Jason's life would be an appropriate assumption supported by his willingness to accept Mrs. Compson's statements as fact. Such statements reaffirm that which she has undoubtedly conditioned him to believe: that no woman will ever be as good for him as his mother has been. When she dies, he will be free to take a wife, but Mrs. Compson has ensured that because of her manipulations, and because of his willingness to accept those manipulations, he will be unsatisfied with any woman with whom he cultivates a romantic relationship and will be just as untrusting of her as he is of Lorraine, of the "good, church-going" (246) women who surround him in town, even of his own sister. His mother is the only woman who can live up to this construct of an "ideal woman" about which Polk writes.

Despite his mother's manipulations, Jason remains blind to her controlling nature and exhibits a childlike attachment to her, coupled with a desire to protect her. When he imagines that Caddy may show up at the house asking to see her daughter, he anticipates the strain this would put on his mother and laments that he "couldn't even get away from the store to protect [his] own mother" (206), as if Caddy's intentions were not based in loyalty to and love for her family but in a desire to physically harm her mother. In the same vein, Jason is angered by the fact that

Miss Quentin has grown up to be such a deviant—not because of any concern he may have for the quality of the family name or out of concern for her well-being, but instead because it causes his mother such distress, as evidenced by the fact that his strongest line of reasoning when trying to discipline Miss Quentin lies in the notion that she should be more concerned with the stress she brings on her grandmother. We can assume that this pattern will continue until Mrs. Compson is gone, as Jason has reassured her that he will never "get far enough from the store [where he works] to get out of [her] reach" (206).

The relationships illustrated in *King Oedipus* and *Hamlet* demonstrate the key aspects of an Oedipal complex as clearly as Jason's relationship with his mother does. Freud's discussion of the plot of King Oedipus in *The Interpretation of Dreams* outlines for his reader a tale that demonstrates the universality of these inherent impulses and proves that they have been present in the lives of men for millennia. Patrick Brady has commented on these similarities, pointing out that Jason "[bears] the same name as his father" and so it seems that he is "predestined to replace him" within the family structure. He is also "'disinherited' by the father (as the infant Oedipus was)" (29) when his father makes great sacrifices to send Quentin to college, leaving Jason with no college education and substantially less land to inherit. Freud also notes *Hamlet* as a piece of literature that demonstrates a man's sexual longing for his mother and harbored hatred for his father, but argues that in this case the title character demonstrates semi-functional repression. Hamlet is initially unable to exact revenge upon his uncle for killing his father and marrying his mother, but Freud argues he is not *incapable* of action, as criticism will often suggest. After all, we see him murder Polonius in a sudden fit, but his abundance of analytical thought keeps him from acting immediately because to do so would be to avenge a feat (murdering his father so he could cultivate a sexual relationship with his mother) that he subconsciously wanted to commit himself. The difference between the two classic texts is in the title characters' abilities—or lack thereof—to repress their sexual and violent impulses. While Oedipus acts out the unspeakable desires of the so-named Oedipal complex, Hamlet is able to repress them to a certain degree, though he is plagued by their governing power in his life. These Oedipal urges, Freud argues, are generally present in children, so Jason's Oedipal love for his mother is one of which we are all capable. This fact is what allows a reader to detect this type of relationship in a text.

In *King Oedipus* the effects of these impulses are tangible as the actions are carried out, while in *Hamlet* the actions are repressed and we know the desires exist, not because we are able to experience them in action but through the effects these impulses produce on the one who possesses them. The ancient text demonstrates fulfilled desires and their consequences, while the more recent text demonstrates repressed desires and *their* consequences, thus offering a comparison of texts which serves as a statement about society's progression of the unconscious understanding in relation to the need for the repression of these impulses. Freud suggests that the "change in treatment of the same material reveals the difference in the inner life of these two cultural periods so remote from each other: the advance of repression over the centuries in mankind's emotional life" (204).

Drawing similarities between Jason Compson and Oedipus is unavoidable in an analysis of an Oedipal complex, but Jason exhibits a closer similarity to the title character of *Hamlet* than he does to King Oedipus. Unlike Oedipus, Jason does not follow through in his desires to kill his father in order to sleep with his mother, but, very much like Hamlet, his repressive processes work just well enough to keep him from doing that which he desires, while still causing him to be plagued by this lack of action and the presence of his unacceptable longing. Jason's rivalry with his father indicates a desire for murder; however, his father's death has left Jason in a state of limbo in which his murderous desires are not fulfilled and his fixation on his mother cannot be overcome. Much like Hamlet, he will never be able to confront that murderous aspect of his complex, and his father's death does not ensure that the relationship he unconsciously desires to have with his mother will ever be realized. In fact, because Jason's repressive capabilities are still somewhat intact—enough to ensure that he can function within society—he needs a father figure who will surely thwart his desire to cultivate a sexual relationship with his mother. In this sense, Faulkner has thus not produced another King Oedipus in *The Sound and the Fury* because Jason does not act upon his sexual desire for his mother and, as is noted in Kathleen Moore's article, he was not the one who took his father's life. Instead, this novel is more *Hamlet*-esque in that Jason's Oedipal impulses are repressed, and we know of their existence only through the tension exhibited in each exchange of conversation between him and his mother, the disdain he still feels for his father, the rivalry he pursues against Uncle Murray who has become his father-surrogate, and the resulting distrust for and distance from women.

To return to Ritchie Robertson's quote from the introduction to *The Interpretation of Dreams*, Freud's impact on literature has been in the criticism of it, not in the creation. Instead, the appearance of aspects of his theories in a piece of literature points to the author's unconscious sense of the human psychological condition. For this reason, concentrating our efforts on Faulkner's *knowledge* of Freud to explain the appearance of Freudian psychological theory, or attempts at having characters lie on our psychoanalytic couches to pick out their various psychoses, allows little critical progress. The Freudian critic should instead concentrate on Faulkner's intuition of that about which Freud theorizes, thus sticking to one of the basic tenets of Freudian theory. Using Freud's work as a lens through which to view this particular character allows the reader to see Jason as a victim of a manipulative mother afraid of losing control over the one child she feels has done right by her. Faulkner has created a character meant to simultaneously elicit disgust and sympathy from the reader, and one who fits naturally into psychological literature that has spanned several millennia.

Works Cited

Bockting, Ineke. "The Impossible World of the Schizophrenic: William Faulkner's Quentin Compson." *Style* 24.3 (1990): 136-49.

Brady, Patrick. "Birth Trauma, Infant Anality, and Castration Anxiety in *Germinal* and *The Sound and the Fury*." *Excavation: Emile Zola and Naturalism* 1 (1992): 25-30.

Crews, Frederick. *Out of My System: Psychoanalysis, Ideology, and Critical Method.* New York: Oxford UP, 1975.

Faulkner, William. *The Sound and the Fury.* 1929. New York: Vintage, 1984.

———. "Interview with Jean Stein van den Heuvel." In *Lion in the Garden: Interviews with William Faulkner* 1926-1962, ed. James B. Meriwether and Michael Millgate. New York: Random House, 1968. 237-56.

Freud, Sigmund. *The Interpretation of Dreams.* Trans. Joyce Crick. Intro. by Ritchie Robertson New York: Oxford UP, 1999.

Gwynn, Frederick L., and Joseph Blotner, eds. *Faulkner in the University: Class Conferences at the University of Virginia.* 1957-1958. New York: Random House, 1965.

Irwin, John T. "Horace Benbow and the Myth of Narcissa." *American Literature* 64.3 (1992): 543-66.

———. "Not the Having But the Wanting: Faulkner's Lost Loves." In *Faulkner at 100: Retrospect and Prospect*, ed. Donald M. Kartiganer and Ann J. Abadie. Jackson: UP of Mississippi, 2000. 154-64.

Kartiganer, Donald M. "Introduction." In *Faulkner and Psychology*. Jackson: UP of Mississippi, 1994.

Moore, Kathleen. "Jason Compson and the Mother Complex." *Mississippi Quarterly* 53 (2000): 533-50.

Polk, Noel. "Faulkner and Crime Fiction." *Philological Review* 29 (2003): 1-26.

———. "Testing Masculinity in the Snopes Trilogy." *Faulkner Journal* 16.3 (2001): 3-22.

Storhoff, Gary. "Jason's Role-Slippage: The Dynamics of Alcoholism in *The Sound and the Fury*." *Mississippi Quarterly* 49 (1996): 519-35.

Weinstein, Philip M. "'If I Could Say Mother': Construing the Unsavable about Faulknerian Maternity." In *Faulkner's Discourse: An International Symposium*, ed. Lothar Hónnighausen. Tübingen: Niemeyer, 1989. 3-15.

Some Medical History Embedded in Faulkner's Jason Compson

Medical science sometimes reveals the secrets about how human behavior can be triggered by human physiology. For instance, we owe much to the medical sciences for exploring the brain functions behind aberrant behavior, like gambling; for mapping the biochemistry of depression; for following the chemical memory prompts involved in Post-traumatic Stress Disorder (PTSD); for tracing post-partum depression to a poor hormonal switch between placenta and pituitary gland; for locating the ever-hungry neural receptors that addicts are devoted to filling. In short, medical science provides complex approaches to explicate our human natures.

While literary authors illustrate characters with odd or peculiar traits, medical scientists (including those in the relatively young sciences of psychology and psychiatry) gather evidence to examine and expose the causal details that combine to develop such human portraits. Underlying physiological roots to our emotions and behaviors are fascinating enough on their own merit, but they are especially so when unearthed in some of Faulkner's fictional people.

We can safely gamble that most MDs loathe the idea of English professors "playing doctor," offering diagnosis, quoting from the *Physicians' Desk Reference*, or abusing medical Latin, but since we can "do no harm" to literary characters, I propose that we allow some literary characters to be "pretend patients." First a little medical history, then onto the patient: youngest sibling Jason Compson from *The Sound and The Fury*.

Medical History

William Faulkner wrote his early novels just after a major divide in American medicine. Homeopathy, an alternative medical treatment sometimes summarized by the dictums that "like cures like" and that "less is more," dominated American medicine in the nineteenth century. Its pharmacopeia—the cause of the medical dispute—is comprised of ultra-diluted chemical remedies of naturally-occurring substances that would effectively produce the very same set of ill symptoms if given to a healthy person. Though widely practiced, revered by the well-educated, and endorsed by virtually all the Transcendentalists, it was effectively driven underground by the newly-powerful American Medical Association, which prohibited regular doctors from treating patients who had formerly consulted homeopaths or risk losing their licenses.

Despite having founded the nation's first medical teaching hospitals in America (Philadelphia, Michigan, and New York), homeopathy lost the battle for dominance in American medicine, though homeopathic doctors did not completely disappear from the culture. Instead, they continued to develop new remedies. In the early decades of the twentieth century, physician (and devoted Swedenborgian) James Tyler Kent expanded homeopathy by introducing new remedies at even higher dilutions that he believed treated deeply emotional and psychological symptoms coupled with, and manifested in, the physical ones.[1] Constitutional or Kentian homeopathy took a developmental leap forward, and it claimed to be able to reach deeper into a patient's psyche in order to treat both body and soul. It described various archetypes or portraits evident in human nature, and, in this way, it expanded on the foundation of homeopathy as medical treatment previously founded in Germany by physician and medical translator Samuel Hahnemann in the late eighteenth century. Near the close of the nineteenth century and well into the twentieth century, homeopathic doctors routinely published manuals or repertories further defining their Latin-named remedies and further describing and listing their extensive and now far-reaching nomenclature for each of the homeopathic archetypes, which numbered about fifty. These doctors included James Tyler Kent, Constantin Hering, Douglas Borland, H.C. Allen, Margaret Tyler, and Clemens von Boenninghausen, among others not mentioned here, and their contributions to homeopathic repertories have recently been compiled, referenced, and edited by the prominent homeopathic doctor and author, Catherine R. Coulter, whose work I will soon draw from to suggest Faulkner's plausible source of inspiration for the fictional Jason Compson.

Jason is but one example in my larger argument that the cultural scene of medicine's divided legacy informed William Faulkner's character conceptions and portrayals. In their psycho-biological traits, some of his characters represent homeopathic descriptions of the human portraits quite accurately, allowing readers to find ample parallels between Faulkner's fictional people and concurrently published descriptions of homeopathic archetypes. This convergence prompts several questions: Could Faulkner have been attentive to the period's medical literature, especially the repertories which described a range of some of the very same peculiar symptoms and odd traits that Faulkner delighted in reproducing and fictionalizing? What signs of homeopathic typology are written on his characters' bodies or embossed on their behaviors, not only as the effects of a character's underlying illness, but simply as general predispositions, the constitutionally weak and strong areas that defined each archetype?

When we consider the era's medical division, Faulkner's family history of serious illness and alcoholism, family visits to "cures," and his own reading about psychological and physical health, especially hormonal health, we find that medical influences likely informed his creation of characters. A study of Faulkner and his fictional people—from the perspective of medical history—further suggests that the unorthodox ideology of homeopathy continued to play a role in the culture through literature, even as it lacked legitimate authority from the newly established medical community.

For instance, I argue in unpublished research, that all the main characters depicted in *The Sound and The Fury* are, in significant ways, fictional renditions of concurrently published homeopathic remedy-portraits. Quentin Compson and his father Mr. Compson are incarnations of the portrait known as *Lachesis*. Benjy Compson demonstrates signs from the portrait known as *Phosphorus*, and his brain damage symptoms probably from measles exposure are generally described by the portrait known as *Calcarea Carbonica*. Though the youngest brother Jason shares combined signs with Benjy's *Phosphorus* nature mixed with some of Quentin's *Lachesis* undertones, his nature is most precisely matched to the portrait *Nux Vomica*. The Compson parents present a mix of symptoms that sometimes obscure the underlying portraits of their children. Faulkner's depiction of mother Caroline, for instance, corresponds thoroughly to the homeopathic portrait *Sepia*. When *Sepia* is ill, as Caroline is typically portrayed, and co-parents with an ill *Lachesis* (Mr. Compson), the effects on the family can be especially venomous. I find it also fascinating to point out that each family members' remedy-portrait, with the notable exception of Caddy, are fictional renditions of remedies formulated from poisons, conceivably bringing additional meaning to Quentin's lament, "Done in mother's mind though. Finished. Finished. Then we were all poisoned" (126).

Perhaps it is not so surprising that Faulkner was attuned to medicine of his day when we consider that the writer and his family knew local Oxford doctors quite well, some who were old enough to be trained in the former mainstream homeopathic hospitals, including his paternal great-grandfather Dr. John Young Murry, medically educated in Philadelphia in 1855, a time and place brimming with homeopathic understanding (Williamson 38). Faulkner and other men in his family were frequent patients of the Keeley Cure for alcoholism, which used injections of homeopathic medicines, and members of the older generation visited hot spring spas where homeopathic medicines were routinely available (Williamson 55).

Further compelling evidence points to the period's many publications not only in constitutional homeopathy, but of other innovative medical theories popular during Faulkner's writing years. In fact, Faulkner owned a bestselling medical book describing the newly-discovered role hormones play on body and mind. At the same time, in his literary creations, the writer's characterizations show us repeatedly that the mind and body are not only connected, but deeply manipulate each other. He may have drawn from this rich medical or alchemical knowledge to construct his characters, just as he often drew from mythology or psychology to construct plot, characterization, or theme.

The Keeley Cure for Alcoholism

From taking the Keeley Cure, which employed homeopathic medicines at the nearby Memphis Institute for several weeks at a time, Faulkner would have heard the assertion that alcoholism could be treated as a disease, not a moral weakness. Dr. Leslie E. Keeley (1832-1900) claimed to treat and cure lingering morphine and opium addiction caused by their abuse during the Civil War. Biographer Joseph Blotner writes that Keeley's publications were probably known to Sallie Murry Falkner, the wife of Faulkner's paternal grandfather and "the main force behind J. W. T. Falkner's trips to the Keeley Institute" (Blotner 56).[2] By the end of the nineteenth century, Keeley Institutes in America totaled 370 chapters, claimed $2.7 million in revenues, and treated 30,513 addicts in 1900 alone. Every state had at least one institute; many states boasted two or three (Trice and Staudenmeier 15).

Dr. Keeley was among the first to classify alcoholism as a disease capable of responding to medical intervention. This was extraordinary for a time when both popular and academic opinion about alcohol abuse was planted firmly in a person's morality or will-power. The Keeley Cure's chemical tonic and injections substituted the "poison of alcohol" with other chemicals similar to the poison, without causing drunkenness. The Cure used common remedies straight from the homeopathic pharmacopeia: strychnine and medicinal gold (Tracy 82-86).[3] Strychnine (known by its homeopathic name *Nux Vomica* once it is diluted and potentized) remains in homeopathic use today as both a common constitutional remedy, especially for alcoholism, but also as an acute remedy to relieve the alcohol hangover. Medicinal gold (known by its homeopathic name

Aurum Mettalicum) claims a long history in healing, rejuvenating, and particularly, purifying the body. Patients of the Keeley Cure received mandatory injections four times daily, and every two hours imbibed a liquid mixture of Atropine, an alkaloid made from the homeopathic poison remedy *Atropa Belladonna* (known to folk medicine as Deadly Nightshade) and from the poison remedy *Datura Stramonium* (known in folk medicine as Thorn Apple or Devil's Apple).[4]

At home, alcoholics in Faulkner's family used dilutions of liquor as a home-cure to wean themselves—an adaptation of the homeopathic principle that "like cures like," but also the Falkners [*sic*] had accepted Keeley's theory that the body becomes habituated to a poison and only another similar poison in smaller amounts can replace and subdue the original dependency. This thinking, in a nutshell, clearly demonstrates some grasp of two important homeopathic principles, namely that "like cures like" and that "less is more."

Dr. Berman and Endocrinology

One book in particular in Faulkner's home library would have dramatically informed his general medical awareness: specifically, Dr. Louis A. Berman's 1921 bestseller *The Glands Regulating Personality: A Study of the Glands of Internal Secretion in Relation to the Types of Human Nature*, which has been described as "the intersection between chemistry, physiology, psychology and internal medicine" (Norlund 92). Among other accolades, Berman is credited with "isolat[ing] the secretions of the parathyroid glands . . . the ovaries . . . and the adrenal glands" while pioneering studies to discover the role of the endocrine system for breast cancer and Parkinson's disease. He is famous in medical history for guiding the direction of endocrinology after the initial discovery of the "first chemically isolated hormone"—adrenalin—in New York in 1901 (Norlund 88).

In his book, Berman wrote that his research explained the "chemistry of the soul" (22) and coined the term "psycho-endocrinology," using it as the title of an article he published in the journal *Science* in 1928. He explicitly redirected a great deal of curiosity and attention away from discussions of Freud and Jung with his theories about the psychological effects emanating from secretions in the body's glands (Norlund 94). Even this doctor's physiological explanation for alcoholism agreed with theories promoted by the Keeley Cure. From Drs. Berman and Keeley then, Faulkner was likely exposed to the notion that certain physical attributes, behaviors, and emotions are the result of biology or physiology, particularly the complexities of hormones—the primary site of action for many homeopathic medicines.

If Faulkner read and didn't just own *The Glands Regulating Personality*, he would have learned this new medical theory that hormones greatly influence, and often determine, individual behavior and psychology. Dr. Berman's proposals for subsequent hormone therapy gained immediate mainstream notice as early as 1921 when the insulin-deficient pancreas was isolated as the cause for diabetes, earning its researchers the Nobel Prize for Medicine in 1923 (Norlund 88). Hormone therapy continued and, some might say, now dominates current medicine in the form of birth control pills, hormone replacement therapies, the human growth hormone, and steroids.

Dr. Berman's book, coupled with Faulkner's several visits to the Keeley Institute for Alcoholism, and perhaps his early and life-long fraternity with local doctors, all gave the writer the opportunity to study and re-imagine direct medical practice and principles. By way of the Keeley Cure and Dr. Berman's theory about glands driving behavior, Faulkner was perfectly situated to absorb two progressive and enduring innovations concerning health and medicine in America: hormone therapy and Alcoholics Anonymous. Faulkner's readers may find it fascinating that both innovations, the disease-model explaining alcoholism and the role of endocrinology, intend to clarify and elucidate the compulsions of the body as they interact with and often combat (as in the case of Faulkner's people) attempts by the mind to control, manage, or determine one's outward behavior, emotions, and personality. In this way, Faulkner's recurrent theme of compulsion vs. free-will can be said to be seated squarely in the medical setting of his times. If Faulkner was indeed thinking along these lines of physiological compulsions challenging man's independent free will, it is likely Faulkner would have also been curious about the concurrently published homeopathic archetypes that this mind-body system established.

In 1971, British scholar Mick Gidley identified characters in Faulkner's work that appear to carry the unmistakable features of Dr. Berman's personality types, formed, as Berman first proposed, by their particular glandular dominance and inferiority. To mention a few parallels between Dr. Berman's endocrine types and some of Faulkner's fictional people, Gidley writes that Berman's patients with thyroid deficiency exhibit some of the physical traits Faulkner attributes to Benjy Compson from *The Sound and The Fury* (1929), patients with overactive adrenal glands tend to match the physically precocious traits manifested in Eula Varner from *The Hamlet* (1940), and the sub-thyroid types share a similar endocrine system with Anse Bundren from *As I Lay Dying* (1930). Other physiologic theories of glandular activity included many characteristics readers of Faulkner will no doubt recognize: "popping eyes, chinlessness, hairlessness, and, even, 'delinquency' itself" (Gidley 85).

Additionally, Faulkner scholars André Bleikasten and Walter J. Slatoff chronicle Faulkner's preoccupation, as they sometimes call it, with depicting several specific bodily actions that I think further indicates he may have been familiar with homeopathic ideology, especially in Faulkner's signature descriptions of traits that include all sorts of stillness, frozen action, paralysis, immobility (especially when furious); loquacity and silence; amplified sounds (characters hearing their thoughts as if spoken by another or listening to pulsating sounds within their bodies); all kinds of bleeding, discharging, hemorrhaging; all throat sensations including suffocation, wheezing, talking, swallowing, moaning, bellowing. These traits in Faulkner's fictional people are, in fact, keynote symptoms found in repertories to describe the homeopathic *Lachesis* archetype. I suggest in my unpublished research that Faulkner was fascinated with this particular archetype which suits both the menopausal Joanna Burden and her younger male version Quentin Compson. But that is beyond the scope of this argument, so let us now turn to "our patient," Jason Compson.

The Patient: Jason Compson

Jason prides himself in abstaining from alcohol, but instead he indulges in excessive and constant anger. Jason's fury can be explained best by a contextual analysis of his homeopathic *Nux Vomica* portrait, one of the same medicines Faulkner himself likely took at the Keeley Institute. Using anger, Jason reproduces his father's tendency to indulge, soothing himself not with his father's whiskey but with an indulgence in unrestrained anger, anger that is probably worsened by the debilitating physical side effects from his many chemical sensitivities and allergies that have created in him, as in his alcoholic father, a physically addictive cycle.

Jason is a victim of constant, intoxicating, self-indulgent anger. The primary result is a constant splitting headache, similar to an inebriate's protracted hangover. It is in one of Jason's furious rants that we see clues to his physical and emotional addictions. Jason thinks "just to look at water makes me sick and I'll just as soon swallow gasoline as a glass of whiskey and Lorraine telling them he may not drink but if you don't believe he's a man I can tell you how to find out" (291). Here, Jason remembers Quentin's drowning, Mr. Compson's drinking, and his own need to defend his gender identity or sexual adequacies with Lorraine. These powerful emotional issues are mixed with the noxious fumes of the car's gasoline which he indeed inhales in great amounts throughout the final two sections of the novel. Perhaps he inhales so much of it that he feels *as if* he swallows it. Nevertheless, gasoline appears to be associated in his mind with his father's alcoholism and Quentin's indulgent suicide. But can one indulge in gasoline?

Jason is apparently overdosing himself with the toxic fumes to which he has had a life-long allergy. The reader learns later from Caroline that "'gasoline always made [him] sick . . . Ever since [he was] a child'" (296). Thus, in buying a car and inhaling its fumes, Jason is either punishing himself in a self-destructive quest, or attempting to fight, ignore, or otherwise overcome his distress by perversely following the dictum (itself a misunderstanding or subversion of homeopathy) that "what does not kill you makes you stronger."

But another argument from medical physiology is also likely. Jason essentially craves the very thing he is allergic to (gasoline fumes, in this case) because his body has become addicted to the cycle of allergic reactions.[5] Jason's familiar and habitual physiological reactions to his allergy explain much about his behavior. Allergies cause a histamine release in the brain as the body attempts to defend itself against what it *perceives* to be an alien invasion. In fact, the allergic response is the result of the body's overreacting, releasing more histamine than needed for a reasonable defense. Since histamine releases an organic stimulant similar to adrenaline, an addictive cycle can soon develop. According to his mother, the addictive-allergic pattern developed early in Jason's life and his habitual response over time explains Jason's ingrained defensiveness verging on paranoia, his overstimulated, oversensitive senses, and his hyperactive, unfocused hurry, resulting in headaches, irritability, overreactions, and a desire to fight. All symptoms point to adrenal failure. In short, alcohol or stimulant abuse suppresses functioning of the adrenal glands to regulate adrenaline. The manuals are clear that the *Nux Vomica* type does not manage stimulants well, describing excessive agitation from even small amounts of caffeine or nicotine. Jason need not look for environmental stimulants when his own body is providing the chemical stimulant in the form of histamine produced by his life-long allergic response as he regularly doses himself with gasoline fumes. Consider too this odd sentence about the portrait *Nux Vomica,* noted by the nineteenth century homeopath Constantin Hering: fainting or dizziness can occur "when many gaslights are burning" (qtd. in Coulter 2: 12). Of course, gaslights in the nineteenth century were not fueled with car gasoline, but it is tempting to see some suggestion that Jason's allergy to gasoline is so nearly identified in Hering's repertory.

It is also possible Jason has been unintentionally drinking alcohol, if he has been imbibing the patent medicines provided by his mother, Caroline. Benjy has collected the empty bottles for his "play" cemetery, thus providing what may be a revealing clue about a family addiction dilemma. In his interior monologue, as if addressing Caroline, Jason thinks: "I says you always talking about how much you give up for us when you could buy ten new dresses a year on the money you spend for those damn patent medicines. It's not something to cure it I need it's just an even break" (298).

Alcohol supplied the main ingredient in patent medicines of the day, and these tonics were marketed to women specifically as "female remedies to calm the nerves." Many women who abstained from drinking liquor became addicted to Peruna (containing 19 percent alcohol and creating what came to be known as the "Peruna drunk") or the infamous Lydia Pinkham's Vegetable Compound (Anderson 36). If Jason were taking some of the patent medicines he says his mother provided (and likely took herself), then he might have been drinking mixtures of up to 40 percent alcohol, along with several other chemical ingredients that patent medicines contained: heroin, morphine, chloroform, opium, turpentine, and kerosene (Anderson 36). This easily accounts for his many hang-over symptoms and further complicates what now appears to be a multiple-drug combination.

The homeopathic remedy *Nux Vomica* is indicated *precisely* to alleviate such a muddled and chronic drug exposure, and it would have been the ideal homeopathic remedy for Jason's symptoms. In fact, in a literary example of the homeopathic dictum of "like curing like," Jason appears to be unconsciously attracted to poisons in the botanical form (like *Nux*'s origins from the strychnine nut) when he puts his "hand right on a bunch of poison oak" and "couldn't understand why it was just poison oak and not a snake . . . So I didn't even bother to move it" (300), or when he fantasizes about poisoning the swallows that crowd the courthouse square (309), or becomes distracted at the dinner table by the female Quentin's mouth "like it ought to have poisoned her, with all that red lead" (323).

To complicate Jason's problems with chemical exposure, he is also repeatedly dosing himself with camphor (294). In a series of self-punishing acts, Jason says he is allergic to the smell of gasoline, though he buys a car with his embezzled money, and then ironically uses camphor on a rag to counteract the effect of the smell of gas.[6] In doing so, Jason shares with his mother Caroline an appetite for camphor. To cite but one instance, Dilsey notes the "pervading reek of camphor" when she checks on Caroline left alone in her dark room after the Easter Sunday church service (373).

Jason's sort of violent, explosive anger is described in the homeopathic manuals under *Nux Vomica* as reason to prescribe *Nux* as "temper medicine" (Kent), and the manuals use the favorite mnemonic phrase: "Nasty *Nux*" to capture the primary symptom of this portrait (Coulter 2: 4). The hotheaded and sadistic anger evident in the patient requiring *Nux* is described this way:

> "insolent" (Boenninghausen), "fiery and hot-tempered" (Hahnemann), "a victim of his own hysterical outbursts" (Kent), . . . refusing to even try curbing his temper . . . indulging himself in outrageous behavior for the release or sense of power that it gives . . . an expert at making scenes . . . sensitive pride . . . unable to bear the least contradiction . . . cannot abide being corrected. (Coulter and others qtd. in Coulter 2:15-45)

Insecure feelings about his own power and authority drive Jason. As a child, he refuses to take direction from Caddy, the leader. The childhood scene when the children are to abide by what Caddy says is especially imprinted on Jason. Young Jason protests: "'I'm not going to mind you . . . Frony and T. P. don't have to either'" to which Caddy replies: "'They will if I say so. . . . Maybe I wont say for them to'" (39). "Saying" becomes the method to implement power for Jason, so he is constantly "saying" as an adult in his attempts to control the adolescent Quentin: "'You've got to learn one thing, and that is that when I tell you to do something, you've got to do it'" (267). When Jason sells Caddy her chance to see the baby Quentin, Caddy must agree several times to follow his strict directions, "'just like you say to do it'" (253).

The signature grasp for control as an indication of a *Nux* diagnosis is well documented in the homeopathic manuals: homeopath Catherine R. Coulter writes: "A discussion of power relationships is central to any analysis of *Nux Vomica.* . . . In the home, his [authoritarian] nature insists that others live according to his principles, respect his wishes, and defer to his opinions. For, once having laid down the law, he requires unquestioning obedience" (2:43-4).

Some of the older manuals use the terms "despotic, tyrannical, intolerant of opposition, unable to bear the least contradiction . . . does not suffer the most reasonable representations to induce him to alter his conduct. 'I said this is how it is, and that's the way it will be, even if I'm mistaken'" (Hahnemann qtd. in Coulter 2:45).

The single most pervasive physical symptom Jason suffers is all sorts of headaches usually brought on from anger. To give just a few examples, when Jason sees his niece Quentin in a dress he thinks is too revealing, he thinks: "It made me so mad for a minute it kind of blinded me" (233). And as he chases Quentin around town, the headache is so painful he imagines that "with every step [it was] like somebody was walking along behind me, hitting me on the head with a club" (299). The pounding aspect to his headaches is again emphasized when he thinks: "It felt like somebody was inside with a hammer, beating on it" (297).

In the homeopathic manuals, Hahnemann, homeopathy's founder, lists nearly one hundred headache symptoms; Allen identifies over one hundred, and Hering fills three pages. Borland writes that the headaches typically occur from overeating, overdrinking, using any stimulant, or undergoing sensory overload, describing a general "fullness in the head . . . feeling of congestion and pressure, usually on the upper part of the head, often in the higher frontal region, associated with eye pain." Headaches are present from waking, "aggravated by mental concentration or any noise," and *made worse by eating* (emphasis mine, Coulter 2:41-2), shedding light on food contributing to the several arguments Jason provokes with niece Quentin at the lunch and dinner table. *Nux* suffers from poor digestion, and while he is "sensitive to the most trifling ailment . . . continues to eat what does not agree" (Kent qtd. in Coulter 2:12). In the same self-punishing manner bringing on his ailments, Jason rushes around town in search of Miss Quentin, missing work and stock market deadlines. His battle against time is an accurate depiction of these *Nux* traits when ill, as excerpted from the manuals: "always in a hurry" (Kent), "often his dreams are full of bustle and hurry" (Boericke), "preoccupation with punctuality and the scarcity of time" yet he manages to "fritter away his time in meaningless activity" (Kent and others qtd. in Coulter 2:33).

Furthermore, the homeopathic manuals indicate that *Nux* can be "gratuitously destructive . . . vengeful, malicious"; and Hering includes this interesting sentence: "wishes to commit suicide but is afraid to die." Boenninghausen writes, "When looking at a knife, he is inclined to stab himself, when at water to drown himself" (qtd. in Coulter 2:20-21). Perhaps this attitude toward suicide reveals in Jason a secret envy that Quentin's suicide and Mr. Compson's self-destructive drinking were brave attempts to face death, which Jason fears that he cannot. Lastly, with regard to Jason's well-remembered lost bank position promised years ago from Caddy's husband Herbert Head, the manuals include this: "Melancholy in consequence of losing [a business] position" (Hering qtd. in Coulter 2:21).

The very complaints Jason lodges against his niece Quentin are his own: lies, forgery, absence from required duties (228, 285), and "hanging around in alleys" (234, 269); although Jason lies to his mother, sister, and niece, forges Caroline's name, is absent from his job, and knows enough about spending time in alleys to accurately describe them and their denizens. The homeopathic manuals include this sort of hypocrisy in the *Nux* portrait: "criticizes others whose faults mirror his own" (Hahnemann qtd. in Coulter 2:40). Jason is incensed to find out that Miss Quentin has stolen from him, but his stealing throughout the years the checks Caddy has sent for Miss Quentin's welfare also demonstrates the *Nux* "fear of poverty" (Coulter 2:56), another trait he shares with his ill *Sepia* mother Caroline whom he gratuitously torments each month by having her burn what she thinks are Caddy's checks.

Conclusion

So many of Faulkner's characters are intriguingly ill. In novel after novel, readers are tempted to go inside the minds and bodies of characters portrayed with peculiar symptoms that resonate through a text. Familiar aspects of the human condition are amplified in the lives of ostensibly ordinary individuals. But the ordinary is soon paradoxically elevated as Faulkner delivers idiosyncratic patterns of mind and body that always hint at some classic inner distortion. It is their illnesses that somehow elevate Faulkner's fictional people to reveal their embodiment of a particular archetype or remedy-portrait that fits homeopathic nomenclature, and these illnesses or traits often lead to dramatic dénouements. Especially in early landmark novels, as he is succeeding in his efforts to understand his characters in complex ways, Faulkner appears to present and diagnose characters according to these archetypal patterns. Faulkner's tragic figures remain out of tune or ill, recognizable but distorted. They suffer from some powerful alteration of their very essence as they obey their own type's default pattern of illness—perhaps Faulkner would call this one's own fate—resulting in manifestations of deeply ingrained symptoms where mind, body, and spirit suffer inner disharmony and external conflict.

As Faulkner himself struggled to manage, understand, evade, or conquer his own addiction to alcohol, often with medical assistance, he must have had the occasion to reflect on the notion that attempts at recovery involve a powerful mind-body consciousness. This direct experience may have contributed to the writer's remarkable talent to notice and consequently portray complex interactions between body and mind, suggesting perhaps that Faulkner's substance abuse allowed him some first-hand familiarity with body-mind struggles that all forms of energy medicine, including homeopathy, tackle as they attempt to strengthen the psyche through integration.

It seems plausible too that Faulkner simply borrowed what he liked from homeopathic constitutional descriptions, and he mixed the traits from the various portraits like a painter mixes colors. We know that he was a voracious reader and a silent, musing observer of the human scene. So while readers might accept that Faulkner's eye for detailed traits and his ability to portray and reveal character types could have emerged and evolved organically from his own gifted imaginative and observational powers, given the times, his small-town, but academic, environment, and his family's known medical history, it is reasonable to suppose that he may have been aware of the constitutional portraits and the rich alchemical history supporting such therapeutic thinking as it is manifested in homeopathy, and consequently that he may have drawn from this knowledge to construct his characters, just as he often drew from mythology or psychology to construct plot, characterization, or theme.

Notes

1. The remedies are so diluted, in fact, that modern science detects no molecule of the active substance in the remedy itself, fueling skepticism about homeopathy's efficacy. Homeopaths counter that the dilution holds the memory of the substance, the essence, or energy, of the substance that can now perhaps be detected by nanopharmacology, and this essence is enough to balance the body's disturbed healing powers or vital force.

2. Sallie Murry, raised by her physician father, Dr. John Young Murry, is also credited with successfully saving her son's life using the natural remedy of asafedita, which provoked the vomiting of a bullet lodged in Murry's throat (Blotner 54). Sallie Murry also subscribed to the health philosophy of Kellogg of Battle Creek, Michigan, famous for specially prepared foods, when she was diagnosed with catarrah of the stomach, a homeopathic term for the diagnosis of cancer. Sallie Murry's daughter, Holland, Faulkner's paternal aunt, married a well-established doctor, James Porter Wilkins, who practiced with Dr. T. D. Isom, Ripley's oldest citizen, possibly portrayed as one of the doctors in Faulkner's *Flags in the Dust* (Blotner 98).

3. The use of medicinal gold was not the secret ingredient. The Cure was also named Bi-chloride (or double-chloride) of Gold remedy.

4. Stubborn alcoholics at Keeley Institutes were allowed and even encouraged to drink liquor, but were then "unknowingly given a vigorous emetic, apomorphine, at the same time" provoking frequent vomiting to perform what we would now call aversion treatment. Many patients took pride in being "manly" enough to

endure the frequent injections, oral medications, and perhaps repeated vomiting. Eventually, patients received the sedative and hypnotic Paraldehyde, still used medically for epileptics and commonly used in psychiatric hospitals until the 1960's to induce sleep (Tracy 86).

5. The body will not become addicted to fatal allergies.

6. Besides the toxic effect such large doses of camphor have on the body, even in small amounts it is known to be one of several universal antidotes to almost all homeopathic medicines. Camphor would make any homeopathic remedy inert, and it is pervasive in the novel from the Compson family's earliest history.

Works Cited

Anderson, Ann. *Snake Oil, Hustlers and Hambones: The American Medical Show.* Jefferson, NC: McFarland P, 2000.

Berman, Louis. *The Glands Regulating Personality: A Study of the Glands of Internal Secretion in Relation to the Types of Human Nature.* 1921. College Park, MD: McGrath, 1970.

Bleikasten, André. *The Ink of Melancholy: Faulkner's Novels from* The Sound and The Fury *to* Light in August. Bloomington: Indiana UP, 1990.

Blotner, Joseph. *Faulkner: A Biography.* Rev. ed. New York: Random House, 1984.

Coulter, Catherine R. *Portraits of Homoeopathic Medicines: Psychophysical Analyses of Selected Constitutional Types,* Vol. 2. St. Louis: Quality Medical Publishing, 1998.

Faulkner, William. *The Sound and The Fury.* 1929. New York: Random House, 1954.

Flinn, John J. "The Keeley League and Its Purposes." *American Journal of Politics* 1 (1892): 654-66.

Gidley, Mick. "Another Psychologist, a Physiologist and William Faulkner." *Ariel: A Review of International English Literature* 2 (October 1971): 78-86.

Keeley, Leslie E. "Drunkenness, A Curable Disease." *American Journal of Politics* 1 (1892): 27-43.

Kent, James Tyler. *Lectures on Homeopathic Philosophy.* 1900. Berkeley, CA: North Atlantic Books, 1993.

———. *Reparatory of Homeopathic Materia Medica.* 1900. New Delhi: Jain Pub., 2001.

Nordlund, Christer. "Endocrinology and Expectations in 1930's America: Louis Berman's Ideas on New Creations in Human Beings." *British Journal of the History of Science* 40.1 (2007): 83-104.

Slatoff, Walter J. *Quest for Failure: A Study of William Faulkner*. Ithaca: Cornell UP, 1960.

Tracy, Sarah W. *Alcoholism in America: From Reconsruction to Prohibition*. Baltimore: Johns Hopkins UP, 2005.

Trice, Harrison M., and William J Staudenmeier, Jr. "The Keeley Cure." In *Recent Developments in Alcoholism: Treatment Research*, Vol. 7, ed. Marc Galanter. New York: Plenum P, 1983. 12-15.

Williamson, Joel. *William Faulkner and Southern History.* New York: Oxford UP, 1993.

Moving Beyond Acceptable Boundaries: Another Critical Awakening

Little argument can be made that Kate Chopin's novel *The Awakening* awoke what Per Seyersted called a "female realism," or that since 1969, this literary work has indeed "broken new ground in American literature" (134). Additionally, there is little question that Chopin's novel dispelled the myth that the neatly packaged—and only—role assigned by patriarchy to a woman as a "mother-woman" was a good fit for all women. Even so, *The Awakening* also created an opening to discuss yet another patriarchally imposed role—one that is just as myopic, one that is just as neatly packaged, and one that is just as limiting—to be scrutinized. And the study of this seldom-questioned role—that of the ideal man—is just as critical in moving beyond yet another accepted and expected social behavior.

Although there has been little scrutiny focused on the role of men in society within *The Awakening*, there are many instances throughout the text that show that all men are not driven to live by their imposed societal role, nor do they care to live by it. Whereas Léonce Pontellier, husband to Edna the protagonist in the novel, depicts patriarchy's ideal man (one who is emotionally distant, the head-of-household, the breadwinner, the decision-maker, husband, and father), Robert Lebrun, Edna's confidante, lover, and the catalyst for Edna's profound sensual, sexual, and self-awakening, does not. And just as there is a continual disparity within Edna Pontellier as to who she is and who she is expected to be, this same disparity lies within Robert Lebrun. Likewise, just as Edna is continually contrasted to her friend, Adele Ratignolle, the ideal "mother-woman" (10), Robert is juxtaposed to Léonce, the ideal man.

Robert, unlike Léonce, strives toward none of the societal aspirations most often relegated to men. Neither does Robert view Edna as an ornament that will elevate him on society's pedestal as an ideal man, husband, and father. Rather, unlike the relationship between Edna and Léonce, Robert and Edna are able to make not only small-talk, but relish the intricacies of making something enjoyable out of something seemingly unimportant. This is something Léonce Pontellier, on the other hand, cannot grasp. Léonce, in all respects, lives up to his role as patriarchy's ideal man. Whereas Robert, in some respects, transcends his role as an ideal man and awakens to his inner self, Léonce never does. In fact, it seems that Léonce never envisions or desires to throw away what he sees as his rightful place in society.

Without question, *The Awakening* is not written in a "linear" fashion, that is, a model focused on "a masculine model of incremental public success"; rather, the novel is "lyrical, epiphanic, concerned with moments of consciousness rather than upward striving" (Ammons 76). Even so, I believe both models are clearly evident. For example, the static nature and "linear" lifestyle Chopin assigns to Léonce Pontellier—head-of-household, provider, decision-maker, husband, and father—portray the epitome of the patriarchal vision of success for a man. In direct contrast, Robert—who dabbles at both work and play—demonstrates that "moments of consciousness" drive him, rather than the "upward striving" sought by Léonce (Ammons 78). In juxtaposing these two men to one another, Chopin creates an avenue to dispel another of Western ideology's truths, that is, that men like Léonce are *not* the only ideal—for women, for men, or for society. In so doing, Chopin raises additional questions: Is this masculine ideology, that is, the conventionally assigned white, Western-male truth, which we all live by, just as repressive for men as women? If the role of "mother-woman" is not right for all women, is this patriarchal model of man right for all men? This raises still another question: Possibly, could there, should there be a male-uprising against their self-inflicted patriarchal confinement? That is yet to be seen. However, one thing is certain—whereas questions such as these have been the sparks that have ignited the change that has taken place in the lives of women, as well as the criticism directed toward them in society and in literature, these same inquiries could open up other previously unknown or unrecognized possibilities for men.

Although Robert awakens to his love for Edna, and to a small degree rebels against societal norms, ultimately, the spark that ignites Robert Lebrun's own awakening is doused by his inability to rebel against society's accepted expectations of him as a man. Léonce, on the other hand, continues in the only world he knows, or cares to know. Questioning that world never occurs to him. And if there ever was a flicker of doubt in his mind as to his assigned role, he does not, I think, even consider it. Even so, both Léonce and Robert open another door for understanding the intricacies of something both men and women can identify with: that of being human.

Initially we are pulled into the world of Léonce and Edna Pontellier. Léonce is trying unsuccessfully to read his paper without interruption, but because of the repetitive "*Allez vous-en! Allez vous-en! Sapristi!*" of Madame Lebrun's parrot and the "maddening persistence" of her mocking-bird, he retreats to the isolation of the Pontellier's summer cottage (1). Here, and throughout the novel, Léonce, unlike Robert, remains isolated from the intricacies of personal relationships—with friends and family, and especially his wife. Additionally, unlike "young Robert Lebrun," Léonce is a "man of forty"—twelve years Edna's senior—whose life surrounds the "market reports" and "editorials" of his business (2). The all-encompassing importance of his work, as well as his opinion of his wife's duties as a mother, are shown when he scolds Edna for not properly attending to their children when "he looked forward to a lively week in Carondelet Street" back home in New Orleans (8).

Additionally, Léonce's tendency to be an "outsider" is revealed as he watches everything from a distance. And unlike his wife and the other vacationers on Grand Isle, Léonce finds no meaning in trivial exploits. This becomes clear whenever Robert and Edna exchange a mutual glance surrounding a personal moment after returning from their mid-day swim. When they fail to explain their amusement satisfactorily, Léonce rises, "yawn[s] and stretche[s] himself" and decides to seek the company of other men and "play a game of billiards" (3). By the same token, Léonce's opinion of his wife's activities, and his wife in general, is in sharp contrast to his own acceptable practices. Robert and Edna's return from their mid-day swim at a "snail's pace" contrasts sharply with both Léonce's need of a "lively week" in New Orleans as well as his notion that his "plunge at daylight" was the only acceptable time to swim. Moreover, once they approach and sit on the porch steps, Léonce chastises his wife with mild condemnation. "What folly!" Léonce views his wife as "a valuable piece of personal property which has suffered some damage" and which has been "burnt beyond recognition" (3). He not only disapproves of his wife's lack of societal sensibilities in swimming at an unacceptable hour, he finds it even more distasteful that her actions and her appearance directly affect how society might very well view him. On the other hand, even though Léonce says nothing directly to Robert, when Robert tells him quite pointedly he was content to stay and spend time with Edna, Léonce's words to his wife reveal that he thinks of Robert as nothing more than a mere distraction, certainly not a man's man, and certainly not a threat to him as a husband.

In another instance, Chopin further reveals society's acceptance and expectation of little boys' behavior. Although Edna's sons most certainly would be affected by her suicide, we find initially that these two children, who, if either of them "took a tumble whilst at play . . . [would not] rush crying to his mother's arms for comfort" (10). Granted, it can be said they wouldn't go to their mother because she would not know to soothe them or because she was too self-consumed to do so, but by the same token, Chopin has subverted society's doctrine that big boys (meaning all boys—big and small) don't cry.

Inasmuch as Edna's awakening is foreshadowed, so too is Robert Lebrun's. Pearl L. Brown reveals this dual awakening. She pointedly asserts that some men, like Robert Lebrun in Chopin's fiction, experience their own rebelliousness against culture. They too are liberated from cultural restrictions in connection to their relationship with women in Chopin's fiction. She cites that "Just as a woman in an intimate moment with a man awakens to an inner self buried beneath a culturally sanctioned social one, so does a man ['s] subjective self buried beneath a public persona . . . [awaken and] defy that culture's masculine norms" (69).

Although neither Robert nor Edna seems to be cognizant of their imposing connection and mutual awakening, this duality is evidenced when Edna, after putting her wedding rings back on her finger, turns to Robert and laughs, and Robert "sent back an answering smile"(3). Léonce, openly puzzled, elicits an attempt by Edna and Robert to articulate the intimate, pleasurable, and seemingly innocent moment they had shared on the beach, to no avail. Neither does Léonce understand, nor care to understand. Nor, at this moment, does Robert or Edna, for they are merely taking pleasure in the simplicity of the moment. However, in this instant, unknowingly to all parties, a "[love] triangle" has formed (Eble 263). Herein, Chopin foreshadows not only the inherent connection Robert plays in Edna's awakening, but his own as well. She also shows that because Léonce is unwilling to move beyond his static sense of self, his emotional distance, and his manhood, he too plays an even more important role than Robert in Edna's demise. Here too, as Brown further reiterates, Chopin has awakened to "the importance of social and psychological awakenings in men as well as in women" (70). However, Léonce does not realize that his societal expectations for Edna are detrimental to him and his life, as well as to the life of his sons, not just Edna's. In adhering to his prescribed life of work, he misses the opportunity to connect with his wife on a more intimate level, and thus is missing a most critical piece of the puzzle that catapults his marriage and his wife toward destruction. Whereas Léonce remains the "ideal man," Robert realizes his own confinement within societal regulations. This contrast between the two men most influential in Edna's life enables Chopin, in addition to subverting the patriarchal ideology, to reveal that patriarchy is not all things to all men.

In contrast to Léonce, Robert is young, attractive, and attentive to Edna. Léonce, on the other hand, is unavailable, emotionally as well as physically, to his wife. There is no connection on any level between them. When the "utter nonsense" about Edna and Robert's "adventure out there in the water" begins to bore Léonce, he yawns and says "he ha[s] half a mind to go over to Klein's hotel and play some billiards" (3). As is often depicted, fictional male characters hold to the ideology that men prefer the company of men.

In addition, the relationship between men is markedly different from that of women, says Nina Auerbach. Even though Auerbach focuses on female bonding in her book *Communities of Women: An Idea in Fiction,* Gail Keating points out that Auerbach touches on the differences between "male and female communities." Whereas men "possess a grandeur and a magnitude and aim to leave their imprint on the world, . . . women have no such lofty aspirations" (Keating 239). Instead, she says, a woman's focus is her home. Additionally, just as Léonce is inattentive to things that concern his wife, he finds her "little half utterances" to the details of his conversations with his male compatriots at Klein's disconcerting (5, 6). He does not make the connection that things that concern Edna should, to some degree, concern him, and vice versa. On the contrary, Robert "chats incessantly" (5) with Edna, about everything and nothing. He has little interest in spending his free time with other men and is uninhibited to voice this profound bit of information to either Léonce, another man, or in front of Edna.

In *The Awakening* Chopin also paints the picture of the "power" and "symbols" important to man's identity (Keating 239). Léonce's need for grandeur is further identified as Chopin describes the Pontelliers' "very charming home on Esplanade Street" after they return home to New Orleans (66). The descriptions detailing the exterior and interior of their home characterize Léonce's power and stature within the community because of his possessions. Léonce's interest in his societal stature is further indicated when he chastises Edna after finding she did not follow "*les convenances*" (68) and receive guests as had been her custom on Tuesday afternoons. As it is, however, Léonce is more concerned with the monetary worth of the Belthrops and the father of "The Misses Delasidas" (69) and how these families can improve his position in society, rather than with mere politeness. In addition, his statement to Edna that the way to riches is "to make money, my dear Edna, not save it" (71), gives evidence to the force societal expectations play on man. As is noted by Auerbach and Keating, to men "such things [*do*] count" (69).

To Robert, however, these things don't count. When Léonce offers an invitation to Robert to come along to Klein's, Robert says "quite frankly" he "preferred to stay where he was and talk to Mrs. Pontellier" (3). In this instance, in relation to the aforementioned patriarchal assumption that men prefer the company of men, Robert stands in marked contrast to Léonce. A conventional male, like Léonce, prefers "the company [of men] . . . and the size of 'the game,'" rather than passing the time with his wife (4). In other words, men like Léonce concern themselves with their public life and how it elevates them in stature within their own minds and within society. This is not to say that this male aspiration is seen as noble by men alone. Chopin is aware that women, too, assign value to "the size of 'the game'"—even in the most minor intricacies. When Mr. Pontellier had left the following morning after his chastisement of Edna for her "neglect of the children" (7), he sent her a gift of sweets. The women whom Edna shared her husband's token gifts with "all declared that Mr. Pontellier was the best husband in the world" (9). Thus, appearances, for all intents and purposes, are important to women and men alike.

Unlike Léonce, Robert has no concern of duties as a husband. And unlike Léonce, Robert speaks of finding his fortune in Mexico, only he chooses instead to hold "on to his modest position in the mercantile in New Orleans" (5). Robert's preference to stay with Edna and keep a mediocre job further enable Chopin to subvert the accepted patriarchal ideology that the identity of all men is centered in a man's ability to hold a position that makes as much money as possible in order to be successful in his eyes, as well as society's. In addition, Chopin achieves the means by which Robert, as well as Léonce, has the potential to his own "epiphanic moments . . . that [are] as liberating and thus life altering as the moments women [in this case Edna] experience" (Brown 70). Since Robert has yet to establish his own role within the patriarchal society, he further lends himself as a foil to Léonce and to his own awakening. This, in itself, offers the possibility of a non-gender specific, universal awakening rather than just a female awakening. And with that there is a further possibility for men also to question what is expected of them by society, and if, in fact, that expectation is immutable.

After they spend the day together at the Chenière Caminade, and Robert awakens to his feelings for Edna, realizing he has fallen in love with her but that he is incapable of questioning or ignoring societal rules of fidelity, he leaves for Mexico. Additionally, he is unable to tell Edna directly; instead, she finds out at dinner just before he leaves. Herein, he falls in line with Léonce in his inability to discuss his inner feelings and intimacies between them. He comes closest to revealing his feelings when he comes to say good-bye to her. Edna tells him "of how pleasant it would be to see you in the city next winter." His reply, cut short, in essence revealed he had awakened to his feelings, but could not act upon them. "So was I," he blurted. "Perhaps that's the—" (60). Continuing would have been the point of no-return, which Robert has found himself unable and unwilling to do. Robert, Donald Pizer says, is living by a "Creole masculine code governing a gentleman's behavior in relations with married women of his own class" (12). Whenever Robert moves beyond the then acceptable boundaries as an "unmarried man . . . [merely] flirt[ing] with a married woman" (12) and falls in love with Edna, he knows those boundaries have been breached. Unwilling to cross those boundaries and in order to protect Edna's reputation, Robert abides by societal rules and leaves. Even after Robert returns, he does not seek Edna out. Only when he meets her by accident at Mademoiselle Reisz's apartment, and then accompanies her home, do both his and Edna's awakening come to fruition. Only when Edna kisses him and her "voluptuous sting penetrated his whole being" does he succumb to his desires and love for her (145). However, before Edna is called to go to Adele who is giving birth, Robert too learns that his feelings for the "sanctity of the marriage bond" do not mirror Edna's (Pizer 11). When he speaks of Léonce setting her free, he too sees Edna as a possession ruled by her husband. When she replies, "I am no longer one of Mr. Pontellier's possessions to dispose of or not. I give myself where I choose. If he were to say, "Here, Robert, take her and be happy; she is yours," I should laugh at you both'" (146). Herein, the "societal consciousness" that no longer affects Edna reinforces its hold on Robert. Edna's total awakening and complete withdrawal from society's expectations puzzles and distresses Robert (Pizer 11). Unlike Edna, Robert cannot throw caution to the wind. Therefore, inherently, Robert awakens to another realization: not only does he love Edna but he must say "Good-by—because I love you" (152).

In the end, unable to transcend societal rules, Robert, in essence, begins to march in step with Léonce and his role as an ideal man. That is, even though Robert understands "the social identity . . . [he has] accepted from [his] culture is not compatible with [his] newly discovered psychological needs," he cannot move beyond society's demands (Brown 69). However, unlike Léonce, Robert's motives are not entirely selfish. He is not looking to enhance his social standing nor take his place in society as an ideal man. In one sense, he is thinking of Edna; on the other hand, he is thinking of himself—and society's acceptance and expectations of him. Inasmuch, he is still bound to his role in society, just as Edna was, only she extinguished society's hold on her when she swam to her death. So, even as Brown cited that "awakened men [and women] cannot always effect a permanent change in their lives . . . their moments of self-revelation are important because they provide . . . a more integrated, fuller life for [themselves]" (82).

Even so, some, like Robert, choose to remain true to society's expectations of them. Léonce, having never awakened, has never had a chance for a life that may have been better than he imagined for him and Edna. By the same token, he has never considered the possibility that he should—or could—do anything differently as a husband, a father, or a man. And just as Robert is Edna's "spark" that ignites her awakening, she too is his "spark." And even though Léonce never experiences an awakening—and Edna chooses to extinguish hers in death and Robert, his, in leaving—these characters, thanks to Kate Chopin, continue to spark additional criticism in an attempt to move beyond a conventional ideal assigned not merely to a woman, but to a man as well.

Works Cited

Ammons, Elizabeth. *Conflicting Stories: American Women Writers at the Turn into the Twentieth Century*. New York: Oxford UP, 1992.

Auerbach, Nina. *Community of Women: An Idea in Fiction*. Cambridge: Harvard UP, 1998.

"The Awakening." *Public Opinion* 22 June 1899: 794. *Twentieth-Century Literary Criticism* Vol. 14. Detroit: Gale Research, 1984. Literature Resource Center. SEMO Kent Library, Cape Girardeau, MO 19 Apr. 2008 <http://go.galegroup.com>.

Brown, Pearl L. "Awakened Men in Kate Chopin's Creole Stories." *American Transcendental Quarterly* 13.1 (1999): 69-82.

Chopin, Kate. *The Awakening and Selected Short Stories*. New York: Bantam Dell, 2003.

Eble, Kenneth. "A Forgotten Novel: Kate Chopin's *The Awakening*." *Western Humanities Review* Vol. X (Summer 1956): 261-69.

Inge, Tonette Bond. "Kate Chopin." In *American Women Writers Bibliographical Essays*, ed. Maurice Duke, Jackson R. Bryer, and M. Thomas Inge. Westport: Greenwood Press, 1983. 47-69.

Keating, Gail C. "Sarah Orne Jewett." In *Encyclopedia of American Poetry: The Nineteenth Century*, ed. Eric L. Haralson. Chicago: Fitzroy Dearborn, 1998.

Pizer, Donald. "A Note on Kate Chopin's *The Awakening* as Naturalistic Fiction." *Southern Literary Journal* 33.2 (2001): 5-13.

"Recent Novels: *The Awakening.*" *The Nation* 3 Aug. 1899: 96. *Twentieth-Century Literary Criticism.* Vol. 5. Detroit: Gale Research, 1981. Literature Resource Center. SEMO Kent Library, Cape Girardeau, MO. 19 Apr. 2008 <http://go.galegroup.com>.

Seyersted, Per. *Kate Chopin: A Critical Biography.* Baton Rouge: Louisiana State UP, 1969.

———. "Kate Chopin: Overview." Reference Guide to American Literature. "The Awakening." *New York Times Book Review* 24 June 1899: 408. *Twentieth-Century Literary Criticism*, vol. 14. Detroit: Gale Research, 1984.

Music as a Motif in *The Awakening*

The Awakening echoes a theme common throughout literature. In the ancient *Antigone*, the modern *Madame Bovary*, and countless other works, strong female characters have subverted the standing social order in an effort to gain the freedom to carry out their intentions, and often enough, the tale ends tragically for its protagonist. Although *The Awakening* falls within this tradition of narrative, Kate Chopin distinguishes her novel from similar works by employing a consistent use of musical allusions to form a dominating conceit. In Frédéric Chopin and Richard Wagner, she chooses composers who were well known among the aristocracy of nineteenth-century New Orleans. Chopin's waltzes and preludes could be heard at the salons of the Creoles, who fashioned themselves after the tastes of Parisian high society, and the operas of Wagner were not an uncommon feature at the French Opera House of old New Orleans. But the author does not use the works of these two great composers merely to add texture to the novel's setting; the musical allusions reflect Edna Pontellier's struggle toward individuation by illustrating the conflict between selfhood and community. The allusions at first may seem simple, as they are often followed, even overshadowed, by overt changes in Edna's disposition. But in four scenes in particular, the pieces to which Kate Chopin alludes not only reveal the alteration of Edna's attitudes but they also illuminate the deeper theme of the novel, namely the clash between the self and the society. Before examining these scenes, however, let us first explore the milieu in which Chopin locates her allusions.

That milieu, being rooted in the Romantic Movement, valued most what appealed to the imagination and the emotions. In the art of music, this transformation becomes apparent in the works of both Frédéric Chopin and Richard Wagner. Chopin moved from Poland to Paris to make his living and there produced waltzes and mazurkas in the style of his native tradition. His mastery of the ballad and the prelude won him adoration in the salons. Nicole Camastra observes Chopin's ability to negotiate between "the 'classical' concern for form and the 'romantic' urge of inspiration" (160). His music embraces both the freedom of the Romantic and the structures set by the Neoclassical, symbolizing the union of personal freedom and societal boundaries. This is Chopin's distinct genius. Camastra describes his pieces as particularly evocative: "[his music is] written in such a way as to inspire improvisation and, ultimately, can be understood as tonal conversations between a performer and an audience" (157).

The style of Wagner, though still Romantic, marks a further shift from the concern for form. Known for the use of German myth and bold compositional techniques such as tonal shifts, leitmotifs, and discord, Wagner rejects the balance of Chopin between form and inspiration in favor of new sounds and new music. His pieces express bold emotions untempered by traditional molds; his tragic opera *Tristan und Isolde* contemplates the association between love and death and explores new musical ground in striking a dissonant chord within the first few bars that continues unresolved until the last song of the composition. Morris Dickstein explains his influence on the novel: "In the Wagnerian, *fin-de-siécle* world of *The Awakening*, passion is a form of dissolution, an erasure of boundaries closely akin to death." By rejecting the classical forms, Wagner ignores the limitations that Chopin incorporates into his music, and this charges his compositions with a tragic sublimity. As can be seen from the example of Chopin and Wagner, Romantic styles are various, but beneath them all is a concern for affecting the primal emotions that underlie human nature. A sophisticated audience seeks an interaction with powerful feelings and a sublimated sense of the self. This demands isolation and reflection, which can be difficult to find in characterizations of the casual salons of the period.

Madame Ratignolle's *musicales* display this difficulty most clearly. In the language that Kate Chopin first uses to describe them, we have an immediate sense of their utility: "The Ratignolles entertained their friends once a fortnight with a *soirée musicale*, sometimes diversified by card-playing" (52). Chopin continues by noting the "various degrees of taste and agility" of the musicians and ends the passage with a comment on the audience: the "*soirées musicales* were widely known, and it was considered a privilege to be invited to them" (53). The aesthetic moments of the evening are undervalued by the minds of the audience in attendance, for sometimes a game of cards begins in preference to the performance; visiting the Ratignolle house every two weeks is merely a routine, though it serves a social purpose. The invitees attend only because it is an honor and because it is one known beyond the circle of guests. As the hostess of a *musicale*, Mme Ratignolle wants to arrange an evening that will flatter the visitors and provoke envy in those not invited. Interestingly, Mr. Pontellier, with a rare insight, dismisses them as bourgeois, indicating that they fall short of their presumed artistic merit, and claims, ironically, that with deference to the *musicales*, he prefers the distractions of the club

(66). The club and the *musicale* are fundamentally similar; both provide the necessary respite from daily concerns and a chance to converse with a handful of the city's elite.

This becomes particularly apparent when Edna's father, an austere colonel of the late Confederacy, accompanies her to a *musicale*. They "made much of the Colonel, installing him as the guest of honor and engaging him at once to dine with them. . . . Madame coquetted with him in the most captivating and naïve manner, with eyes, gestures, and a profusion of compliments, till the Colonel's old head felt thirty years younger on his padded shoulders" (65). The Ratignolles' adorations are out of politeness, of course, as they have never met the man before the party. But behind their kindness lies the insinuation that they are impressed merely with his stature. The man is named only "the Colonel," and he still retains the "military bearing which had always accompanied [his title]" (65). Given such a formal description, the reader can understand why the Ratignolles were so delighted to entertain him and why Mlle Reisz rejected Edna's request to meet and play for him. Reisz refuses to condescend to diversions of this kind and deigns only to play for those who will appreciate music for its aesthetic power.

Indeed Chopin implies sympathy for this opinion of the social sphere. Having a strong concern for taste and appearance, Chopin presents this world as a sensory or, better still, a sensual one. Without a doubt, Alcée Arobin moves through social circles with greater ease than any other character, and so we can expect in him, as the prime representative of the community, taste and elegance. Introducing Arobin, Chopin writes, "He possessed a good figure, a pleasing face, not overburdened with depth of thought or feeling; and his dress was that of the conventional man of fashion" (71). The disconnected and disinterested life, which Arobin typifies, could be seen throughout the city, "at the race course, the opera, the fashionable clubs" (70). Arobin possesses a great deal of surface but little depth, and Edna's attraction fades as she realizes that he cannot give her love but only sensual pleasure. The failure of their affair is foreshadowed the night that they first meet. Edna, Arobin, and the Highcamps listen as their daughter, Miss Highcamp, plays the piano: "[She] seemed to have apprehended all of the composer's coldness and none of his poetry. While Edna listened she could not help wondering if she had lost her taste for music" (72). As her impression of the performance shows, Edna has glimpsed the cheapness of social ostentation, a feeling that anticipates her final thoughts on Arobin.

Where Edna perceives shallowness and tastelessness in the public sphere, she finds passion and depth in her isolated selfhood. She allows herself to be overcome by music; Mlle Reisz sees as much and invites Edna alone to hear her play. In a role similar to that of a prophetess, Mlle Reisz becomes a guide to Edna's awakening, leading her through a labyrinth of ideas and emotions and warning her of the dangers within it. But the cautions of others amount to little in Edna's search, as the end of her awakening is ultimately to stand alone "as an individual to the world within and about her" (14).

During the summer at Grand Isle, the Lebruns' guests take turns teaching Edna to swim. Although they all take her into the water to offer a few techniques, Robert Lebrun spends more time with her than the rest. But she remains incapable of swimming without the aid of someone nearby until one night when Mlle Reisz entertains the group in the community room with a composition by Frédéric Chopin. Before she plays the piece, the narrator informs us that "musical strains, well rendered, had a way of evoking pictures in [Edna's] mind" (25). Well-played pieces can guide her thoughts and stimulate her imagination, but when the virtuoso plays, something unprecedented occurs:

> The very first chords which Mademoiselle Reisz struck upon the piano sent a keen tremor down Mrs. Pontellier's spinal column. It was not the first time she had heard an artist at the piano. Perhaps it was the first time she was ready, perhaps the first time her being was tempered to take an impress of the abiding truth.
>
> She waited for the material pictures which she thought would gather and blaze before her imagination. She waited in vain. She saw no pictures of solitude, of hope, of longing, or of despair. But the very passions themselves were aroused within her soul, swaying it, lashing it, as the waves daily beat upon her splendid body. She trembled, she was choking, and the tears blinded her. (26)

This scene immediately precedes the moonlight bath, when "intoxicated with her newly conquered power, she swam out alone," (27), and this proximity forms a thematic association between the music played by Reisz, which simulates the waters of the Gulf, and the Gulf itself with everything it comes to symbolize for Edna's individuation. After returning to shore, while she and Robert walk up the beach, she explains, "A thousand emotions have swept through me to-night. I don't comprehend half of them. . . . I wonder if I shall ever be stirred again as Mademoiselle Reisz's playing moved me. . . . It's like a night in a dream" (28). Her description of the experience as a dream is apt, for this is the beginning of her awakened individuality, and its formation is a struggle between her hazy, half-realized self and the tumultuous emotions swirling within her.

Her reaction to the music and the water carries a greater sense of her fate than she realizes. In it we recognize the universality of her plight and notice a resemblance between this scene and the aesthetic philosophy of Friedrich Nietzsche in *The Birth of Tragedy from the Spirit of Music.*[1] Nietzsche conceives of artistic representation as a struggle between Dionysus, who represents ecstatic impulse, and Apollo, the restraining force of the "*principium individuationis*, in whom the eternal goal of the original Oneness, namely its redemption through illusion, accomplishes itself" (33). Nietzsche argues that in striking a balance between Dionysus and Apollo, a work of art forms the nexus for tragedy:

> We might picture to ourselves how the ["dream and ecstatic artist"], in a state of Dionysiac intoxication and mystical self-abrogation, wandering apart from the reveling throng, sinks upon the ground, and how there is then revealed to him his own condition—complete oneness with the essence of the universe—in a dream similitude. (24-5)

The principle of Apollo is that of "the individual—or, more precisely, the observance of the limits of the individual" (34), and these limitations are illusions that only separate one from the emotion and passion of Dionysus. The two forces are engaged out of necessity in an eternal battle, and its skirmishes provide the motifs of drama. The struggle between Apollo and Dionysus, mirroring that between the individual and the community, continues until the individual either accepts the limits of her person or she succumbs to the power of her passions. For Edna, every intimation of selfhood comes during a moment when she can "wander apart from the reveling throng" and look inward, and music provides her with the opportunity. But even in a world of sound she is confronted by both Dionysus and Apollo, by the passions provoked by Reisz's skill and the illusions of taste and elegance that organize the Ratignolles' salons, though she does not recognize the universality of her conflict.

But the choice is not one between passion and superficiality; even Mlle Reisz controls the depth of her playing with some restraint, and as a prophetess, she attempts to teach this lesson of control during one of Edna's visits to her apartment. Robert has sent a letter, a symbol of restrained passion, to Reisz, though Edna learns of it during their conversation. She demands that Reisz give it to her and play the Chopin

Impromptu. Reisz consents but surprises her with an improvisation on the piece, in which she subtly incorporates advice into "the tonal conversation," to return to Camastra's phrase. After playing an interlude of her own composition and then "the soft opening minor chords of the Chopin Impromptu," she "glided . . . into the quivering love-notes of Isolde's song, and back again to the Impromptu with its soulful and poignant longing" (61). In this chapter the author skillfully applies the motifs of restraint, illusion, and passion to the symbol of the letter and to the structure of the performance. In sending the letter to the pianist, Robert exercised restraint, for the content of the letter, which was "nothing but Mrs. Pontellier from beginning to end," would have made it scandalous to send to her directly (60). But to heighten the effect of the letter's indirect communication of passion, Kate Chopin interweaves the motifs into the aural fabric of the scene. By beginning and ending her performance with the Chopin Impromptu, Reisz emphasizes the balance that the composer strikes between "the 'classical' concern for form and the 'romantic' urge of inspiration," accentuating the idea of limitation, which can and should govern individual passion. Reisz places inside this frame the "Liebestod," the love-death, from Wagner's *Tristan und Isolde*, an opera that tells the story of two lovers who die as a consequence of their affair. Reisz attempts to warn Edna with this contrivance, but she does not heed the advice. Instead, she leaves weeping "just as she had wept one midnight at Grand Isle when strange, new voices awoke in her" (62). Although this warning fails, Reisz makes another attempt by describing the pathos of an injured bird, an image that reappears with several others in the final chapter of the novel.

This last chapter, not only resolving the heroine's turmoil, brings the rest of the book into thematic focus by recalling a few well-chosen images, one of which is an amalgamation, which combines imagery associated with two previous musical performances: "A bird with a broken wing was beating the air above. . . . For the first time in her life she stood naked in the open air, at the mercy of the sun, the breeze that beat upon her, and the waves that invited her" (108). Here Edna stands completely alone for the first time, outside her home and away from the conventions and expectations of New Orleans, and it is through this seclusion that she finds herself disenthralled for the first time. Her sense of freedom is clear in comparing the following passages: first, "[Mr. Pontellier] could not see that she was becoming herself and daily casting aside that fictitious self which we assume like a garment with which to appear before the world," and second, "she cast the unpleasant pricking garments from her" (55, 108). The second refers back to the first, but it also verifies its implicit presage. When Edna drops her faded suit on the sand, she frees herself from social reservation and stands naked, unburdened by responsibility. The image does not contain the exuberance of triumph, and when compared with its referent, the reason is clear. In chapter nine, Chopin explains Edna's ability to see pictures upon hearing well-played pieces of music. Mme Ratignolle plays a piece which Edna, despite knowing the title, names "Solitude." As she hears the notes, "there came before her imagination the figure of a man standing beside a desolate rock on the seashore. He was naked. His attitude was one of hopeless resignation as he looked toward a distant bird winging its flight away from him" (26). The images are not exact—Edna is not near a desolate rock, and the bird in her imagination is uninjured. The broken wing, although not found within this image, fulfills the last of Mlle Reisz's warnings: "The bird that would soar above the level plain of tradition and prejudice must have strong wings. It is a sad spectacle to see the weaklings bruised, exhausted, fluttering back to earth" (79). Edna does not realize this, and we are aware of it only through Chopin's high and fatal irony, but there will be no return to the community and no "redemption through illusion" (Nietzsche 33). Edna, bare and despondent, in "hopeless resignation" (26), returns to the sea, where she first experienced the autonomy of individuation, and she submerges her body so that the waves may again sway and lash her soul as they had done before. Recalling the "night in a dream" when "a thousand emotions" (28) ran through her, when she felt "the very passions themselves" (26) arise during Reisz's performance, and when, exhilarated, "she swam out alone" (27) into the Gulf, Edna returns to the water to recapture the feeling of "complete oneness with . . . the universe" (25). Instead of attaining a renewed sovereignty, Edna's mind is invaded by thoughts of Léonce, Robert, her children, and her childhood. She tries to outswim them but only becomes fatigued. And she realizes that she is beyond help as she remembers Dr. Mandelet. She comes to recognize the empathy and the possible resolution offered by him; Mandelet "would have understood if she had seen him—but it was too late; the shore was far behind her, and her strength was gone" (109). The sea, once provoking a profound insight into her own being, now consumes her in a state of despondency, loneliness, and despair after generating passions with which she is unable to live.

Edna, once among the many, has strayed away from them. She has seen herself as an individual in discord with the rest. In struggling to define her individuality, Edna repeatedly returns to the moment when she first recognized it, at first with music, evoking emotional and sensual responses, and then with a trip to Grand Isle, where she first felt control over her body. But she arrives alone, not realizing that there are some who could have taught her how to integrate an individual freedom into the timbre of the whole. And for that mistake she pays dearly. Chopin's talent, especially her usage of musical allusions, redeems the plot from the commonplace and illuminates the universal and fundamental struggle between the self and the society, rendering it with a singular originality.

Notes

1. Although Chopin benefited from the German influx to St. Louis during the nineteenth century, it is unclear whether or not she knew German. In her youth she did not attend public school, where German was compulsory, but she did join a German Reading club in 1868. After her return to St. Louis, Chopin and Frederick Kolbenheyer renewed their friendship which had been interrupted while she lived in New Orleans and later, Cloutierville. Patricia L. Bradley argues that Kolbenheyer could have introduced her to the philosophy of Nietzsche (Bradley 43-4).

Works Cited

Bradley, Patricia L. "*The Birth of Tragedy* and *The Awakening*: Influences and Intertextualities." *Southern Literary Journal* 37.2 (Spring 2005): 40-61. *Project Muse*. Edith Garland Dupré Library. 30 July 2008. <http://muse.jhu.edu/>.

Camastra, Nicole. "Venerable Sonority in Kate Chopin's *The Awakening*." *American Literary Realism* 40.2 (2008): 154-66. *Project Muse*. Edith Garland Dupré Library. 30 July 2008. <http://muse.jhu.edu/>.

Chopin, Kate. *The Awakening*. 2nd ed., ed. Margo Culley. New York: Norton, 1994.

Dickstein, Morris. "*The Awakening*: Between Feminism and the Fin-de-Siécle." (paper presented at the University of Louisiana at Lafayette. November 2004).

Nietzsche, Friedrich. *The Birth of Tragedy and the Genealogy of Morals*. Trans. Francis Golffing. Garden City, NY: Doubleday Anchor, 1956.

Kate Chopin and "Super-Spiritual Superior" Influences

When Kate Chopin published *The Awakening* in 1899, St. Louis was a city ripe for spectacle. Missouri had been the site of conflict for decades: divided by pro-slavery and anti-slavery forces (indeed, the Missouri Compromise of 1821 made Missouri's statehood a pivotal point in the balance of Congress), Missouri would rank "third among the States with the most [recorded] battles and engagements in the War Between the States" (Bartles 1). This official record did not of course take into account the tremendous number of brutal guerrilla skirmishes that also dominated life in Missouri during the Civil War.

Even prior to the war, Missouri was marked by unrest. The trial of Celia, a slave from Callaway County who stood accused of murdering her master and burning his body in her fireplace, began on October 9, 1855, when Kate Chopin was five years old. The Dred Scott case, argued at the Old Courthouse in St. Louis and begun before Kate Chopin was born, was not ultimately decided until March 6, 1857.[1] Both of these trials were covered extensively in St. Louis newspapers such as the *Daily Missouri Democrat* and the *Republican*, and it is reasonable to assume that the Chopin family, as other citizens of St. Louis, were aware of and discussed these trials. New scholarship about these lawsuits, however, have begun to consider them from the angle of gender politics.

Melton McLaurin writes that "It [Celia's challenge to her master's power] was unacceptable because gender mattered in both the social conventions and in the laws that upheld slavery. To have empowered slave women in the domestic arena, to recognize their *right to control their sexuality* [emphasis added], would have undercut the power of the master to a degree that would have threatened the very survival of the institution" (138).[2] Authors Lea VanderVelde and Sandhya Subramanian claim, in "Mrs. Dred Scott," that the "intersecting subordinations of race and gender not only impelled Harriet toward freedom but also effaced her role in fighting for that freedom" (VanderVelde).

In addition, in 1870, St. Louis was the first city to establish a system to regulate prostitution (D'Emilio and Freedman 139). Although a bill repealed the plan four years later, the recognition that sexuality existed beyond the domestic sphere had been exposed in a public arena.[3] In all of these cases, the ownership and commodification of women's bodies was the subtext. Spiritualism, a landmark religious movement that developed at the same time as these landmark legal cases, vigorously addressed the issue of ownership over women's bodies, regardless of the institution that claimed that ownership. Free Love activist and radical Victoria Woodhull ran for president of the United States in 1872. Finally, the impending millennium was a time of great excitement in the city.[4] All of these contextual factors made St. Louis susceptible to the lure of Spiritualism, and Kate Chopin had returned to St. Louis after the death of her mother in 1885.

Whether the Spiritualist movement did actually begin with the rappings in the Fox house in Hydesville, New York, on March 31, 1848, exactly one hundred and fifty-nine years before the writing of this sentence, will always remain an unresolved matter and is clearly out of the scope of this article.[5] What is significant, however, is that the rappings of the Fox sisters, although ultimately proven to be a hoax, began a movement that brought women into a position of empowerment and, for the first time, gave women a voice in a major religious movement.[6] Spiritualism spread with tremendous force across the United States and was the fastest-growing religious movement at the time. From 1850 to 1863, according to Victoria Woodhull biographer Barbara Goldsmith, its following grew from 2 million to 7 million (78).[7] Ann Braude contends that the number is impossible to determine, since the Spiritualists were a group that would defy organization (a tendency that probably contributed to the downfall of the movement). However, after the 1890 census, 45,000 individuals officially considered themselves part of the Spiritualist movement (already in decline), while contemporary estimates ran as high as 11 million out of a total population of 25 million (25). Perhaps the ferment in St. Louis made that city predisposed to the cataclysmic social changes implied by the Spiritualist movement; medium Emma Hardinge commented about the remarkable support for the movement she experienced in her travels there.[8]

Perhaps Kate Chopin, a citizen of St. Louis, thought about the movement while she was writing her novel *The Awakening*, and her character Edna Pontellier was thinking of it when she made the choices that she did. Dr. Mandelet, the one person Edna thinks might have understood her, immediately thinks of the Spiritualists when he asks a concerned husband who stands to lose his "valuable piece of personal property," Léonce Pontellier, "Has she . . . been associating of late with a circle of pseudo-intellectual women—super-spiritual superior beings?"[9] Indeed, Léonce did consider his wife his property (and was within his legal rights to do so), and he "greatly valued his possessions, chiefly because they were his" (50). However, his wife also had her possessions: her "thoughts and emotions . . . and she entertained the conviction that she had a right to them and that they concerned no one but herself" (48). The fact that her husband sees Edna as an external object and she clearly perceives herself as intangible and non-objective is a key factor in her final meeting with Robert (the man she has chosen as her beloved) and her rejection of him: "I am no longer one of Mr. Pontellier's possessions to dispose of or not. I give myself where I choose" (106-7).[10] The question of ownership of the body was, as discussed above, quite overtly the major focus of the day. In more modern systems, interpretations of the placement of power transfer the location of control from the containment of the body in older systems of authority to the control of the subject's mind.[11] As Sandra Lee Bartky explains it, "Power now seeks to transform the minds of those individuals who might be tempted to resist it, not merely to punish or imprison their bodies," a shift that requires a finer knowledge of the subject as an individual (40). The discussion of Edna as a "possession" clearly articulates both corporeal and mental control by an outside force, one which Kate Chopin investigated in earlier writings.

Although Kate Chopin's collection *Bayou Folk* (1894) was hailed as a masterpiece of local color, some of the stories in that collection hint at those dark and serious issues that were occupying the American mind at that time. Her story, "La Belle Zoraïde," narrated by a "black as the night" woman who recounts only "true" stories to help her mistress sleep, tells of the life of a beautiful mulatto who is both serving maid and godchild to her Madame and "even had her own little black servant to wait upon her."[12] "La Belle Zoraïde" conveys a shaded layering of complex relationships, a tangle of ownership and affection.[13] Madame Delarivière wants to marry Zoraïde to another mulatto, whom Zoraïde detests. She falls in love instead with Mézor: "That Negro! that Negro!" Madame exclaims, as though he could never be good enough for her goddaughter. However, when Zoraïde asks her mistress, "Am I white?" we have to wonder whether she was forcing her mistress to confront the truth or whether she simply does not know how to define herself. Such was the nature of confused identities and relationships. Madame leaves no doubt about Zoraïde's identity, however: "You deserve to have the lash laid upon you like any other slave; you have proven yourself no better than the worst" (137). Perhaps Madame was equally "speechless with rage" at Zoraïde's suggestion that she had any right to choose for herself from her "own race" and her own "heart" (137).

In *The Awakening*, we certainly see Léonce attempt to control Edna throughout the novel as he tries to force her to keep up appearances and her Tuesday afternoons at home. He attempts to control her every physical movement. When Edna is lying outside on the hammock, feeling rather than thinking of that night when she had for the first time felt unafraid of swimming alone, Léonce returns home: "I can't permit you to stay out there all night. You must come in the house instantly" (32). Edna wonders whether her husband has ever spoken to her in that commanding voice before, and, realizing that of course he had but that she had always yielded, refuses to obey or even to respond. In fact, the next day on a spontaneous trip with Robert, Edna becomes aware of her own physicality and the power it implies as she "looked at her round arms," observing "as if it were something she saw for the first time, the fine, firm quality and texture of her flesh" (37). However, her continued refusal to act the way Léonce wishes her to act leads him "to wonder whether his wife were not growing a little unbalanced mentally" (57). He can see that Edna "was not herself"; what he will not see is that Edna is becoming a new person entirely, "casting aside that fictitious self that we assume like a garment" (57). Her husband simply cannot make her care about the fixtures in the house or its visitors the way that he does.

One method in which women who did not behave were handled was through the vehicle of the insane asylum. According to an unpublished report about the insane asylum of the city of St. Louis, the number of people hospitalized for mental disorders grew from 74,028 to 187,791 from 1890 to 1910, paralleling the growth in population from 78,000 in 1850 to 311,000 in 1870 (3, 5). The overcrowding of the facilities made quality care almost impossible, regardless of the sex of the patient. However, the authors state that one reason for the hospitalization of women was their inability to adjust to the social behaviors that were expected of them. In fact, the "recovery of women patients was often equated with their acceptance of prescribed female roles and behavior" (3-4). In other words, the women would be more likely to be discharged when they convinced the doctors that they were capable of assuming their feminine duties once more.

Kate Chopin certainly was aware of the association of women with mental illness, whether real or fabricated. At the end of the nineteenth century, the Louisiana Code, an American adaptation of the *Code Napoleon*, legally considered married women, babies, and the mentally deranged incapable of making contracts (Dyer 10-11; Rheinstein 147). In her story of "La Belle Zoraïde," Chopin clearly feels compassion for the deranged Zoraïde and may therefore be shifting responsibility for her condition onto the society she is forced to inhabit, while at the same time commenting on the infantilizing and degrading of women by the

Louisiana Code. When Zoraïde chooses Mézor anyway and becomes pregnant, Madame instructs his owner to sell the slave, so infuriated is she that Zoraïde has disobeyed. She has their child sold as well, telling Zoraïde that her baby has died, and a bundle of rags becomes Zoraïde's baby. From that day Zoraïde is "demented" (139), ostensibly driven to madness with her grief, although it is the "wicked falsehood" that actually changes Zoraïde (138). When we return to the frame story, the mistress says to the narrator that it would have been better if the "little one" had died. Clearly, she is impervious to sympathy for Zoraïde, who has gone from "la belle" to "la folle," a woman no one wants to marry. The responsibility for her own madness falls on Zoraïde. However, it is clear that the reader will feel sympathy for the young woman and antipathy for the mistress who demands a tale to help her sleep with no compassion for its tragic figure.

In addition, the prevailing medical theory at the time attributed further female "weakness" to the reproductive system and to the fact that females menstruate. In 1871, Dr. Edward Clarke published *Sex in Education, or a Fair Chance for the Girls*, in which he argues that because females were particularly vulnerable during this time of "weakness," they should avoid rigorous studying.[14] He warned that ignoring this advice could lead to infertility. Ultimately, then, it would be advisable that girls did not pursue learning as vigorously as boys, since it might damage their bodies and affect their ability to produce healthy children (Rury 49).[15] Just as the number of women in mental hospitals grew when women did not obey proscribed gender roles, such essentialist medical arguments became more strenuous against those forces that threatened "existing social arrangements" (Rosenberg and Rosenberg 332). Women were both the "product and prisoner" of their reproductive systems (335). Paradoxically, women who did not marry or who remained childless were at even greater risk of dying young or suffering more traumatic illnesses (336). Following the writings of Clarke, R. Frederic Marvin went even further to assert that "utromania," hysteria having its origins in the female reproductive system, leads to other forms of hysteria, including "Mormonism, Mesmerism, Fourierism, Socialism, oftener Spiritualism. She becomes possessed by the idea that she has some startling mission in the world. She forsakes her home, her children, her duty . . ." (Braude 159-60). A safer—and infinitely more socially acceptable and physically healthy—choice is implicit in these pronouncements: young women should accept their inferiority rather than try to compete with men. Marvin even coined a new name for the disease: "Mediomania, or the insanity of mediums ... a very ancient form of derangement'" (Braude

159). Indeed, in the Evans and Johnson sample of the St. Louis Insane Asylum, seven women were admitted because of religious excitement or spiritualism (12). Other women were admitted for other unruly behaviors: Louisa Burkhardt "has always been very jealous towards husband, consulted numerous mediums, fortunetellers, etc. about her husband." Mrs. Burkhardt, Case #6267, asked for medicine because she thought she was going "insane." Katie Jacobs, patient #6570, identified herself as a Spiritualist. Lillie Roth spent around six months in the asylum; she used to be "industrious," but grew "careless in habits and manners." On October 9, 1899, her husband George took her home, hopefully improved.[16] Patient #6429, Eliza Rheim, was admitted for the Probable Predisposing Cause of a "Disorder of Menstruation."

The case page of Katherine Blum, patient #6313, was offset by a small, pasted article from a local newspaper recounting Mrs. Blum's disheveled hair and manners. Comments about Mrs. Blum included the information that she had "a sudden notion to read novels" (St. Louis Insane Asylum Patients [sic] Historical Register, 6200-6699). Mrs. Blum was committed to the Insane Asylum of St. Louis the same year that Kate Chopin would publish *The Awakening*.[17] In that novel, when Edna chooses to move into her own little house and Mademoiselle Reisz asks her "What does your husband say?" Edna realizes that he probably will consider her "demented" (79).[18] Perhaps Chopin is revealing a sympathy for women who are judged as mad (similar to her sympathy for Zoraïde) when they are simply exhibiting emotion: Edna pities Adèle's contented but "colorless" life, devoid of "anguish" and "the taste of life's delirium" (56).

Asylum superintendent Edward C. Runge addressed the particular needs of his female patients in his 1896 annual report of the St. Louis Insane Asylum: "Much could be done if I had one good woman physician on the staff, and I shall recommend the appointment of one at the very next time a vacancy occurs" (Evans and Johnson 20-21).[19] Dr. Runge was very progressive in his thinking. In 1867, when Elizabeth Stuart Phelps wrote an essay about "weak-minded" women in *Harper's New Monthly Magazine* in response to Dr. Clarke, several hundred women were practicing medicine, "despite widespread and frequently venomous opposition" (Wegener 1).[20] Violent argument also ensued in the medical community over the efficacy of allopathic medicine versus homeopathic therapies.

Hydropathy, or the "water cure," one homeopathic reform embraced by the Spiritualist movement, encouraged the use of looser, lighter clothing and healthy diets, and "contradicted convention" by suggesting a respite from the care of the family (Braude 154).[21] Edna "loosened her clothes" as she lay on Madame Antoine's "high, white" bed (37). The night before, learning to swim had given her a sense of exultation and strength (28-9). Hydropathy encouraged women not to perceive their condition as pathological (unlike the repressive views of the medical establishment) and also to be vigilant about themselves apart from others, suggesting a new idea—a certain ownership of self. Edna, while not conscious of the change, goes through this evolution: "She could only realize that she herself—her present self—was in some way different from the other self" (41). Clearly, Edna's independence from her perceived responsibilities are marked by her connection with water and the liberty it gave her, "leaving her free to drift withersoever she chose to set her sails" (35). Learning to swim (and to walk into the sea at the end of the novel) has given Edna a taste of free will.[22]

In order to retain the power of the medical community, allopathic organizations such as the American Medical Association fought the presence of women.[23] Some men, like Spiritualist Andrew Jackson Davis, "read the Book of Nature with a different light" and suggested female birth attendants who would not see childbirth pains as a reflection of "original sin" (Braude 155). Kate Chopin's friend, Dr. Frederick Kolbenheyer (also the man who suggested she try her hand at publishing to support herself), famous for his "radical political views" (Toth and Seyersted 123; Toth 131), probably shared the unorthodox medical views circulating at the time. Attending to the birth of Adèle Ratignolle's fourth baby, Edna reacts with a "flaming, outspoken revolt against the ways of Nature … a scene of torture" (109). As they leave together, Dr. Mandelet encourages Edna to speak to him. "I know I would understand," he says, "and I can tell you there are not many who would" (110). Not "given to confidences" (15), Edna does not invite his friendship; however, one of her final realizations is that he indeed might have helped her (114).

Edna does see Adèle Ratignolle as one of the "ministering angels," women who "idolized their children, worshipped their husbands, and esteemed it a holy privilege to efface themselves as individuals" (10). Although Edna tries to develop a friendship with Adèle, "the two women did not appear to understand each other or to be talking the same language" (48). Edna, on the other hand, is "fond of her children in an uneven, impulsive way" and feels that she "assumed" the role of motherhood without choosing it (20). She tries to appease her friend but ultimately comes to pity Adèle's life of "appalling and hopeless ennui" (56). Even if social norms perceived as the wife's calling the production of healthy children (if she had shielded her reproductive organs from too much damaging knowledge), the dangers of childbirth were well known and imminent.[24] Sexuality and birth control were common medical concerns.[25] Certainly these concerns, as well as the attraction of Spiritualism, added to the development of the Free Love movement.

To the Claflin sisters, Victoria and Tennessee, a man's privilege to demand sexual submission from women was the basis for all opposition to the enfranchisement of women and the extension of women's involvement outside of the home (Rosenberg and Rosenberg 347n.). Unlike the *"feminine—*negative and passive" qualities desirable in most mediums, the Claflin sisters were the opposite, although they were used as money-making tools by their father when they were quite young and did operate under the influence of other men throughout their lives. When Victoria Woodhull ran for President in 1872, she declared, "To preach the doctrine you must live the life" (qtd. in Showalter 17).[26] Although a strong advocate of Free Love, which encouraged true love and desire rather than reproduction as the basis for sexual union, she certainly was not its only adherent. Lois Waisbrooker offered this quotation to explain the confusion many women must have felt: "I came to womanhood with the idea that purity was without desire, and when my own nature awoke I despised myself because I could not subdue it" (qtd. in Braude 138). It was society's insistence that she deny these feelings that truly compromised a woman's purity, Waisbrooker contended (138). It is precisely this hypocrisy that the woman's movement railed against. Demanding a revision of divorce laws, Elizabeth Cady Stanton wrote in 1867: "Marriage today is in no way viewed as an equal partnership, intended for the equal advantage and happiness of both parties. Nearly every man feels that his wife is his property, whose first duty, under all circumstances, is to gratify his passions . . ." (qtd. in Goldsmith 206). Articles in *Lucifer, the Light-Bearer*, a Spiritualist newspaper, were filled with observations such as this: "Is it slavery to keep the house clean? Is it drudgery to cook nice victuals? Certainly not if the person who cleans house and cooks victuals cleans and cooks from choice. But if the cleaning and cooking be compulsory, it then becomes slavery, and society has no more right to force a woman to do it than a man" (1). While on a trip to New York in 1870 with her husband Oscar, Kate Chopin met "Miss Claflin, the notorious 'female broker' of New York."[27] After discussing business with her husband, "Miss Claflin" (whether Victoria or Tennessee is not specified) entreats the newly married Mrs. Chopin "not to fall into the useless degrading life of most married ladies—but to elevate my mind and turn my attention to politics, commerce, questions of state, etc. etc." (Rankin 61). Certainly Kate Chopin was aware of Victoria Claflin Woodhull's campaigns for the White House, even if she did not see Thomas Nast's cartoon of the candidate in 1872. (By the 1890s, Kate Chopin was submitting stories to *Harper's Weekly*, where the cartoon appeared, so she certainly was aware of that periodical.) Although Woodhull's relationship with the established woman's suffrage movement was volatile, "Mrs. Satan" was transformed into a martyr in Elizabeth Cady Stanton's defense of her: "When the men who make laws for us in Washington can stand forth and declare themselves pure and unspotted from all the sins . . . then we shall demand that every woman . . . shall be as chaste as Diana. . . . If Victoria Woodhull must be crucified, let men drive the spikes and plait the crown of thorns" (Goldsmith 282; Harper 279).

Susan B. Anthony declared to defend any prostitute from the unfair laws that placed her "at the mercy of manhood" (Goldsmith 282). Emma Hardinge, speaking at the Polytechnic Institute of St. Louis on Saturday, April 13, 1867, spoke in defense of "fallen women." She spoke to a "full house" (*Banner of Light* 1). Clearly, the double standard that existed in most marriages was a sensitive and topical issue, especially in a city that in three years would be the first to regulate prostitution, regardless of how Victoria Woodhull and Tennessee Claflin were reviled and ridiculed in the popular press.

After a personal encounter with Alcée Arobin, Edna senses the hypocrisy in her own marriage, feeling "like a woman who in a moment of passion is betrayed into an act of infidelity," but she is still under the influence of the kiss he gave her. She thinks of Robert, whom she believes she truly loves, and Léonce seems to her "like a person whom she had married without love as an excuse" (77). Although she responds to Arobin physically, Edna realizes that it was not love that "had held this cup of life to her lips," and it is that realization that causes regret, not her actions. The Free Love platform found sexual union without love as immoral, even within marriage. That Kate Chopin had been influenced in her development of Edna Pontellier by Victoria Woodhull and the Free Love movement is not possible to say with certainty, but it seems likely to assume that she was aware of the unorthodox attitude toward marriage held by its followers. Kate Chopin held one of the most intellectual salons in St. Louis; her friend Vernon Knapp said of her that she possessed the "mentality and wit" essential to a "brilliant social circle" (Toth 257).[28] As an author, Chopin implies that Edna was becoming aware of the changing attitudes toward sexuality when Edna reads a book that she feels compelled to read "in secret and solitude," although no one else seems bothered by its contents (11). However, right after Edna learns to swim, and she is sitting on her hammock with Robert seated beside her, the silence is "pregnant with the first-felt throbbings of desire" (31). Only the present is significant to her (46). Overcoming her fear of the sea made Edna aware of other boundaries that she needed to breach.

Ultimately, Spiritualism became a type of Bakhtinian force, inverting the familiar into something unrecognizable, perhaps even alien or grotesque. Mary Russo remarks that she always considered spectacle a "specifically feminine danger . . . a kind of inadvertency and loss of boundaries" breached, perhaps by showing "dimpled thighs" or a "sliding bra strap" stepping "into the limelight out of turn" (318-19). Spiritualism brought women into the limelight for the first time, and the impact was terrific. The eroticism aroused by the self-fashioned, virginal Cora Hatch, who wore ringlets and a white rose, or Achsa Sprague, who wore "flashy ribbons," did provide men "with a rare opportunity to look unrestrained at an unknown woman," and the mediums did manipulate their public images (Braude 107-8). This new public way of female spectacle, however, also sent the message to women that they, too, might exceed the boundaries "that hedged her life in with limitations" (111). Rosemary Betterton suggests that the grotesque body extends the boundaries "between performance and material embodiment" in a manner that is uncomfortable for the viewer (95).[29] Certainly Katherine Blum was considered a grotesque as she was dragged off to the St. Louis Insane Asylum with her hair streaming wildly. The eroticism implied by a virginal medium and the grotesque spectacle of a woman stepping into the limelight caused an awareness of change in the perception of sexuality as well as a reaction against that change. Spiritualists sensed the undercurrents of change in American society caused by slavery, war, and repressive public policy. American life had undergone devastating changes, and Spiritualism was the religious force that provided the forum for a new type of expression, as Oliver Wendell Holmes observed as early as 1859:

> Spiritualism is quietly undermining the traditional ideas of the future state which have been and are still accepted . . . to a larger extent than most good people seem to be aware of. It needn't be true, to do this, any more than Homeopathy need, to do its work. The Spiritualists have some pretty strong instincts to pry over, which no doubt have been roughly handled by theologians at different times. And the Nemesis of the pulpit comes, in a shape it little thought of, beginning with the snap of a toe-joint, and ending with such a crack of old beliefs that the roar of it is heard in all the ministers' studies in Christendom! (90)

Many changes were still to come, begun by the force of Spiritualism. Laurence Moore writes that the mediums persisted in their cause, despite "the double stigma of doing something most women did not do in the service of a cause that many people laughed at" (221). The medium served as a catalyst for the transformation of women's lives. Many women, like Edna Pontellier, were to agree with Helen Wilmans: "It is the being forced that I object to" (*Lucifer* 1). Just as Edna "began to look with her own eyes" (93), Spiritualism forced Americans to probe very fundamental questions about their society, "undermining the traditional ideas," influencing women like Kate Chopin of St. Louis to make a difference in the world.

Notes

1. In Daniel Rankin's biography of Chopin, he quotes her lifelong friend Kitty Garesché on the subject of slavery in St. Louis: "I never went to slave sales, nor do I think Kate ever did, though we wanted to" (38). Rankin lists Sister Garesché's memory among the friends' other "delights and activities." St. Louis was a deeply divided city under Union rule; the Chopin family members were Confederate sympathizers. Kate's half-brother George O'Flaherty died a Confederate soldier. In Jeb Sharp's series on Public Radio International, October 8, 2008, political scientist Stephen Biddle discusses the persistence of the Civil War, long after Lee surrendered to Grant at Appomattox: ". . . So if you think of the war as being something other than just the battles on the battlefields but what caused it, what it was for, what its consequences were, then it took a very long time for the Civil War to come to anything like an end" (http://www.theworld.org/?q=node/21456).

2. Edward E. Baptist contends that the purveying of "fancy maids," attractive slave women held for sexual pleasure by the master, defined the identity of both: "Like ideas about honor and manhood, independence, and whiteness, the collective sexual aggressiveness enabled and valorized by the slave trade helped form a group identity for slave-owning white men. Market participants were all greedy [for field and reproductive slave labor], but also for 'fancy maids'" (1640).

3. "Symbols of vulnerable womanhood," virgins dressed in "pure white" gowns, delivered the petitions of 100,000 opponents' signatures in a "white-ribboned wheelbarrow" (139).

4. See Joseph Heathcott about the plans for the 1904 Louisiana Purchase Exposition being made as early as 1890 (11); see Emma Hardinge, *Modern American Spiritualism*, for the "fervid enthusiasm" of St. Louis Spiritualists for the "immediate millennium" (364).

5. Henry Blinn claims that the Shaker community had experiences such as visitations and trances at least ten years prior to the Fox sisters' celebrity in 1848.

6. Elizabeth Cady Stanton, Susan B. Anthony, and Matilda Joslyn Gage recognized that Spiritualism was the only religious sect that recognized the equality of women (*History of Woman Suffrage* 530).

7. Contacting spirits was not just a parlor game for the common folk: some very prominent figures—Mary Todd Lincoln, Cornelius Vanderbilt, and Harriet Beecher Stowe among them—depended on mediums to contact their dead loved ones.

8. "In the history of Spiritualism, then, St. Louis must either have played an important part, or the movement itself would have lacked the vast power in the West which has been attributed to it. The former is the case" (*Modern American Spiritualism* 354).

9. Chopin, *The Awakening* (66). All subsequent references to the novel appear parenthetically in the text. Dr. Mandelet is sympathetic to Edna, but his use of the prefix "pseudo" and the fact that he continues his question to add, "My wife has been telling me about them," indicates that the concerns of the women are somewhat beneath his personal recognition. See below for the influences of the medical profession on women's minds and bodies.

10. Per Seyersted sees this speech as an indication that Edna "demands in part to be 'a Free Lover,' as Victoria Woodhull had termed it" in 1871 (144). I agree that Kate Chopin was influenced by Victoria Woodhull but also had other very local influences as well that contributed to her sense of independence. See the discussion of the free love movement below.

11. See Wood's argument countering this "social control model" in more recent scholarship as more complicated than it appears on the surface (3-5).

12. "La Belle Zoraïde" (136). All further references to the story appear parenthetically in the text.

13. According to Baptist, the trade in light-skinned "mulatto" women in the nineteenth-century South was significant, and the systematic rapes of these women appear frequently in existing correspondence (1619-1621). Interestingly, much is made of Zoraïde's smooth skin the color of "café-au-lait," her "elegant manners," and her "svelte and graceful figure" that Madame's visitors envy. However, it is precisely these features that make Zoraïde more valuable and more vulnerable.

14. Rosenberg and Rosenberg quote Clarke on the results of study on a young girl's body: "monstrous brains" might cause "puny bodies"; "flowing thoughts" mean "constipated bowels" (340). Clarke's manual went through eleven printings.

15. Rury makes a significant observation: this view of women's sexuality as debilitating was not shared by members of the working class, especially among immigrants and African Americans (50). See Braude (30, 78) for a discussion

of African American involvement in the Spiritualist movement; also see John Kucich, *Ghostly Communion.*

16. According to Evans and Johnson, the average stay was 677.2 days (14).

17. In 1860, the wife of a Massachusetts state senator and the sister of a state senator from New York [Phoebe Harris Phelps] begged Susan B. Anthony to hide her and her child from her abusive husband, who wanted to commit her to an insane asylum for disobeying him. She did so, despite "continuous persecution from the Massachusetts Senator and his wife's brothers" and from abolitionists William Lloyd Garrison and Wendell Phillips, who feared that Anthony's actions would damage the cause for abolition and women's rights. "You would die before you would deliver a slave to his master, and I will die before I will give up that child to its father" (Dorr 139-140). According to Ida Husted Harper, Anthony never relented, but detectives tracked the woman, took the child, and they were never reunited (205). See Alex Owen on the British Married Women's Property Act of 1882, prior to which a woman who wished to contest her incarceration in an asylum could not do so without her husband's permission and support (152).

18. Moving into the "pigeon" house moved Edna closer to the behavior suggested by homeopathic healers of the era: "Every step which she took toward relieving herself from obligations added to her strength and expansion as an individual" (93). See discussion of homeopathy and hydropathy's prevailing philosophies below.

19. Patience Worth, a Puritan English girl who spoke through the St. Louis medium Pearl Curran, dedicated a series of poems to Mrs. Edward C. Runge, dated January 11, 1926, that are in the archival collection of the Missouri Historical Society.

20. Thomas Hazard of Rhode Island warned about doctors and ministers incarcerating "innocent healing mediums" in insane asylums (Braude 145). See about Dr. Marvin, above, who characterized mediumship as a disease. See Moore: Emma Hardinge had a man confined to an asylum when he persisted in writing love letters to her and following her everywhere in his "astral body" (210).

21. "Dress reform to us is synonymous with health reform," Lydia Sayer Hasbrouck wrote, and the long dress prevented women from being equal with men in "political, professional, or business relations" (qtd. in Donegan 136, 165).

22. Of the women in the St. Louis Insane Asylum sample, 31.7 percent were suicidal (11).

23. Braude 143; although Howard University had hired Dr. Isabel Barrows to lecture in ophthalmology in 1873, the AMA prohibition against female medical professors forced her resignation two years later (Wegener 3 and n.14). Mary Gove Nichols, pioneer hydropathist, served as a "role model" for women who

hoped to have a career in medicine (Donegan 30). Hydropathists recognized childbirth as a natural (albeit dangerous) process and encouraged "women to counteract debilitating influences by taking charge of their own bodies" (Donegan 193). Also see Wegener and Phelps for insight into the allopathic/homeopathic battle.

24. See, for example, Rosenberg and Rosenberg 345-6. These dangers were complicated by the husband's control over his wife implied by numerous children (Rosenberg and Rosenberg 346 *n.*).

25. See Rosenberg and Rosenberg 347-8, or Daniel Scott Smith.

26. The reader is encouraged to view Thomas Nast's 1872 *Harper's Weekly* cartoon of Victoria Woodhull as "Mrs. Satan," available through the Library of Congress and other sites.

27. Victoria Woodhull and her sister were lampooned in another *Harper's Weekly* cartoon in 1870 as "The Bewitching Brokers.—Women on Change."

28. In an article printed in the St. Louis *Republic* on September 11, 1910 (a paper that Knapp's family owned and edited), he was to bemoan the lack of a salon and say, "Since the death of Mrs. Chopin, some five years ago, St. Louis has lacked anything that savors of a true salon where one can meet interesting people."

29. Louise Pratt suggests that the figure of the grotesque, aging woman Bakhtin reacts to with ambivalence might not be "as bleak . . . as previous scholarship has tended to suggest. Old women retained a social function with the intention of bringing them much affection and some respect" (62).

Works Cited

Baptist, Edward E. "'Cuffy,' 'Fancy Maids,' and 'One-Eyed Men': Rape Commodification and the Domestic Slave Trade in the United States." *American Historical Review* 106.5 (Dec 2001): 1619-1650. JSTOR. Web. 19 Mar. 2007.

Bartels, Carolyn M. *The Civil War in Missouri Day by Day 1861-1865*. Independence, MO: Two Trails, 1992.

Bartky, Sandra Lee. "Foucault, Femininity, and the Modernization of Patriarchal Power." In *The Politics of Women's Bodies: Sexuality, Appearance, and Behavior,* ed. Rose Weitz. NY: Oxford UP, 1998. 25-45.

Betterton, Rosemary. "Promising Monsters: Pregnant Bodies, Artistic Subjectivity, and Maternal Imagination." *Hypatia* 1.1 (2006): 80-100. Project MUSE. Web. 27 Mar. 2007.

Blinn, Henry. *Spiritualism Among the Shakers 1837-1847.* East Canterbury, NH: [n.p.], 1899.

Braude, Ann. *Radical Spirits: Spiritualism and Women's Rights in Nineteenth-Century America.* 2nd ed. Bloomington: Indiana UP, 2001.

Chopin, Kate. *The Awakening.* Norton Critical Edition. Ed. Margaret Culley. New York: Norton, 1976.

———. Commonplace Book. Kate O'Flaherty Chopin Papers. Missouri Historical Society. St. Louis, MO.

———. "La Belle Zoraïde." *"The Storm" and Other Stories with* The Awakening. Ed. Per Seyersted. New York: The Feminist Press, 1974. 135-140.

D'Emilio, John, and Estelle B. Freedman. *Intimate Matters: A History of Sexuality in America.* New York: Harper & Row, 1988.

Donegan, Jane B. *"Hydropathic Highway to Health": Women and Water-Cure in Antebellum America.* New York: Greenwood, 1986.

Dorr, Rheta Childe. *Susan B. Anthony: The Woman Who Changed the Mind of a Nation.* New York: Frederick A. Stokes Company, 1928.

Dyer, Joyce. The Awakening: *A Novel of Beginnings.* New York: Twayne, 1993. 3-17.

Evans, Carol J., and Mary E. Johnson. "Women in the Asylum at the Turn of the Last Century: An Examination of the 1895-1905 Casebooks of the Insane Asylum of the City of St. Louis." Unpublished Paper. 08 Jan. 2004.

Goldsmith, Barbara. *Other Powers: The Age of Suffrage, Spiritualism, and the Scandalous Victoria Woodhull.* New York: Alfred A. Knopf, 1998.

Hardinge, Emma Britten. *Modern American Spiritualism: A Twenty Years' Record of the Communion Between Earth and the World of Spirits.* New York: Self-published, 1870. 353-80.

———. "Fallen Women." *Banner of Light.* 13 April 1867: 1.

Harper, Ida Husted. *The Life and Work of Susan B. Anthony.* Volume 1. Indianapolis: Hollenbeck Press, 1899.

Heathcott, Joseph. "Out of the 'Wilds': Visions of an Urban Order." *Gateway Heritage* (Spring 2004): 10-19.

Holmes, Oliver Wendell. "The Professor at the Breakfast Table." *Atlantic Monthly* 3.5 (January 1859): 85-97. <http://cdl.library.cornell.edu/moa/>. 27 Mar. 2007.

Knapp, Vernon (Bunnie). "Is There an Interesting Woman in St. Louis?" [St. Louis] *Republic* 11 Sept 1910: 5.1.

Kucich, John J. *Ghostly Communion: Cross-Cultural Spiritualism in Nineteenth-Century American Literature.* Hanover, NH: Dartmouth College P, 2004.

McLaurin, Melton. *Celia, a Slave.* New York: Avon, 1993.

Moore, R. Laurence. "The Spiritualist Medium: A Study of Female Professionalism in Victorian America." *American Quarterly* 27.2 (1975): 200-221. JSTOR. Web. 27 Mar. 2007.

Owen, Alex. *The Darkened Room: Women, Power, and Spirituality in Late Victorian England.* Chicago: U of Chicago P, 1989. 139-201.

Phelps, Elizabeth Stuart. "What Shall They Do?" *Harper's New Monthly Magazine* 35 (June-Nov 1867): 519-523. < http://cdl.library.cornell.edu/moa/>. 27 Mar. 2007.

Pratt, Louise. "The Old Women of Ancient Greece and the Homeric Hymn to Demeter." *Transactions of the American Philological Association (1974-).* 130 (2000): 41-65. JSTOR. Web. 23 Mar. 2007.

Rankin, Daniel S. *Kate Chopin and Her Creole Stories.* Philadelphia: U of Pennsylvania P, 1932.

Rheinstein, Max. "The Code and the Family." In *The Code Napoleon and the Common-Law World*, ed. Bernard Schwartz. New York: New York UP, 1956. 139-161.

Rury, John L. "'We Teach the Girl *Repression*, the Boy *Expression*': Sexuality, Sex Equity and Education in Historical Perspective." *Peabody Journal of Education* 64.4 (1987): 44-58. JSTOR. Web. 29 Mar. 2007.

Russo, Mary. "Female Grotesque: Carnival and Theory." In *Writing on the Body: Female Embodiment and Feminist Theory*, eds. Katie Conboy, Nadia Medina, and Sarah Stanbury. New York: Columbia UP, 1997. 318-36.

Seyersted, Per. *Kate Chopin: A Critical Biography.* Baton Rouge: Louisiana State UP, 1969. Inscribed copy, property of the Wednesday Club, St. Louis, MO.

Showalter, Elaine. *Inventing Herself: Claiming a Feminist Intellectual Heritage.* New York: Scribner, 2001.

Smith, Daniel Scott. "Family Limitation, Sexual Control, and Domestic Feminism in Victorian America." *Feminist Studies* 1:3/4 (1973): 40-57. JSTOR. Web. 22 Jan. 2007.

Smith-Rosenberg, Carroll, and Charles Rosenberg. "The Female Animal: Medical and Biological Views of Woman and Her Role in Nineteenth-Century America." *Journal of American History* 60.2 (1973): 332-356. JSTOR. Web. 23 Jan. 2007.

Stanton, Elizabeth Cady, Susan B. Anthony, and Matilda Joslyn Gage, eds. *History of Woman Suffrage.* Vol. 3, reprint. 1876-1885. NY: Arno & the *New York Times*, 1969.

Toth, Emily. *Kate Chopin*. New York: William Morrow & Company, 1990.

Toth, Emily, and Per Seyersted, eds. *Kate Chopin's Private Papers*. Bloomington, IN: Indiana UP, 1998.

VanderVelde, Lea, and Sandhya Subramanian. "Mrs. Dred Scott." *Yale Law Journal* 106.4 (1997): 1033-1122. Proquest. Web. 31 Mar. 2007.

Wegener, Frederick. "'Few Things More Womanly or More Noble': Elizabeth Stuart Phelps and the Advent of the Woman Doctor in America." *Legacy* 22.1 (2005): 1-17. Project MUSE. Web. 29 Mar. 2007.

Wilmans, Helen. "Strike Off Our Fetters." *Lucifer: The Light-Bearer.* 24 April E.M. 285 [C.E. 1885].

Wood, Mary Elene. *The Writing on the Wall: Women's Autobiography and the Asylum.* Urbana: U of Illinois P, 1994.

Contributors' Notes

Victoria M. Bryan earned her M.A. at the University of Tennessee at Chattanooga and is currently working on her Ph.D. in nineteenth- and twentieth-century American literature at the University of Mississippi. She has a special interest in the work of William Faulkner and the social construction of race and sexuality.

Jessica Copous currently resides in McKenzie, Tennessee, where she teaches English and art at Bethel University.

Ryan Crider is a Ph.D. candidate in English at the University of Louisiana at Lafayette, where his research interests include American realism, early modernism, and Southern regionalism. He has taught English and creative writing at several universities, and his fiction has appeared in a variety of literary journals.

Donna J. Essner received her M.A. in English with a focus in Creative Writing in 2009. Currently she is the office manager and assistant editor of Southeast Missouri State University Press. Publication credits include *Journey*, *Big Muddy*, *Newpages*, and the *Southeast Missourian* newspaper.

Barbara C. Ewell is the Dorothy H. Brown Distinguished Professor of English at Loyola University New Orleans, where she has taught since 1984. She is the author of *Kate Chopin* and numerous essays about Southern writers, as well as co-editor of *Louisiana Women Writers* (with Dorothy Brown) and *Southern Local Color: Stories of Region, Race and Gender* (with Pamela Menke).

Geri Harmon studies how medical theories, especially homeopathy, influenced Modernist literature. She is an Assistant Professor of English at Georgia Gwinnett College near Atlanta.

Robert W. Hamblin is Professor of English and Director of the Center for Faulkner Studies at Southeast Missouri State University. His most recent of several Faulkner books are *Critical Companion to William Faulkner* (co-edited with A. Nicholas Fargnoli and Michael Golay) and *Faulkner and Twain* (co-edited with Melanie Speight).

Brian Daniel Howton received a Bachelor of Arts in English from the University of Louisiana at Lafayette. He is currently studying at the

Graduate Institute at St. John's College in Annapolis, Maryland, where he will earn a Master of Arts in Liberal Arts.

Julie Kares is completing her Ph.D. in American Literature at Southern Illinois University–Carbondale. Her research interests include Southern studies, cultural theory, and film.

Gretchen Martin is an Associate Professor of American Literature with special interest in Southern literature at The University of Virginia's College at Wise. She also teaches African-American literature and Literary Theory. The author of *The Frontier Roots of American Realism*, she has also published essays in *The Southern Literary Journal*, *Mississippi Quarterly*, *South Atlantic Review*, *Southern Studies*, *The North Carolina Literary Review*, and *Studies in American Humor*.

Caroline S. Miles, an Assistant Professor at the University of Texas-Pan American, has published on issues related to labor and gender in William Faulkner, Rebecca Harding Davis, Dime Novels, and Latin American literature. Her most recent articles appear in *The Mississippi Quarterly*, *Hispanic Newsletter*, *American Transcendental Quarterly*, *Dime Novel Round-Up,* and *The Faulkner Journal*. She is currently working on a book-length manuscript that examines Faulkner's representations of capitalism and the blue-collar South.

Kathleen Butterly Nigro is an Assistant Teaching Professor in the Department of English and Program Advisor for Women's and Gender Studies at the University of Missouri-St. Louis. Much of her research focuses on Missouri women's history, most recently on Missouri slave narratives. She is President of the Kate Chopin Society of North America and serves on the executive board of the Kate Chopin International Society.

Shiela Pardee is an independent scholar residing in Oregon. She is interested in nineteenth- and twentieth-century fiction, anthropology, and permanent peace in the real world.

Christopher Rieger is an Assistant Professor of English and Assistant Director of the Center for Faulkner Studies at Southeast Missouri State University. He is the author of *Clear-Cutting Eden: Ecology and the Pastoral in Southern Literature*, as well as essays on Erskine Caldwell, Zora Neale Hurston, and Larry Brown.

Alisa M. Smith-Riel is currently enrolled in the Ph.D. program at Northern Illinois University, focusing on African-American and American Literature since 1865. Her extensive work on Faulkner motivated her upcoming dissertation work on the "gaze" and its effects on both women and men within texts of the twentieth century.

Jeremy Wells is currently a Visiting Assistant Professor of English at Allegheny College. He is the author of *Romances of the White Man's Burden: Race, Empire, and the Plantation in American Literature, 1880-1936*, forthcoming from Vanderbilt University Press.